# Praise for
# *SUGARS AND FLOURS:*

---

"This book is a comprehensive, and well-researched self-help tool. It offers easy-to-follow solutions to a set of increasingly common problems that baffle 'mainstream' physicians. The guidelines offered in this book are the same that I use for a variety of treatments, as well as for promoting and enhancing overall health, vitality and mental stability."

Gilbert Manso, M.D.
Assistant Professor
University of Texas Medical School

"This food plan is life-transforming. I have a vastly improved sense of physical, mental and emotional well-being."

Cylette Willis, PhD Biology
Professor, California Polytechnic

"Because of this book, I am now encouraging patients to consider eliminating sugars and flours from their food. Every therapist needs this information."

Susan Price, MSW, author, *The Female Ego*

"This book has a lot to offer for keeping temperament and energy even and for keeping toxins from packaging foods out of our system."

Janet Keeney-Valenza, Podiatrist, 2:48 Marathoner
Gulf Athletic Congress Runner of the Year

"Throughout my whole life, I have been either starving or binging. This book has given me a workable plan for sane weight maintenance. I immediately ordered three more copies for friends who suffer."

Cynthia Hughes
Financial Executive

*SUGARS AND FLOURS*
*How They Make Us Crazy, Sick and Fat,*
*And What to Do About It*

## is the only book that. . .

Identifies all of the relevant reactive substances in our foods and all of the benefits from eliminating them

Provides a workable implementation plan for the whole family from a mother's perspective

Provides workable plans for handling shopping, food storage, travel, restaurants, holidays, entertaining, schools and family relations

Shows the medical theory for why this food plan could improve the life of almost any American

Provides analysis of American patterns of refined carbohydrate consumption

Discusses a national support system based on the 12-step model

Describes how to start a support group

Discusses how to work the 12-steps to recover from refined carbohydrate addiction

Shows how food enhances spirituality

Provides real-life stories of recovery from refined carbohydrate abuse

# COMMENTS FROM READERS

"The most incredible part of this food plan is that I have actually developed a revulsion towards sugars and flours. I keep cookies in the house for my husband and I have no desire for them whatsoever. I am still in awe over how simple it was to end years of misery."-Thea

"I am 65 years old. By eliminating sugars and flours, I lost 25 pounds, but more important, I haven't had interim weight gain in almost four years. I have been free of depression and headaches for the first time that I can remember. I am grateful that my old age will be vigorous and happy."-Nora

"I am 48 years old. I have never attracted so many men. It's not just the weight loss. It's the health and confidence that I radiate."-Nancy

"Over 12 years, I had gradually gained 50 pounds. Eliminating sugars and flours made it possible for me to lose that 50 pounds seemingly effortlessly in about 9 months. I had given up acting, feeling ashamed of my body, but now I have resumed my career with more success and energy than ever before."
-Randy

"I had already attempted suicide twice. Now I know that the powerful effects of refined carbohydrates had created false despair in me. I don't like to think where I would be today without the information in this book."-Lynn

"My acne cleared up and I got my first A on a science test."-Heidi

"My 2 year-old has avoided sinus surgery because we took her off sugars and flours. Her formerly uncontrollable asthma has not flared up for months. As for myself, I thought my feelings about food were the result of being emotionally messed up. Now I know that it was the other way around. I was emotionally messed up because of the foods I ate."-Barbara

# SUGARS AND FLOURS
## *HOW THEY MAKE US CRAZY, SICK, AND FAT*
## *AND WHAT TO DO ABOUT IT*

# SUGARS AND FLOURS
## *HOW THEY MAKE US CRAZY, SICK, AND FAT AND WHAT TO DO ABOUT IT*

By

**Joan Ifland**

# ABOUT THE BOOK

*SUGARS AND FLOURS: How They Make Us Crazy, Sick, and Fat, and What to Do About It* is the only book that treats carbohydrate addiction with the decades-old methods of recovery from addictive behavior, i.e. elimination of the addictive substances. It is the only book that identifies both refined carbohydrates and other triggering foods as the source of abnormal eating behavior. Thus it is the only book that identifies a broad range of emotional, mental, behavior, and physical benefits. Benefits include relief from

| | | | | |
|---|---|---|---|---|
| Weight gain or loss | Despair | Allergies | Attention deficit | High cholesterol |
| Cravings | Shame | Headaches | Hyperactivity | Numbness |
| Hunger pangs | Anger | Sinus pain | Compulsive behavior | Fatigue |
| Anxiety | Mood swings | Coughing | Obsessing | Mental fogginess |
| Depression | Humiliation | Congestion | High blood pressure | Type B diabetes |
| Confusion | Critical nature | Asthma | Low self-confidence | Anorexia |
| Fear | Tension | Infection | Pre-menstrual | Bulimia |
| Restlessness | Irritability | Swelling | syndrome | Acne |

*SUGARS AND FLOURS* is unique among diet books because it provides a practical implementation plan for the whole family from a household perspective. It provides practiced plans for handling shopping, food storage, travel, restaurants, entertaining, schools, and family relations. It covers the holidays in detail. It explains the medical theory for why this food plan could improve the life of almost any American. It shows how American patterns of refined carbohydrate consumption have skyrocketed to create a health crisis. It gives information on a national support system based on the 12-step model. It describes how to start a support group for recovery from over consumption of carbohydrates. It discusses how to work the 12-steps to recover from refined carbohydrate addiction. It shows how non-reactive food enhances spiritual life. It provides real-life stories of recovery from refined carbohydrate abuse.

# ACKNOWLEDGMENTS

This book is a synthesis of thought from three important areas of research. The first is substance abuse and the work of Kay Sheppard, LMHC, CEDS. Kay Sheppard's book *Food Addiction: The Body Knows* started me on my path of recovery from reactive foods. I cannot overstate the importance of her book in saving my life. The second author and activist that I must recognize is Nancy Appleton, Ph.D. Her book *Lick the Sugar Habit* reassured me that medical research exists to explain the miracles that I witness daily. The last group is the food allergists Theron Randolph, M.D., William Philpott, M.D., and Doris Rapp, M.D. They have labored for decades to understand food allergies and to persuade traditional allergists to adopt a broader view of allergies. Their work is finally gaining recognition in a country desperate to understand why it is so sick.

The doctor/writer who pulls it all together for me is Abram Hoffer, M.D. His reputation as the father of orthomolecular medicine is well deserved. His books are so clear and sensible. His many decades of experience give his recommendations unassailable credence. I was astonished at how he closely describes my own experiences and observations.

I would also like to honor the courageous work of Gary Null whose book, *Good Food, Good Mood* started me on my quest for information. His later book, *Nutrition and the Mind* is quoted repeatedly herein. I am grateful for his unflagging interest in bringing information about orthomolecular treatments into public awareness.

I would be remiss to leave out the highly persuasive writings of Robert Crayhon, M.S. and Lendon Smith, M.D. Their views on the role of nutrition and well-being are based on extensive clinical work and are highly credible.

The last author I would like to acknowledge is Candace Pert, Ph.D. *Molecules of Emotion* took my breath away in its ability to elucidate the mysteries of biochemical communication.

I hope that my sapling of a book will one day grow to stand in the grove of giant oaks that these works represent.

I am especially grateful to Gilbert Manso, M.D. who took time to read and reread the chapters on theory and related conditions. Also, Chip Slauter and Jess Hawkins were generous with their knowledge of allergy treatments.

I thank all of those who shared their experiences and ruminated with me on the nature of sugars and flours, especially: Libby Edson, Cynthia Grady, Cynthia Hughes, Laura Mirsky, Carol Newberry, Joan Nuber, Susan Price, M.S.W., Mary Anne Stanphill, R.N.M.S., Nita Verges R.N., and Cylette Willis, Ph.D.

Most importantly, I would like to acknowledge my very fine family. Without their patience and willingness, this book would not have been possible. Their courage to be different from their culture and to have compassion for those who suffer touches me deeply.

*To my Tuesday friends*
*and to Scott, Claire, Camille, and Jane*

# Disclaimer

I am not a trained or licensed nutritionist or dietician. All of the information in this book is based on my personal experience or on experiences relayed to me first hand. Please confer with your health professional before you change your diet, especially if you are on *any* kind of medication.

# GENERAL CONTENTS

# TABLE OF CONTENTS

## RECIPES

### BREAKFAST RECIPES

### BASIC LUNCH AND DINNER MENUS

### FAVORITE LUNCH AND DINNER MENUS

# HOLIDAY RECIPES

# TABLE OF CONTENTS

# IMPLEMENTATION TOOLS

# INTRODUCTION

This book is about how to recover from the most widespread, most ignored disease of the twentieth century: carbohydrate sensitivity and addiction! It is not a diet book rather a life time plan for recovery.

Throughout my adult life, I have had numerous physical and emotional problems. I have been overweight. I have been hungry and tired most of the time. A daily nap has been imperative. My sinuses have been chronically painful and frequently infected. I have had severe respiratory allergies that could not be controlled by drugs and that did not respond to shots. I have had temper tantrums, and bouts of depression and anxiety that therapy and prayer helped but did not cure.

> **Early in 1996, within a few weeks of a change in my diet, these weight, infection, allergy, fatigue, and mood problems were GONE or GOING. I was never hungry. My sinus pain was rare and manageable. Allergic reactions were unusual. My disposition was even. I knew consistent serenity for the first time in my life. I had enough energy to get me through my day. Within a year, I had lost the thirty pounds that had plagued me for thirteen years.**

How did these changes come about? **I eliminated all forms of sugar and flour from my diet** and stopped nourishing myself poorly. I joined a support group that taught me how to look for sugars and flours in my food, and how to replace them with whole foods. I learned how to solicit emotional and spiritual guidance in taking care of myself. In short, I made peace with my food.

I took my family off sugars, flours, and wheat. They experienced needed weight loss and reduction in headaches, coughing and allergies, respiratory infections, tension, fear, and irritability. In 1995, I filled eight prescriptions for antibiotics for myself and my family. In 1996, the first year that we were off sugars and flours, I filled none. I noticed decreased hyperactivity and increased attention span in my teen-aged children. Their study habits improved. In addition to the effects that I observed in my family, I heard from members of my support group that they experienced increased confidence, greater intellectual clarity and memory, decreased cholesterol, lower blood pressure and less hypoglycemia.

> The over-consumption of refined carbohydrates has resulted in the astonishingly broad range of physical, mental, and emotional illnesses that are endured by millions.

How could such results be possible? I searched the literature and discovered that researchers have known for twenty years that over-consumption of a single food can cause a break down in the functioning of specific organs and that quite different organs can be affected from individual to individual.[1] Refined carbohydrates are absorbed quickly into the system and can overwhelm the body's biochemical balancing capabilities.

I told everyone I knew about my experiences in eliminating sugars and flours. They always replied, "What's left to eat?" I conceived of a seminar which would show people that there are a

---

[1] William H. Philpott and Dwight K. Kalita *Brain Allergies* (New Canaan, Conn.: Keats Publishing, 1980) 15.

zillion other foods to eat. I gave the first one in July, 1996. The "how-to" manual that I prepared for the seminar was the first version of this book.

Carbohydrate sensitivity and addiction are tricky to treat because we still need to eat whole carbohydrates while breaking the habit of getting "high" from refined carbohydrates (sugars and flours). No other treatment for sensitivity or addiction faces this challenge, nor the problems associated with social acceptance (even encouragement) of the addiction, nor the practice of hiding the addictive substances in otherwise normal food. The mechanics are pretty simple, but the style of eating is so different from the practices of this society that education and support are essential to long term success and recovery.

It absolutely thrills me to share my experiences and techniques through the "how-to" manual that has grown into this book. I have heard the excitement in readers' voices as they experience their first days without depression, as they experience new mental clarity and creativity. I have witnessed tears of relief as they shed the burden of obesity or anorexia and began a life of normal appetite and hunger. It has been a limitless blessing for me. My life has been transformed. The light that God has chosen to shine through me, and the light that begins to shine from people as they recover from the devastating effects of sugars and flours, combine to create divinity on earth.

*Notebook*:

## WHAT BRINGS YOU TO THIS BOOK?

Dear Reader,

Before you start reading, write down your own reasons for interest in changing your diet.

# PART I

## SITUATION ASSESSMENT

Reactive foods are any foods that create an adverse reaction in the body. Industrialized countries consume them in horrific quantities. This book focuses on refined carbohydrates, specifically sugars and flours. But reactive foods also include allergenic foods, foods that result in malnutrition, and foods like red food dye and aspartame that are simply toxic. They also include foods that create adverse reactions when over-consumed. In this latter category, you will read about wheat and dairy in particular.

Refined carbohydrates such as sugars and flours are the most prevalent reactive foods. (Honey is included because it acts on the system like a refined carbohydrate, even though it is not one.) Sugars and flours are manufactured under a great variety of names. The following list of names for sugars, flours was developed by an organization dedicated to helping people escape the addictive power of sugars and flours. Food Addicts in Recovery (FAIR), is a successor group to Recovery from Food Addiction and Food Addicts Anonymous. These are the substances that they believe cause the body to react negatively.

> ### THE NAMES FOR SUGARS, FLOURS, AND WHEAT
>
> Refined carbohydrates include all substances with any of the following words in their names: sugar, molasses, syrup, caramel, concentrated juice, sweetener (except pure saccharine), dextrose, saccharide, honey, fructose, alcohol, galactose, glucose, Jaggery, lactose, levulose, malt, manitol, nectars, ribose, sorbitol, succanat, wine, and sucrose. The flours include any product with the word "flour" in it, as well as corn meal.[2] Wheat, one of the most common allergic foods, is also called couscous and bulgur. Buckwheat is NOT wheat, so it is OK. Tortilla chips and tortillas have corn flour in them, even though it does not say so on the package. Breakfast cereals are also made from flour.

I recommend adding saccharine and aspartame to FAIR's list for reasons I will explain presently. Like FAIR, this book considers wheat products to be a common reactive food. All flours, including "whole grain" flours, are considered reactive because research has shown that they all create a brain chemical response in the form of increased serotonin levels. This serotonin 'high' is thought to contribute to the creation of refined carbohydrate addiction.

Other common reactive foods are corn, coffee, beef, pork, yeast, dairy products, eggs, yeast, and food additives. This book will address how to find out if you have a problem with these common allergic foods, but they are not necessarily eliminated from recipes and suggestions.

The reason FAIR does not have saccharine on its list is that when the first support group for refined carbohydrate addiction was formed, it was believed that saccharine did not cause a

---

2  Food Addicts in Recovery, "A List of Names for Sugar, Flour, and Wheat" (Houston: Food Addicts in Recovery, 1998).

reaction like refined carbohydrates. Specifically, it was believed that it did not trigger the pancreas to release insulin because saccharin does not convert to glucose in the bloodstream. However, Dr. Nancy Appleton, a prominent nutritionist, has a different view:

"In a number of laboratory tests, rats were given saccharin. Their bodies were fooled into thinking the sweetener was sugar, and they produced a boost of insulin. This is one reason why artificial sweeteners are poor aids for weight watchers and sugarholics; they are not good substitutes for sugar."[3]

Saccharin is used by people in recovery from refined carbohydrate addiction. Later in the book we will discuss how you can tell if its usage is appropriate for you.

In addition to the arguments against artificial sweeteners in general, the case against aspartame contains more serious elements: "...the methanol in aspartame may be dehydrogenated by fermentation into formaldehyde (embalming fluid) and attaches itself to protein. It can thus destroy the myelin around the nerve cells."[4] Dr. Doris Rapp, leading allergist writes that "some investigations indicate that aspartame can damage the nervous system or brain, not only in rats but also in humans. It is said to cause mood and behavioral changes, epileptic like seizures, insomnia, depression, headache, and even menstrual disorders. The use of this substance during pregnancy is questioned."[5] Since 1980, when the FDA set up its Adverse Reactions Monitoring System, 72% of problems reported concerned aspartame. The complaints are of headaches, dizziness, and vomiting. Need I say more?

Are there any sweeteners which can safely be used by a person wishing to recover from the devastation of refined carbohydrates? Some researchers feel that any sweetener can trigger a pancreas which has been sensitized through prolonged use of refined carbohydrates. The release of insulin is the beginning of the devastation caused by refined carbohydrates and it must be avoided at all costs by the recovering refined carbohydrate user. For the most sensitive, the answer may be that no sweetener can be used safely. For people who have been in recovery from some time, the pancreas may be somewhat desensitized and a substitute sweetener may be considered. However, never again can a refined carbohydrate be used because the presence of glucose in the system *always* triggers the pancreas. We will come back to this topic when we discuss how to shop for non-reactive foods.

You may be thinking at this moment that the list of substances to be avoided is long. But hold on. We are coming to an even longer list: the list of benefits that come from removing reactive substances from the diet. Can you do this food plan? Yes. I know you can. Will you reap the benefits? Yes. In some way, shape, or form your life will change significantly for the better. Discovering the array of positive results that will accrue to you specifically are part of the joy and surprise of eliminating reactive foods.

---

[3]  Appleton, Nancy, Ph. D., *Lick the Sugar Habit.* (Garden City Park, NY: Avery Publishing Group.1996) 178.

[4]  Smith, Lendon, H. M.D., *Feed Your Body Right.* (New York: M. Evans and Company. 1994) 186.

[5]  Rapp, Doris, M.D. *Is This Your Child?* (New York: William Morrow. 1991) 573.

# Chapter 2
## THE BENEFITS FROM ELIMINATING REACTIVE FOODS

In the years that I have been studying reactive foods, I have either experienced for myself, or witnessed in my family, friends, or support system, relief from *all* of the following symptoms:

| | | | | |
|---|---|---|---|---|
| Weight gain or loss | Despair | Allergies | Attention deficit | High cholesterol |
| Cravings | Shame | Headaches | Hyperactivity | Numbness |
| Hunger pangs | Anger | Sinus pain | Compulsive behavior | Fatigue |
| Anxiety | Mood swings | Coughing | Obsessing | Mental fogginess |
| Depression | Humiliation | Congestion | High blood pressure | Type B diabetes |
| Confusion | Critical nature | Asthma | Low self-confidence | Anorexia |
| Fear | Tension | Infection | Pre-menstrual | Bulimia |
| Restlessness | Irritability | Swelling | syndrome | Acne |

Precious reader, I know it is hard to believe that all of these conditions can be aggravated by sugars and flours. The most difficult aspect of my mission is to convey to my listeners and readers the breadth of the problems that refined carbohydrates create. Sometimes I would like to compare refined carbohydrates to a poison, but I cannot because, in small, infrequent quantities, sugars and flours do not hurt us. However, in the vast quantities that we Americans consume them, these substances affect our whole physical being. At an average consumption of one pound per person per day, we are soaked in sugars and flours. Our systems are literally being worn out from the effort to process this huge quantity of sugars and flours.

I have personally heard the stories of recovery from the effects of refined carbohydrates over and over. Many medical studies have been done to supply the theory to support these results. In the next chapter, *Medical Research and Theory*, I present the explanations for why sugars and flours cause such a huge variety of problems. For the moment, let me invite you to suspend disbelief and just share the joy and wonder at the relief from suffering.

## WEIGHT CONTROL

I suspect that most of you will try replacing reactive foods because of weight problems. That is certainly why I started it. You can expect to lose two pounds per week like clockwork, especially if you are comfortable without the lunch starch. (If this is not happening, look at the chapters on *It's Not Working* and *Support* in this book.) At this writing, I have eliminated reactive foods for three years and have lost the thirty pounds that I wanted to lose without gaining any back. I know that I will not eat reactive foods for the rest of my life. For almost everyone, this is an overwhelming thought. I keep myself from being overwhelmed by focusing on my food program only one day at a time. I am glad to have the weight problem under control now, but I am even more motivated to stay away from reactive foods for all of the reasons listed below.

> When serotonin wears off, the brain demands that it be restored, and a candy bar, for example, becomes irresistible. Will power is not an issue. The allure of the candy bar has the force of a powerful addiction.

**Cravings** An unhealthy drive to eat is created from the brain chemical reactions described in the next chapter. The net result of eating refined carbohydrates is that the level of a brain chemical, seratonin, rises in the brain.

Serotonin swings explain why we think about food when our mind should be on something else. Without reactive foods, these serotonin swings do not occur, so the brain is not demanding a new high, and the cravings are GONE. Also, because our bodies are very well nourished, we do not have the restless feeling that we still need something to eat. Our bodies are at peace.

Many weight specialists have recognized the relationship between refined carbohydrates, serotonin, and weight cycles. Few have realized that the relationship extends to all sugars and all flours, not just white refined sugar and flour. Cutting out just white sugar and flour leaves us helplessly in the grip of the serotonin cycle as we continue to use such substances as dextrose, maltodextrose, fructose, honey, molasses, sucrose, corn flour, and whole wheat flour.

**Inappropriate hunger pangs** In addition to cravings, the brain also signals demand for a fresh supply of serotonin through hunger pangs. Even when we've eaten all the food we need, if the brain is withdrawing from serotonin, it will send the signal to create hunger pangs. Without reactive foods, we no longer experience these hunger pangs unless it is truly time to refuel our body. **As long as we eat on time and eat everything on the list, hunger pangs are GONE.**

Paradoxically, this food plan has also worked for other eating disorders, such as anorexia and bulimia, where weight gain is desirable. This is because these eating disorders are also rooted in abnormal serotonin levels. Without the influence of refined carbohydrates, serotonin levels become normal along with appetite. Appropriate hunger is restored. For me, it is just as thrilling to witness an anoretic experience her first normal hunger, as it is to witness a compulsive eater lose the relentless cravings.

## EMOTIONAL BENEFITS

The scientific theories on why replacing reactive foods provides emotional benefits are fairly simple. There are four of them and they concern the serotonin and glucose cycle, polypeptides, malnutrition and allergies.

> Most people *start* eliminating reactive food to control weight, but they *stay* on the program because of the emotional benefits.

The serotonin cycle theory described above, and in the next chapter, argues that mood swings are related to the raising and lowering of serotonin levels in the brain and fluctuations in blood glucose levels. Lethargy and confusion can occur when high levels of serotonin and glucose are present, whereas depression, irritability, and anxiety occur when levels are low.

The second theory concerns the creation of polypeptides in the course of the digestion process. Polypeptides are partially digested foods that escape into the bloodstream and wreak havoc with the personality. Polypeptides are carried throughout the body, including the brain, and cause irritation and inflammation. Without the disruptive presence of, particularly, sweeteners, our blood stream is clear of polypeptides and we enjoy a stable personality.

The third theory on why replacing reactive foods helps emotional states relates to vitamin and mineral deficiencies. Doing away with reactive foods paves the way for truly complete nutrition. If mood swings are the result of malnutrition, eating a variety of whole foods will alleviate this problem. The use of mineral and vitamin supplements to cure even severe psychic disorders dates back to the 1930's. Today, the most sophisticated schizophrenia clinics emphasize diet and mineral and vitamin supplements in their treatment programs. Taking vitamin supplements helps me to keep a positive outlook. Release from fear, irritability, depression, and anxiety is very common among people who have replaced reactive foods with a complete regimen of whole foods.

The fourth reason is not completely understood, but is thoroughly documented. It relates to food allergies. Many people react to certain foods with dramatic mood swings. The most common allergies are to wheat, corn, sugar, coffee, chocolate, malt, barley, yeast, and dairy items. Allergies may develop in response to frequently eaten foods. However, another theory states that food allergies develop in the presence of sugar, as a reaction to the presence of polypeptides. In fact, addictions are the physiological manifestation of an allergic reaction. We keep wanting addictive foods, because even though they make us a little sick all of the time, withdrawal is worse in the short-term.[6]

No matter what the physiologic basis, the emotional results of eliminating reactive foods from the diet are very dramatic. In the chapter *Stories of Personal Triumph*, you will see that recovering victims of sugars and flours dwell on the release from emotional suffering more than any other benefit.

**Anxiety** A body that is constantly wondering about its next fix of serotonin is anxious about it. The brain worries, and this anxiety spills over into all parts of our lives. It is also possible that while we are eating a lot of refined carbohydrates, the rest of our nutritional needs are neglected. This undernourishment also makes the body anxious about its well-being.

Worrying is a very draining, destructive thought pattern. I always thought that I worried because something was wrong. Either there wasn't enough time or money, or someone wasn't doing their job, or I was about to be in trouble because I hadn't done my job well enough. It still stuns me today to think that worrying was the result of food, specifically sugars and flours, but also, in my case, caffeine and peanuts. Anxiety leads to many destructive behaviors, including unjustified criticism and temper tantrums. I am so grateful for the peace I now experience in its place.

One of the lovely ways that release from anxiety shows up is in the feeling that we have enough time for whatever we need to do. In my own case, I used to worry that projects would not be completed in time. I endured the constant stress of rushing to be on time for meetings. Today, I relax into the security of knowing that whatever happens is OK. I will have the strength and presence of mind to deal with it.

> I no longer live in the constant company of my long-time companion IDA - Irritability, Depression and Anxiety.

My anxiety about money has also vanished. I know that no matter how little money my family has, we are capable of making adjustments to fit within our means. My sense of well-being has improved so much that I know that material goods will not make me happy. I do not fear going without.

**Depression** can be experienced when the brain runs out of serotonin. We may still experience depression after replacing reactive foods, but it will be related to a real event, and not a chemical state. For the first time in my life, when I lie down at night to sleep, I sometimes think, "This has been a really nice day." I have often heard recovering friends say that their lives used to be bleak, but are now filled with optimism. During withdrawal from reactive foods, some people experience depression as a symptom. This will last only a matter of days.

---

[6]  William Vayda, *Mood Foods* (Berkeley: Ulysses Press, 1995), 113.

**Fear** Our fear is diminished as we experience a new sense of connection and balance. Because we are stable, we no longer have to wonder how we will feel. Our lives become more predictable. The loss of fear promotes more honest and open relationships with friends and family because we are no longer afraid of the consequences of our honesty. Without the chemically induced sensation of fear, we do not tend to seek ways to numb our feelings, including other substance and behavioral addictions and compulsions.

**Despair** At the bottom of the cycle is despair. I experienced despair over the loss of control over my body. I had despair over my appearance. But I also experienced a chemically induced despair when the high from the serotonin ended and dumped me off. We may experience despair after taking up whole foods, but it will come from real life, not chemicals.

The force of the despair that refined carbohydrates induces is hard to comprehend. At its most powerful, despair generates thoughts of suicide. Whenever I hear people talk about how worthless their lives are, I make a point of asking if they've noticed any particular food consumption patterns. Inevitably they reply that all they want to eat is some kind of high-sugar-content food such as ice cream. I try to offer them the hope that their suffering can be relieved and that there are lots of people who will support them while they withdraw from refined carbohydrates.

A word of caution here. Often, reintroduction of refined carbohydrates after a period of abstinence brings on more severe reactions than those that which were occurring before the person withdrew from the substances. Thoughts of suicide are no exception. If a person has eliminated refined carbohydrates because of suicidal thoughts, and then has reintroduced sugars and flours, he or she may need close monitoring until withdrawal has been completed.

**Shame** Shame is perhaps the most powerful of the negative emotions. It thrives in hiding. When we eat privately because we are too ashamed to show the world that we have no control, shame thrives. It binds us. After I replaced reactive foods, my sense of self-confidence was restored. I looked better, and because I talked about my problems with an accepting friend or support group, I overcame my shame to experience a new sense of joy, serenity, and freedom. In support groups, I have heard others talk about their problems and noted the absence of judgment from the group. We were all encouraged to do the same. When we experience acceptance regularly, shame loses its grip.

**Anger** After I eliminated refined carbohydrates, my anger, like other emotions, derived from real life events and not from a chemical cycle. I no longer have to be angry at myself for being unable to control myself. My anger does not spill out inappropriately at my friends and family. I do not need to use anger to shield myself from my fear and pain because I experience less fear and pain. Because I am a former rage-aholic and am also the daughter of a rage-aholic, the cessation of temper tantrum, yelling, screaming, and slamming doors is the most precious gift that I have received from eliminating refined carbohydrates.

**Mood Swings** Without the chemical cycle, my mood is more dependable. A calm enfolds me. My mood swings used to drive my husband crazy. One day I would be ready to file for divorce and the next I would think he was the greatest guy in the world. He is grateful that now I have a nice, steady respect for him.

About three weeks after I replaced reactive foods, my sister came for a visit. She had asked me not to try to talk her into replacing reactive foods. I had agreed. After she had been here for four days, she said that she had never seen me in a good mood for four days in a row in our whole lives together. Two days later, she started replacing reactive foods.

**Humiliation** occurs when we have eaten, but are still hungry. It occurs when we want to control our appetite and cannot. We experience increasing helplessness in the face of recurring

8

defeat as we try yet another diet. Because hunger and cravings disappear when we eliminate reactive foods, we regain our dignity and humiliation is banished.

**Spirit** Something absolutely wonderful happened to my spirit on this program. It used to be buried under fat and negative feelings. Now my spirit is free to guide me. I am conscious of walking in divine light so much of the time. I hope this happens to you too.

## PHYSICAL BENEFITS

The physical benefits of replacing reactive foods are explained by the same theories supporting the emotional benefits. Malnutrition causes our organs to perform poorly. Poorly digested foods (polypepetides) cause swelling wherever they lodge in the body. Allergic reactions abound. The overworked immune system fails. Replacing reactive foods solves these problems.

**Allergies** I am not talking now about food allergies *per se*. I am talking about airborne allergies such as hay fever. I am talking about sneezing, itchy, swollen eyes, and runny nose. I am talking about endless prescriptions and doctor visits. I am even talking about abnormally high sensitivity to insect bites and poison ivy. I live in a city that is world- famous for its nearly lethal combination of humidity, pollution, and pollen. Yet whole months go by without so much as a sneeze from my family. In fact, one of the ways I know that I have eaten a hidden reactive food is when my eyes itch. The release from respiratory allergies was a completely unexpected and enormous benefit of eliminating sugars and flours.

An interesting theory proposes that sugar is the cause of food allergies. When sugar is present in the system, it creates mineral imbalances that disrupt the enzyme production necessary for digestion. This in turn results in the release of the partially digested foods known as polypeptides into the bloodstream. When the immune system detects these partially digested foods, it manufactures "antibodies" to dispose of them. These "antibodies" then are left in the immune system to react inappropriately anytime they detect those foods in the bloodstream, whether or not they are properly digested.[7]

**Infections** In the first four years that my family lived in the city where we currently reside, we averaged eight respiratory infections requiring antibiotics per year. These affected ear, nose, throat, and lungs. In the first year on our new food program, we did not fill one prescription for antibiotics. William Philpott, food allergy expert, tells us why:

"... each time there exists an acute allergic reaction resulting from a nutritional deficiency, no matter what the specific reaction is, there simultaneously exists an inflammatory edema causing a local reduction in oxygen supply to tissues involved in the reaction. Once this has occurred, a favorable biological state exists for a flare-up of infection. Infectious microorganisms quickly multiply at staggering rates and become toxin-producing. This infectious toxicity causes the biochemical system to become even more nutritionally deficient, and the end result is a low level of immunological defense which invites even more infectious invasion, since proper levels of antibodies used in the fight against infections cannot be attained unless optimum nutrition is available; a more severe allergic sensitivity also results."[8]

In the face of repeated onslaughts of sugars and flours, the immune system just wears out. Researchers have actually observed that white blood cells are less active and effective in their job of consuming foreign bodies when they are in the presence of sugar.

---

[7]  Nancy Appleton, *Lick the Sugar Habit* (Garden City Park, N.Y.: Avery Publishing Group, 1996), 45-47.

[8]  Philpott and Kalita, *Brain Allergies*, 103.

So, it's not surprising that without these substances, in addition to reduced respiratory infections, I have noticed that all of my family's maladies repair themselves with astonishing speed - from common colds to cuts and insect bites. Everything heals more quickly.

> My family has dropped from eight respiratory infections per year to one or none.

If you are reading this book because you hope to reduce infections in your household, I would suggest that you pay particular attention to the story of Barbara's daughter in the chapter *Stories of Personal Triumph*. This two-year old was slated for sinus surgery before she got off refined carbohydrates. She was taking twelve drugs including steroids for asthma and infections. Her change in diet, plus affirmation work, has eliminated the need for surgery and brought her asthma under control. She is using only one drug at this writing.

**Headaches** My children's headaches are virtually gone. They used to come home from school with severe headaches every day. These are GONE. This phenomenon is mentioned often in the chapter *Stories of Personal Triumph*. It is not surprising, since headaches can be caused by swollen blood vessels.

I find it very ironic that some of the food manufacturers who put sweeteners in their products are diversifying into pharmaceuticals, particularly headache remedies. It is a little like a tobacco manufacturer diversifying into cancer care.

**Sinus pain** I used to have sinus pain that laid me out flat. It was such terrible pain that the simple motion of air back and forth over the sinus surface made me cry. It might last for two to three days at a time. No doctor could diagnose these pain attacks, much less cure them. I was reduced to taking steroids to control the pain, even though I knew that steroids could eventually damage my liver and shorten my life span.

Today, these pains are greatly diminished. They were so severe that release from this sinus pain alone would keep me away from reactive foods. On the day after Valentine's Day, after being on the program for about six weeks, my guard was down because I had gotten through the holiday without eating any sugars. Before I was fully aware of what I was doing, I ate a small chocolate peanut butter cup. Within twenty minutes, my sinuses were swollen, throbbing, and painful. That was the last time I knowingly ate sugar. Believe me, I don't miss it.

**Congestion** In the last year before we started this food program, my family filled sixty prescriptions for antihistamines, decongestants, steroids, nose sprays, and antibiotics related to respiratory distress. (Included in this number is the eight prescriptions for infections discussed above.) During the first year on our food program, we filled half that number. During the second year, the number dropped again to about fifteen.

> Over three years, our family of four has dropped from sixty prescriptions annually to six.

I no longer have constant congestion in my nose. My nasal passages are so clear that if I do get congestion, I know immediately that I have eaten something allergic. In addition to refined carbohydrates, dairy products also produce congestion.

In the worst allergy months, I do still get congestion. These months used to produce reactions so severe that drugs could not control them. Invariably, I would get sinus infections. In the first year after eliminating reactive foods, a routine antihistamine controlled the occasional symptoms, and no infections appeared. In the next year, when I started taking vitamin and mineral supplements and cut back on diary products, antihistamines became necessary only rarely.

**Coughing/Asthma** I had asthma as an adolescent that continued when I was an adult. My asthma improved when I got off sugars and flours, but it was not cured. A number of factors contributed to the improvement in my condition. To some degree, it came about because secretions from my nose were no longer dripping into my lungs. It was due also to the absence of irritating polypeptides in the bloodstream.

However, because my asthma did not improve as much as other respiratory problems, I finally had to conclude that I had other food allergies. About a year after removing sugars, flours, wheat, their accompanying food additives, and yeast from my diet, I had an allergy blood test performed. I found that I had a long list of other minor food allergies that, when combined, caused the asthma to flare up. As I began to avoid over-exposure to these foods, particularly citrus, my asthma improved again.

In addition, there was an emotional component: I was no longer in so much fear and anxiety. Fear and anxiety tend to spasm the little muscles that control the airways in the lungs, thus bringing on an asthma attack. At the end of the second year of eliminating refined carbohydrates, I felt like dark clouds had gathered around my heart. I was sure this mood was not from my food and I wondered if old memories were coming up. My therapist suggested exploring the problem with a new technique called Eye Movement Direction Reeducation. In three sessions, I broke through to old memories and in so-doing released the hold of fear that they had created around my lungs. I was literally free to breathe. My asthma took another leap forward to recovery.

My asthma may not go away completely as long as I live in a high-pollution, high-humidity, high pollen city. However, it is not debilitating and is easily controlled with an inhaler. This is a huge improvement.

**Low energy/fatigue** An increase in energy was perhaps the first effect I noticed from replacing reactive foods. It happened after only three days. It was completely unexpected. The processing of refined carbohydrates takes a lot of energy. It was as if I had been ingesting a toxin that my body tried to process in a way that minimized damage to my systems. The constant effort to bring my body back into balance consumed great resources. No more. My energy is steady through the day.

Have you ever tended a fire? After you get it started, all you have to do to keep it going at a nice steady heat is put another log on it. Now, imagine that you have only newspapers to burn. You must tend the fire constantly, and even so, the newspapers flare up hot and cool down quickly. Whole carbohydrates are like logs, refined carbohydrates like newspaper. When I stopped trying to run my body on refined carbohydrates, I started having a nice steady energy. I no longer had the late morning, late afternoon, and evening fatigues.

The other day, I was talking with my daughter's sports coach. The coach mentioned that she was ready to go on a no-sugar, no-flour, no-wheat program because her brother had lost his body fat and improved his swimming times dramatically on this food plan. I responded that we were doing a similar plan. Her face lit up and she said, "Oh, I just *knew* it, because your daughter is the only one with energy left at the end of a tournament!"

**Numbness** High levels of serotonin leave the brain in a kind of stupor. They create the sleepiness that we sometimes experience after a big meal. Without them, we emerge from a fog. Our thinking becomes sharper. We experience a clarity of thought that is startling.

A note on **diabetes, candida, high cholesterol, hypertension, and high blood pressure:** I have heard repeated, first-hand reports of sudden and dramatic improvements in these conditions after the elimination of sugars and flours. If you suffer from these ailments and are adopting this food plan, please confer with your health professional, as you may need frequent reductions in any medications you are taking. Replacing reactive foods helps **yeast** problems

> Many conditions improve within days after replacing reactive foods. So medications may need significant adjustment.

for three reasons: the replacement food contains no yeast; yeast organisms feed on sugars, which are also eliminated; resistance to all kinds of infections is improved. If you are already receiving medical advice on any of these issues, let your professional know that you are making changes in your diet.

In the case of high blood pressure, please have your blood pressure checked very frequently while you are withdrawing from refined carbohydrates. I have listened to several people relate instances where blood pressure dropped so quickly that medication levels became dangerously high in just a matter of a few days. Also, cholesterol seems to drop by about fifty points within the first month, so you may want to be retested.

If your health professional is not trained to use diet to treat physical, emotional, mental, and behavior problems, help him or her out by providing this book! Seriously, in any event, always let your anesthesiologist know that you are not eating sugars and flours. Like recovering alcoholics, we do not need as much medication as people who are still ingesting reactive foods. See the chapter *It's Not Working* for sources of physicians who will understand the impact of foods on your health.

The common wisdom in my support group is that we need about half of the dosage of medications that the general public takes. So, for example, I take only one aspirin. On a recent trip to Africa, I found that I needed only half of a digestive treatment. Antibiotics are tricky. Because our immune systems tend to function more effectively than those of the general population, I have wondered if we could get away with a smaller dose. I have not had the nerve to try this. However, when my daughter's tonsillitis recurred immediately after the first course of antibiotics, I realized that the normal dose of antibiotics, plus her abnormally strong immune system, had combined to wipe out all of her friendly bacteria, leaving her exposed to reinfection.

The solution to this overdose of antibiotics is to take acidophilus, or whatever your physician might suggest for replacing friendly bacteria after a round of antibiotics.

## MENTAL/BEHAVIORAL BENEFITS

The pesky polypeptides described in the next chapter as partially digested foods can lodge in the brain, cause swelling, and wreak havoc with thought patterns and behavior. Refined carbohydrates also cause increased levels of tryptophan which enter the brain and are converted to serotonin. At the high and low ends of serotonin levels, degrees of confusion and alertness alternate. Sugar has also been linked to irregular brain waves.

Eliminating refined carbohydrates means we stay in the middle of the serotonin range. Our brain waves are stable. Our moods are level and our behavior follows suit.

I have spent a great deal of time in the last several years in personal growth work. I sit in meetings on relationship issues several times per week. I have done therapy off and on for over ten years. I have gone back to heal childhood traumas in extremely intense sessions with a women's healing group and a therapist. I am very fortunate to have a vision of what my relationships should look like. I have known for years what kind of behavior I wanted for myself. But while strong stimulants and depressants from reactive foods were coursing through my bloodstream, I could not put this training into effect. My situation was like that of a drunk person who wants desperately to drive safely, but who is just too inebriated to perform well.

The mental and behavioral impact of refined carbohydrates and other substances, especially caffeine, is very broad:

**Confusion** It is very hard to think clearly when the brain is subjected to chemical swings. When refined carbohydrates are eliminated from the diet, decisions become easier, needs become clearer, and memory becomes sharper. Even test-taking skills improve. Communication becomes easier. Appointments are made and kept with routine ease.

In the early weeks of eliminating refined carbohydrates, it is easy to be confused as the brain seeks to reestablish its fix of serotonin. It's important to discuss decisions, especially food decisions, with someone else during withdrawal.

I had the sensation of a mental fog lifting when I stopped eating sugars, flours, and wheat. My brain became clear, like a TV screen coming into focus. It was such a shift that it was startling. I will never forget the look of pleasure and surprise on the face of a struggling graduate student as she told me about her new-found mental clarity. Her perception of her ability to do well in her graduate program soared. What grace!

Followers of the food plan suggested in this book also enjoy relief from confusion about what to eat. I used to be hungry but not sure about what I wanted to eat. Now, if I leave an item out of the plan and start to feel uneasy, I know exactly what to eat. I never have to wonder if I should have a vegetable or protein or starch. I know to eat whatever I have left out.

**Amends** I am not so afraid of asking for forgiveness for behavior that I regret. I can clear my problems routinely and promptly. Outbursts have become less frequent, so they stand out in my conscience. They hang like a little black cloud over me until I return to the person whom I have wronged and apologize. As a result of this routine, my family and friends find me more trustworthy. Knowing that I will have to make amends also gives me an incentive not to engage in unpleasant behavior in the first place.

I also make amends to myself when I have eaten something off the plan. I know that I have malnourished my body, or have caused an energy-draining reaction. I must apologize to myself for harming my body in this way. This self-apology reminds me that I am a precious person, deserving of the very best.

**Boundary Setting** I used to set limits on behavior around me but I did not have the consistent fortitude to maintain them. My children learned to treat my threats with skepticism. Because I grew up in a chaotic household, I really didn't know what reasonable boundaries were. As an adult, it frightened me to set boundaries because this was done in such a crazy fashion in my family of origin, so I felt crazy doing it for my own children.

Today, with the review of a professional therapist, I have set up expectations and consequences for my children. I enforce limits in a kind, consistent, loving fashion. I no longer need a boost of anger to assert a household rule. The people around me are more secure because they know what is OK and what will get them into trouble. My husband is also better able to set boundaries with clients and colleagues. His communication is more clear and firm, but without the irritability that used to accompany his requests.

**Chaos** Reactive foods stimulated our household into constant scrambling that created chaos. After eliminating sugars and flours, I noticed a big shift towards day-to-day calm that was gradual but ultimately miraculous. My friends who work this program in a family setting note the change in two particular areas: school projects and departures for outings. Prior to eliminating reactive foods, these tasks were completed with great stress. For school projects, books and materials always seemed to be missing. Accusations and recriminations would fly through the air with increasing intensity. Too much was left to do in too little time. Fear and anxiety added fuel to the fire. Inevitably someone would be in tears before the assignment was complete. Today, projects and preparations take place over time. We actually remember to get the supplies we need. Items are assembled and put in order without the yelling that seemed to be necessary in days past. We are available to help each other as needed. This is a huge change.

A similar shift has occurred in preparation for outings such as vacations and trips to the beach. Formerly, the jobs that needed to be done would overwhelm me. Just packing the cooler and a bag for the beach would send me into a dark mood. I would get a siege mentality as if the rest of my family was intent on undermining my efforts. Everyone would accuse everyone else of not doing enough. Shouts of "Hurry up! We're late!" would ricochet through the house with increasing vehemence. It was painful. After we got into the car, many miles would roll by before we could regain our composure.

These days, we all just stay with the preparations until we're ready to go. Everyone moves through collecting their gear and making food at a reasonable pace until everything is done. We've actually gotten into the car in a good humor!

**Compulsive Behavior** With the calm honesty that "being clean" brings, I am less tempted to act out in all areas of my life. I have had bouts of workaholism, for example, that are under better control. I have heard stories of other compulsive behavior, such as shopping and co-dependency, coming under control when reactive foods were eliminated. The shift is like coming through a hurricane on the open deck of a ship. We are in a panic, in high fear, even terror and pain, on the heaving deck that refined carbohydrates make of our lives. We seek out ways to alleviate the pain. But in a calm sea, we are steady and sure of ourselves. We no longer need to numb our pain by engaging in compulsive behavior, because we no longer experience our lives under chemically induced fear.

Control of my angry behavior would be another reason, just by itself, that I would stay away from reactive foods. My children trust me more. I am irritable less often. I physically feel that my face is more relaxed. My family can open up to me. My husband's eyes look bigger because the muscles around them are no longer so tight. Our relationships are warmer, more intimate. This is a very precious gift from replacing reactive foods.

**Attention Deficit** In this area, I would like to share the experience of my children. Before our family replaced reactive foods, they had a hard time sitting still to do their homework. Now, they are much calmer and the homework hours are much smoother. My children have never been diagnosed with attention deficit, but the improvement in their ability to concentrate makes me hope that you will suggest trying the elimination of refined carbohydrates to the parents of children who are taking medication for this condition.

**Hyperactivity** My children used to come home sometimes and literally bounce off the walls. They were absolutely unable to refrain from constantly pestering each other and me until I sent them to their rooms. In the weeks after completing withdrawal from sugars and flours, they still did this when they came home from a birthday party where they'd had cake, ice cream, and sweets. I knew right away from their behavior that they had been eating reactive foods.

I have read about the studies showing that sugar has no effect on the behavior of children. I believe that these studies are seriously flawed in that they did not use an amount of sugar anywhere close to the amount of sugar actually consumed by the average child. The studies also did not control all forms of refined carbohydrates, including all forms of sugars and flours.

One of the most famous of these studies gave children only one extra teaspoon of sugar in a sweet drink following lunch. Of course this is not enough to have an effect on children whose daily intake might be as much as a pound of refined carbohydrates. Also, since the teaspoon of sugar followed lunch, its absorption was slowed. It is very important to look carefully at who is funding the research before making up your own mind about how useful the study might be for your own children.

To find out how your children are affected by reactive foods, you can take them off common reactive foods, especially sugars and flours, for four to seven days. You could try this on a vacation, when their access to food is more under your control. Or follow the simple menus given in this book if your kids eat at home most of the time. Once they have been off the substances for four to seven days, you might be tempted to give them a big slug of sugar or flour

> In truth, you don't have to rely on anyone's study, opinion, or advice to decide if your children are affected by reactive foods. Test them yourself.

14

in isolation (i.e. without other food) to see how their behavior changes. I think you will be absolutely astonished to see them dissolve into restless, angry, or whiny creatures. No matter what you read, or what anyone tells you about the effects of sugars and flours on your children, you can rely on your own experience for guidance by following the project outlined above.

The task of keeping children away from refined carbohydrates is not as difficult as it may seem. See the chapter *Bringing Your Household on Board* for ideas on handling the transition. You may need to go through withdrawal yourself before trying this on your kids. You will have more energy, clarity of mind, and experience in identifying hidden sources of refined carbohydrates. Your chances of being able to withstand their protests will increase commensurately.

**Memory** My memory became sharper when I replaced reactive foods. This was certainly good for short-term functioning. However, I know now that I was attracted in part to the numbing effects of serotonin because I needed to blot out some old bad memories. I cannot adequately emphasize the need for support throughout withdrawal, particularly from refined carbohydrates, which affect brain chemistry so directly. Find a therapist, a clergy member, or other counselor who can at least go "on call" even if you don't need a regular appointment. Find an empathetic friend. Find a support group. See the chapter *Support* for more ideas.

**Critical Nature** With our lives under control, we can stop looking for reasons for why we are in such bad shape. We stop criticizing ourselves and others. We stop blaming our condition on others. Our criticism stops flowing into all areas of our lives. It becomes much easier to accept ourselves and others as we are. We tend to project more benign motivations onto others.

I grew up with criticism. Constant dissatisfaction with my school work, appearance, and friends left a painful spot on my psyche, a feeling of being inadequate. My children also got this treatment until they were in their early teens, when I eliminated refined carbohydrates from my

| |
|---|
| My very nature shifted from critical to approving. |

diet. I am deeply regretful that I was so critical of them. I apologize whenever they remember how rejecting I was. I don't carry guilt, because I simply didn't know what to do about it at the time. I had no idea that my food was making me irritable and critical.

Now, before I comment on their activity or appearance, I try to wait for them to ask me for my advice (unless they're doing something that is very clearly inappropriate). I praise specific acts and details of their work. I avoid over-stating their achievements so they don't carry the burden of thinking they have to measure up to unattainable standards. Some wounds will never heal, but I can go forward with a positive attitude towards my children.

My relationship with my husband followed a similar pattern. As a child, I had only heard my mother criticize my father, so I really didn't know any other way of relating. This conditioning, in combination with the chemical imbalances caused by food reactions, meant that my husband couldn't do anything right in my eyes. Communication between us was minimal, since I jumped on him for almost everything he said.

About three weeks after starting to replace reactive foods in my diet, I had the thought that my husband hadn't done anything annoying for quite a few days. Like a thunderbolt striking, I realized it wasn't so much that his behavior had changed, as that my perceptions had changed. I started to reevaluate my assessment of his routine behavior. For example, before I adopted the food plan, when he was reading in the den, I would think about how he never talked to me and feel lonely. The thoughts were painful and they made me mad. After starting the food plan, I found myself looking at him in the den one evening and thinking, "He's just reading! Nothing more and nothing less. Just reading. He's not ignoring me. He's not avoiding me. He doesn't dislike me. He's just sitting there reading!" Instead of experiencing anger, I felt peaceful. I felt lucky to have a husband who sat in the den and read instead of the zillion other less constructive things he might have been doing.  What a turnaround!

**Tension/Quarreling** Because I am feeling more steady, more uniformly good about myself, I don't tend to erupt into arguments with my friends and family.  Other people's behavior doesn't "push my buttons" the way it used to.  With two teenagers in the house, it is very easy to get pulled into their demands, accusations, manipulations, and general angst.  Whenever I can just acknowledge their emotions and not react with despair or anger, this is a triumph, and I thank the great good fortune that got me off reactive foods.

**Obsessing** Here, I am not just talking about obsessing about food, although that did go away.  I am talking about when the brain is on "spin cycle" for hours on end, thinking the same thoughts over and over again.  This obsessing has been greatly diminished.  My "stress reduction" techniques (meditation, prayer, exercising) are much more effective.

**Lethargy** Many people report that they are more active and productive when they give up the sugars, flours, and wheat.  Their businesses and jobs run better.  They have more "get up and go."  My sister and my husband, both of whom run their own businesses, turned in their best year in the twelve months after they eliminated reactive foods.  Before I eliminated reactive foods, I was so listless that I wondered if I could return to work when my children got into high school.  Now I *am* back at work!

## OTHER

Sugar has been linked to a wide variety of other diseases.  The best book that I have seen on this subject is *Lick the Sugar Habit* by Nancy Appleton, Ph.D.  Dr. Appleton's views are brilliantly supported by an extensive review of the research that has been conducted on the relationship between sugar and an astonishing range of illnesses.  In addition to the maladies listed above, she mentions problems with mineral balance, triglycerides, kidney damage, lipoproteins, chromium deficiency, copper deficiency, and calcium and magnesium absorption; cancer of the breasts, ovaries, prostate, rectum, colon, and gall bladder; eyesight, narrow blood vessels, acidic stomach, childhood adrenaline levels, skin wrinkles, gray hair, alcoholism, tooth decay, colitis, inflamed ulcers, arthritis, gallstones, kidney stones, heart disease, appendicitis, multiple sclerosis, hemorrhoids, varicose veins, periodontal disease, osteoporosis, saliva acidity, growth hormones, protein absorption, food allergies, toxemia during pregnancy, childhood eczema, the structure of DNA, cataracts, emphysema, free radical formation, enzymes' functioning, liver enlargement, fat in the liver, kidney enlargement, brittle tendons, migraines, hormonal imbalance, and blood clots.  Dr. Appleton names seventy-seven conditions that arise from the consumption of sugars and cites at lease one study to support the connection in each case.[9]

> At least seventy-seven illnesses are associated with sugar consumption.

Other very nice benefits of eliminating reactive foods are strong nails, clear skin, and shiny hair.  Dark circles under the eyes disappear.  My sister reported that she had grouted her entire bathroom with her fingernails without breaking a single one.  A teen-age friend saw her acne clear up.  My husband's canker sores and bleeding gums went away.  And so on and so on . . .

Each person's experience with recovery from refined carbohydrates is unique.  However, every person shares the surprise and joy of some highly valuable benefit.  In order of frequency, the top ten benefits are

---

[9]   Appleton, Nancy, Ph.D., *Lick the Sugar Habit*, 69-72.

# TOP TEN (+) MOST TREASURED BENEFITS

These are in order of frequency mentioned in conversations about recovery from refined carbohydrate usage. Weight loss appears fairly low on the list, not because it doesn't happen, but because other benefits are even more important to practitioners of refined carbohydrate elimination.

1. Relief from depression and restoration of optimism

2. Confidence and self-esteem

3. Mental clarity

4. Relief from cravings and obsessing

5. Spiritual development

6. Day to day peace and serenity

7. Relief from headaches and joint aches

8. Weight loss

9. Self-control

10. More energy

(11. Relief from respiratory congestion and infection)

*Notebook:*

## WHICH BENEFITS DO YOU WANT?

Dear Reader,
    Which of the benefits in this chapter could be valuable to you?

*Notebook:*

## CHRONICLE OF BENEFITS

Dear Reader,

As you notice that illnesses fade away, keep track of the relief on this page. Sometimes benefits appear very subtly. You may find yourself in a circumstance under which you would historically get a headache, or binge, or catch a cold, or get depressed, and so on. If the illness does not occur, write it down here.

# Chapter 3
## MEDICAL RESEARCH AND THEORY
**with Gilbert Manso, M.D.**

Everyone who knows anything about publishing health books says that nutrition recommendations must be backed up by medical theory and research. I myself wanted to know everything about the workings of refined carbohydrates when I started experiencing the benefits of eliminating them. But, frankly, many people's eyes glaze over when I start explaining the body's reactions. They say "I really don't care why the food plan works. I'm just real grateful that it does." If this is you, skip this chapter.

But if you can bear with it, aside from curiosity, there are two other good reasons to know the theory. When we reach the details of the plan for replacing refined carbohydrates with healthy, balanced foods, the guidelines of the plan will make more sense. Knowing the rationale may help you see them as useful instead of controlling or even capricious. Knowing the theory may provide answers to the internal voice that says it's not important to follow the rules. The second reason is that many healers find that guided imagery helps focus healing energy in the body. If you have a mental image of what's needed to heal your body, it could be useful in the meditations suggested in the last part of this book. So, here we go. Let's take the plunge.

The long lists of peer-reviewed, prestigiously published studies have been detailed elsewhere and need not be repeated here. For example, Dr. Appleton lists studies connecting sugar usage to 77 different diseases.[10] Dr. Null gives 226 studies that show how nutritional deficiencies and toxic food additives (off-shoots of refined carbohydrate addiction) create 18 mental illnesses.[11] Dr. Doris Rapp lists multiple books on how food creates problems with pregnancy (6), delinquency (2) candida (8), and hypoglycemia and diabetes (3). She references 45 titles on more general food and environmental illnesses. For educating psychologists, educators and physicians, there are 13 books and 81 articles about allergies and how they create illness.[12] One of the most meticulous evaluations of the research in carbohydrate sensitivity, particularly as it relates to alcoholism, is in *Potatoes, Not Prozac* by Dr. Kathleen DesMaisons. She cites 54 studies of impeccable pedigrees.[13]

> The research is astonishingly deep and varied.

The intention here is to lay out the biological reactions to sugars and flours in terms any non-scientific type can understand. The information is sliced two ways. First are biological processes and how refined carbohydrates shake them up. The second slice pulls from the descriptions of the processes and the organs to specifically explain the benefits laid out in the previous chapter.

The ingestion of refined carbohydrates upsets almost every function in the body. In this book, we are only taking a look at the functions which are directly devastated by these substances: (1) blood glucose stabilization, (2) neuropeptide and neurotransmitter function and formation, (3) hormone function and formation, (4) immune system responses, and (5) the elimination of toxins.

---

10 Appleton, Nancy Ph.D., *Lick the Sugar Habit*, 211-239.

11 Null, Gary Ph.D., *Nutrition and the Mind*, 231-286.

12 Rapp, Doris M.D., *Is This Your Child?*, 602-615.

13 Des Maisons, Kathleen, Ph.D., *Potatoes Not Prozac*, (New York, Simon and Schuster, 1998) 197-208.

## BLOOD GLUCOSE STABILIZATION

You will often see this process discussed in the literature as blood sugar stabilization. I vastly prefer the term blood glucose because both sugar and flour turn to glucose in the bloodstream and *any* sweetener, even artificial, has the potential to trigger the pancreas into an insulin release which lowers blood glucose levels. (Even dairy and fruit can produce this result.) Many carbohydrate addict books permit the use of whole wheat flour in their plans. The rationale for this is that whole wheat has fiber and is therefore absorbed more slowly than white flour. While this is true, the absorption is not slow enough to avoid triggering the pancreas into an insulin release. Research has shown that *all* refined carbohydrates trigger the pancreas.[14] In a pancreas which has been conditioned to frequent onslaughts of refined carbohydrates, even the suggestion of in-coming glucose is enough to set off an insulin release. Even a sweet smell can set off insulin releases, such as the case of my friend who developed cravings after installing a sweet scented air freshener in her home.

> Although it is absorbed more slowly than white flour, whole wheat flour can definitely destabilize glucose levels.

The sudden appearance, or *even the threat* of an appearance of a large slug of glucose in the blood stream sets off a chain reaction involving almost all bodily organs and lasts for as long as six hours. It goes like this:

## THE NINE STAGES OF GLUCOSE STABILIZATION

Stage 1.  A person puts refined carbohydrates into the mouth where enzymes start to convert them to glucose.

Stage 2.  When chewed food reaches the stomach, alkaline digestive enzymes complete the conversion of the refined carbohydrates to glucose.

Stage 3.  Glucose is released through the stomach walls in high levels. Some glucose travels through the bloodstream to the pancreas and brain and binds to receptors there.

Stage 4.  Glucose molecules binding to receptors on the outside of the pancreas signal the pancreas to release insulin.

Stage 5.  Insulin molecules bind to muscle and fat cells, instructing them to open up and receive the glucose. Insulin also sweeps small amino acids out of the blood stream. (Amino acids are broken down from ingested proteins. The liver recombines them into peptides. Much more later on peptides.)

Stage 6.  Within a few hours, the insulin has done its job, the glucose is gone from the blood stream, and the brain begins to starve. The brain's only fuel is the glucose present in the bloodstream. The brain does not have any means to store glucose.

Stage 7.  Neuropeptides from the brain travel to the adrenal gland with the message that the brain is starving. DO SOMETHING!

Stage 8.  The adrenal gland secrets adrenaline which binds to receptors on the liver and alerts it to release glycogen (glucose) stores to get glucose back into the bloodstream and feed the brain. This is an all-out panic life-threatening message, just like the flight-or-fight message our ancestors got when faced with a hungry saber-toothed tiger. Our heart pounds, blood is diverted from the digestive organs to the muscles, sweat glands are

---

14  Wurtman, Judith, *The Serotonin Solution*, (New York, Fawcett Columbine, 1996) 20.

activated and glucose pours into the bloodstream to feed muscles and brain. We feel fear and panic, but we survive.

Stage 9. Blood glucose levels stabilize and we get on with our lives until the next ingestion of refined carbohydrates.

This is quite a bit of activity over six hours involving many organs and chemical relations in the body. Let's list the major organs and chemicals involved in the front line response to refined carbohydrates: mouth, stomach, bloodstream (circulatory system), pancreas, brain, heart and liver for organs; insulin and adrenaline for chemicals.

Believe me, this is just the top layer of consequences of the ingestion of refined carbohydrates. Because blood glucose stabilization is a life and death matter and takes priority, many other processes are put on hold during stabilization. If stabilization were taking place infrequently this would not be a problem. But in the American diet with stabilization taking place constantly, there are a host of other consequences.

> Glucose stabilization takes priority so many other biological functions are abandoned with devastating consequences.

For the average American, blood glucose stabilization is happening about eight times per day. So the organs involved gradually wear out. The stomach becomes leaky, the pancreas trigger-happy, the brain foggy, the heart tired and the liver overwhelmed. Obesity, addictive eating, diabetes, hypoglycemia and heart disease are among the results.

The organs involved in recovery from blood glucose destabilization are like soldiers in the front lines of an endless civil war. They are worn down, shell shocked after years of intense combat. But unlike the soldiers, our organs have no troops to relieve them. So what happens as they progressively malfunction? Let's take a closer look at one of the earliest victims, the stomach.

## THE STOMACH

The stomach is assaulted in many ways by the regular ingestion of refined carbohydrates. Its walls are weakened at the same time that important tools are denied to it. It is the first organ to deal with carbohydrate overload and so it is the beginning of a cascade of other problems.

## THE ATTACK ON THE WALLS OF THE STOMACH AND INTESTINES

- When refined carbohydrates enter the system with no protein present, such as when a sugary soda is drunk, or when candy is eaten on an empty stomach, the digestive enzymes generated by the stomach do not have any proteins to adhere to. Instead, they adhere to and dissolve the walls of the stomach.

- Glucose is a favorite food of yeast organisms. "Friendly" bacteria is yeast's enemy. When lots of glucose is present in the intestinal tract and friendly bacteria have been wiped out due to repeated use of antibiotics, yeast flourishes. It eats through the walls of the stomach and intestines and releases toxic substances. Yeast is such a widespread problem in the North American continent that Dr. Hoffer wonders whether humans have domesticated yeast for bread and beer production, or whether it's the other way around and yeast has domesticated humans for food and shelter![15]

---

[15] Hoffer, Abram, M.D., *Hoffer's Laws of Natural Nutrition*, 35.

- The sugars and flours found in commercial baked good are often accompanied by hydrogenated fats instead of essential fats. Therefore, in the addictive quest for refined carbohydrates, hydrogenated fats are consumed at the expense of essential fatty acids. The lack of essential fatty acids makes the lining of the intestines more permeable.[16]

We begin to develop an image of the stomach under great duress. However, that is not the end of its problems.

## HOW THE STOMACH IS DEPRIVED OF DIGESTION TOOLS.

- We saw above that the stomach may have too much or too little sodium bicarbonate and other digestive enzymes from the pancreas because the pancreas is too sensitive and secreting too much or has become exhausted and is secreting too little.
- When life-threatening low blood glucose conditions are present, the stomach is deprived of the blood it needs to take delivery of oxygen, vitamins, minerals and directions from/to information substances. Stress is compounded by the presence of emotional conditions such as depression, anxiety, and anger, further depriving the stomach of blood.
- Because the consumption of refined carbohydrates is increasingly addictive, refined carbohydrates displace other needed nutritional elements, especially high fiber foods. Without fiber, it is difficult for the stomach and the intestines to push food along. Muscles in the walls of the digestive tract tire. Food sits in the system for longer periods allowing the build-up of unfriendly cells including bacteria, yeast and cancer.
- Proteins are also lacking from the diet because of displacement. The few proteins that are consumed are not well employed. Because the digestive system lacks adequate tools, it cannot break down proteins into a form that the body can use.[17] Partially digested proteins escape through leaky stomach walls into the bloodstream. These partially digested foods are called polypeptides (meaning peptides with over 200 strands of amino acids) and we will run into them again and again, especially as we discuss allergic reactions and the immune system.
- Because bicarbonate of soda is not available in the correct dose, the wrong alkaline/acid ratio may exist in the intestines which means that minerals cannot be absorbed and made available for conversion of amino acids into peptides.

One last point about the stomach concerns the brain chemical serotonin. Serotonin generation takes place in the stomach as well as the brain. This is presumably one of the many avenues of communication between stomach and brain. If the user is taking an antidepressant that works by inhibiting reabsorption of serotonin in the brain (Prozac for example), then the stomach will also be awash in too much serotonin.

So out of the long list of benefits described in the previous chapter, which can be explained by improvement to the condition of the digestive system? The first and most obvious is that stomachaches cease because stomach walls are no longer being irritated. Ulcers are repaired. Yeast infections are curtailed as organisms are deprived of their food and friendly bacteria grow again. Even conditions such as a spastic colon are relieved as adequate fiber makes the job of

---

[16] Smith, Lendon H., M.D. *Feed Your Body Right*. (New York, M. Evans and Company, Inc., 1994) 216.

[17] *Ibid*, 182.

pushing food easier. A very common comment from followers early in the plan is delight at relief from abdominal bloating as swelling from stalled food is eliminated. It is truly wondrous.

Secondary benefits accrue to a variety of conditions because yeast toxins and partially digested proteins (polypeptides) are no longer floating through the system wrecking havoc. In their place are properly digested proteins, vitamins and minerals available to make those critical peptides. Swelling and irritation of any body tissue is reduced, sending relief from conditions as diverse as allergies and arthritis.

So, blood glucose stabilization takes its toll on the stomach. As we discuss the other bodily processes most affected, we'll see how other organs fare.

## NEUROTRANSMITTERS AND NEUROPEPTIDES

The effect of refined carbohydrates on neurotransmitters and neuropeptides is huge. There is both immediate direct devastation as well as more subtle, lengthy deterioration. The two neurotransmitters most directly impacted are serotonin and beta endorphins. Excess serotonin is created a process involving insulin release while beta-endorphins are directly stimulated by sugar and flour consumption.

Serotonin is the brain chemical which determines whether we will be optimistic or depressed. It generates our ability to be creative and concentrate. Importantly for the recovering food addict, it drives our appetite.[18]

Beta-endorphins on the other hand are responsible for self-esteem, pain tolerance, compassion, and optimism. Their role in carbohydrate addiction is postulated as follows: people born with too few beta-endorphin receptors tend to try to elevate their mood by making a constant stream of beta-endorphins available to the receptors. People born with a low production of beta-endorphin will try to stimulate more production by eating refined carbohydrates. People born with too many receptors get such a great high from the receptors that the high becomes addictive.

The problem with these approaches to beta-endorphin management through refined carbohydrate consumption is that the brain will shut down receptors which are over-bombarded. This offers one possible explanation for why the disease of carbohydrate addiction is progressive. The sufferer is trying to make fewer receptors absorb beta endorphins to the same degree as a previously higher number of receptors. It may also offer an explanation for why carbohydrate addicts are created, not born, through overly-frequent consumption of refined carbohydrates. Too much stimulation of beta endorphin production through over consumption may cause receptors to shut down.[19]

People who eliminate refined carbohydrates feel better because in the absence of so much stimulation, the brain reopens receptors so the addict ends up getting more beta endorphin action in total. This may also explain why a relapse is so overwhelming. The stimulated beta endorphin production reaches more receptors and the addict gets really high.

> The correlation between refined carbohydrates and mental health is almost painfully simple.

---

[18] Des Maisons, Kathleen Ph.D., *Potatoes Not Prozac. 41.*
[19] *Ibid.* 63.

25

The bottom line is remarkable: when serotonin and beta-endorphin levels are stable and balanced, we have good mental health. When these chemicals are surging and falling, or stuck because of refined carbohydrate usage, mental illness results in some degree.

We would be remiss if we dealt only with the brain when discussing neuro-functions. 'Thinking' happens all over the body! Very recent research performed at the National Institute of Health shows that neuropeptides are manufactured and used throughout the body. (Neurotransmitters are made and used only in the brain.)[20] Both are made from amino acids which are broken down from proteins. The distinction between the brain and the body as the originators of thought and emotion is becoming blurred. Information and instructions are carried by neuropeptides made by the nervous system, immunopeptides made by the immune system, as well as hormones made by glands (the endocrine system). Collectively, they are dubbed 'information substances'.

Information substances are to cells as the central processing unit is to a computer system. Keyboard, monitor, printer, and modem are useless without the central processing unit. So are our tissues without information substances. A better analogy would be a CPU that could travel to peripheral equipment and also knew where and when the CPU was needed. Let's look at an example of how information substances, particularly neuropeptides, work. Then we'll be interested to find out where they come from.

Cholecystokinin (CCK) was one of the first peptides discovered in the early 1900's. It governs hunger and satiety. It is generated by nerves that line the stomach and intestines as well as the gall bladder. When food is moving through the digestive system, CCK is released. CCK has its own special receptors which are located in the brain, the gall bladder, and the spleen. The CCK which travels to the brain delivers the message that we are eating. CCK attaching to the gallbladder gives instructions to secrete digestive fluids to help process the food. CCK travels to the spleen which is the control center for the immune system. Apparently, the purpose of this trip is to tell the spleen not to attack the food which otherwise might look like a foreign invader. Without a good supply of CCK, it's easy to see how our digestive process would be in trouble.

Here's another example of how a neuropeptide connected to digestion works. In addition to CCK, many other neuropeptides are manufactured and received in the digestive tract. Some of these appear to generate and receive emotional information. Scientists have observed that excitement and anger increase spontaneous movement in the gut. On the other side of the same coin, "the movement of the gut as it digests food and excretes impurities can alter your emotional state. 'Dyspeptic' means grouchy and irritable, but it originally referred to having poor digestion."[21] The messages sent between gut and emotional centers in the nerve system are carried by the all-important peptides.

Now that we know what they do, I hope you're keen to find out how to make sure you have a bunch. Most neuropeptides are made from amino acids. The stomach breaks protein down into amino acids. Some neuropeptides are made from fatty acids derived from certain unsaturated fats. Many peptides are made by the liver which binds up individual amino acids into the peptides. Certain vitamins and minerals must be

Every organ and muscle of whatever nature depends on peptides for survival. Every shred of tissue depends on peptides to thrive. Every emotion depends on peptides to be felt. Every sensory contact depends to peptides to be perceived. It's easy to imagine that even spiritual messages depend on peptides to be heard.

---

[20]  Pert, Candace C. Ph.D., *Molecules of Emotion*. 25.
[21]  *Ibid.* 188.

present for the peptides to form. Also, the alkaline/acid balance of the body must be within a certain range for the peptides to be born. That is quite a list of required materials and conditions. Refined carbohydrates can adversely affect them all.

Here are two important examples of neurotransmitter formation. Tyrosine and tyramine are the two amino acids that precede the neurotransmitter epinephrine. The conversion of tyrosine and tyramine to epinephrine can only happen when the minerals magnesium and copper are present, as well as other amino acids and fatty acids, and the vitamins B3 and B6. As another example, tryptophan needs only B3, B6, and certain fatty acids to produce serotonin. Both epinephrine and serotonin have a huge effect on our sense of well-being. The more amino acids and the more vitamins and minerals, the better the neuropeptide production in terms of *both* quantity *and* response time. This has a direct impact on emotional health.[22]

So let's do our list again of the organs and chemicals involved in production of neuropeptides: stomach, liver, and nervous system are the body parts; vitamin and minerals as co-factors and as acidity regulators are the chemical elements. Because refined carbohydrates leach certain vitamins and minerals from our system for processing, and because proteins, good fats, vitamins, and minerals are displaced by compulsive consumption of refined carbohydrates, it is not surprising to see that refined carbohydrates negatively affect formation of neurotransmitters and neuropeptides. This is one of the many reasons that emotional disorders such as depression, anxiety, and psychosis improve when refined carbohydrates are removed from the diet.

## HORMONES

Hormones provide many of the same functions as peptides. They are another type of information substance. Many (but not all) start out as cholesterol and are converted by specific enzymes into specific hormones. Hormones are generated by the endocrine system which consists of glands such as the pancreas, adrenal, thyroid, and pituitary.

For our purposes, let's look at hormones generated by the pancreas and the adrenal gland specifically.

The pancreas not only secrets insulin, but also many other peptides which govern the assimilation and storage of nutrients, all carrying information about satiety and hunger. The pancreas is also instrumental in prompting the secretion of bicarbonate of soda which aids in digestion.

The poor pancreas is one of the saddest victims of repeated glucose deluges. It reminds me of the urban guerilla who is responsible for taking out snipers. He's been at his job for years and he is very tired. Yet, he knows that if he quits, innocent people will die. So he staggers on exhausted, trigger-happy, shooting at just about anything, until he collapses.

In Stage Four of the blood glucose stabilization process, we saw that the pancreas, through glucose receptors on its surface, learns of the presence of too much glucose in the bloodstream. It then secretes life-saving insulin to reduce the glucose levels back to normal. The glucose receptors eventually wear out, becoming either too sensitive or not sensitive enough. In the first case, hypoglycemia results as too much insulin is released and glucose levels become too low. In the second case, diabetes is the problem as not enough insulin releases and glucose levels are too high.

The burden on the pancreas is relieved immediately through the elimination of sugars and flours. The amount of glucose regulating that it is required to do drops and it can begin to repair

---

22  Smith, Lendon H., M.D. *Feed Your Body Right*, 181.

itself as well as begin to perform other tasks more adequately. Most prominent among these is the adequate secretion of bicarbonate of soda for the stomach.

Normalization of insulin and glucose levels has a huge impact on brain chemistry. This in turn heavily promotes weight normalization because low blood glucose levels materialize gradually instead of suddenly. We only experience low glucose levels if we are late for a meal. In this case, low glucose levels are the result of a slow depletion of the fuel we ate at the last meal. We have time to get a meal organized and eaten before low levels make us desperate. This scenario is as opposed to grabbing compulsively for whatever is at hand (almost always a refined carbohydrate) to head off a blood glucose crash which has been instigated by a rush of insulin. Avoiding low glucose panics is one of the reasons eating on time, every four to five hours, or more often if necessary, is a key element of recovery from refined carbohydrate addiction.

When insulin levels fall, weight loss can begin. Until insulin levels are lowered, no glycogen/fat stores will be released. This is the reason weight loss is primarily a refined carbohydrate issue and secondarily a fat consumption issue. Insulin's job is to take glucose out of the bloodstream. So, there is no way it would allow glucose back into the bloodstream while it is trying to clean up an inundation. It would be as nonsensical as a homeowner watering an already flooded flowerbed.

The reduction in insulin also means that a complete range of amino acids are left in the bloodstream. Remember from Step Five in our discussion of glucose stabilization that insulin sweeps out all small amino acids such as tyrosine, leaving the large amino acid tryptophan. It is believed that this is the body's mechanism for triggering the brain to send the signal to STOP EATING. The mechanism works like this: tryptophan enters the brain freely without competition from other amino acids. It converts to the appetite chemical serotonin. The brain senses the surge in serotonin and creates the sensation of satiety. We stop eating (hopefully) and the deluge of glucose into the bloodstream stops.

> Insulin generates surges and depressions in key brain chemicals such as serotonin, epinephrine, dopamine and beta-endorphin.

The process obviously has a tremendous impact on brain chemistry balance and stability. As we saw earlier, a variety of amino acids are turned into a variety of neuropeptides. When only tryptophan is left in the bloodstream, only serotonin is made in the brain. But when tyrosine is also present, it is converted into dopamine and BRAIN CHEMISTRY BALANCE can be achieved. Serotonin makes us feel calm while dopamine makes us feel alert. Serotonin alone will make us feel confused, dazed, foggy and sleepy. Dopamine alone will make us anxious and lower self-esteem. When they are both present, we have an exciting state of confidence combined with intelligent awareness. Our brains are literally resurrected from the serotonin fog.

An important conclusion must be drawn here. The objective of recovery from carbohydrate addiction is to prevent the pancreas from releasing insulin. If we can remember this fact, then making decisions about which foods to eat will make more sense. It will explain why some people can eat carbohydrate rich foods while others cannot. For one person in recovery, just giving up the refined carbohydrates will be enough. For someone else with a more sensitive pancreas, baked potatoes, cooked oatmeal, rice

> Not all pancreases are equally sensitive. So everyone need not give up exactly the same carbohydrates to recover from carbohydrate addiction.

cakes, and even dairy products and fruit will trigger an insulin release and therefore cannot be eaten at least until the pancreas is repaired.

Like the pancreas, the adrenal gland is responsible for a host of functions that must be set aside while it manages the immediate problems of blood glucose stabilization. The adrenal gland is responsible for secreting adrenaline during an external life-threatening situation such as an automobile accident or an internally generated life-threatening situation such as the final step in blood glucose stabilization. The adrenal gland gets low-glucose alert messages from a part of the brain known as the hypothalamus which has glucose receptors on its surface. The hypothalamus has nerve fibers that extend down into the nearby pituitary gland. These fibers secrete a neuropeptide called cortical releasing factor which stimulates the pituitary gland to secret a hormone called ACTH.

ACTH travels through the bloodstream to bind on receptors on the surface of the adrenal gland. Thereby, the orders to release adrenaline are safely delivered.[23] At this time, the adrenal also secrets a healing, anti-swelling hormone corticosterol, presumably in anticipation of the likelihood of a wound. (Corticosterol is only one of about fifty anti-inflammatory peptides. Others are generated by the immune system.) As we learned in the blood stabilizing process, adrenaline is the peptide which attaches to receptors on the liver and orders the release of glycogen stores.[24]

In the person who is eating refined carbohydrates many times per day, adrenaline and corticosterol levels may remain high throughout the day and possibly the night if night-eating is taking place to deal with low blood glucose. The sensation of anxiety and panic will therefore also be present.

Before we leave the adrenal gland, let me mention two other very important adrenal functions, i.e. the production of aldosterone and DHEA. Aldosterone prompts the reabsorption of sodium and thus its presence plays a role in high blood pressure.

DHEA "is the so-called 'mother hormone of the adrenal gland, an antidepressant that seems to be able to counter a lot of the allergic reactions that we see in people who are accumulating toxic insults as they age, decade after decade. . . . DHEA is kind of a baseline hormone. It feeds all the other systems, including the ones that regulate the sugar balance in the body. It can also serve as a precursor to the sex hormones...as well as to the electrolytes, the salt and water hormones of the adrenals. . . . It has an anti-cancer, anti-viral, and anti-depressive effect in animals."[25] DHEA deficiency becomes a problem in people whose adrenal gland has been worn out by constant attempts to stabilize blood glucose levels.

The picture of a system with hormones out of synch is not pretty. Insulin, adrenaline, and corticosterol surge through our bloodstream at the expense of other essential hormones. Exhausted glands include the pituitary, adrenal, and pancreas. And the list of substances that are out of balance include insulin, other emotion-laden peptides governing satiety and hunger, ACTH, adrenaline, corticosterol, DHEA and sex hormones. The conditions that result are fatigue, irritability, high blood pressure, cancer, and viral infections.

## IMMUNE RESPONSES

Laying the groundwork for understanding how the immune system wears out is very satisfying to me. My recurring, painful sinus infections, not to mention friends' sinus surgeries

---

[23] *Ibid*, 271.
[24] *Ibid*, 298.
[25] Null, Gary, Ph.D., *Nutrition and the Mind*, 111- 113.

were monstrous assaults to well-being which were only quelled through elimination of refined carbohydrates from the diet. So how is a strong immune system supposed to work?

Lymph nodes, bone marrow, and spleen are the main components of the immune system. When a foreign invader is detected by roving peptides, the immune system is notified and it manufactures white blood cells which literally engulf and devour the invader, or in some cases escort it off the property.

At some level, this is a never-ending process. Foreign invaders are at us constantly. Viruses and pollutants enter through orifices and breaks in the skin. Bacteria and pesticides are eaten with food. Yeast organisms, as well as other parasites, grow colonies inside the body. Little cancer tumors form constantly. Allergens such as dust, mold, and pollen are also handled by the immune system. White blood cells are generated at any sign of stress, even lifestyle stress. The immune system is normally a busy place, but for the carbohydrate addict the immune system is in overdrive most of the time and trying to function without the tools it needs. At some point, it begins to break down.

For the carbohydrate addict, an especially egregious condition develops whereby the immune system mistakenly perceives food as a foreign invader. This derives from 'leaky gut syndrome,' the condition that results from the constant attack on the stomach walls. Partially digested proteins known as polypeptides, leak through the walls of the stomach. These are very large peptides that the immune system recognizes as foreign invaders. They combine with immune cells to form circulating immune complexes. Their presence explains why some people always feel tired or get a headache after meals. They float through the blood stream lodging in various places, causing swelling which in turn causes pain and sets up membranes as attractive sites for infection. The immune system simply cannot handle the constant onslaught of polypeptides.

In many cases, food allergies result when the immune system becomes too sensitive to the presence of the polypeptides. These allergies can persist even when the food present in the blood stream has been properly digested. The antibodies manufactured by the immune system to handle polypeptides may explain another phenomenon of food allergies. When an allergic food is reintroduced after a number of days of abstinence, the reaction is often much worse than the reaction before the period of abstinence began. The theory for this is that the antibodies to that food have a chance to build up during abstinence and are available in force to react to the reintroduction. However, if the food is eliminated for a longer period, say two weeks, the antibodies dissipate and no reaction may be the result upon reintroduction. The person might even think that the allergy is gone and eat the food in quantity. Unfortunately, this may trigger antibodies to form anew and the person may regretfully re-experience allergic symptoms. Food rotation is one of the answers to avoiding illness from food allergies.

In addition to white blood cells, the immune system also secretes such useful entities as

> Many of the benefits of eliminating refined carbohydrates come from eliminating polypeptides, reducing swelling tendencies, and repairing the immune system to handle the incidental swellings that do occur. This is why conditions as diverse as bug bites and joint aches improve when refined carbohydrates are eliminated from the diet.

interferons (actually made by white blood cells). The immune system can also perform brain and gland functions such as producing the brain chemical endorphin and our old friend ACTH, normally produced by the pituitary gland.[26] The immune system has receptors for *every* brain chemical.

How do information substances work with the immune system? Interleuken-1 (IL-1) will be our example. It is made by macrophages. IL-1 is one of fifty or so peptides that regulate swelling. It causes fever, activates T-cells, induces sleep, and puts the body into a generally healing state of being. Like all immunopeptides, IL-1 has receptors throughout the brain.

Under extreme, prolonged invasions, white blood cells become inadequate to contain the problem. Reinforcements come from macrophages which may travel all the way from the bone marrow to the site of the invasion. Bone marrow macrophages have been found aiding in the counterattack on tobacco use, pollution, and food additives.[27] Dr. Pert found that these macrophages sometimes mutate to become the beginning of cancer. For our purposes here, the constant invaders are food additives, yeast infections, and partially digested foods in the bloodstream leaking from a weak stomach.

The immune system depends heavily on information substances to find out where problems are and how to fix them. The demands that carbohydrate users place on the immune system are tremendous. The restoration of the immune system plays a key role in many of the benefits we've seen to far. The important words for the immune system are white blood cells, circulatory system, bone marrow, lymph nodes, information substances, and macrophages. When we get to the end of this chapter, we will see how malfunctions in the immune system caused by refined carbohydrates play a role in recurring infections, auto-immune diseases, cancer, swelling, colds, allergies, and depression.

## TOXIC ACCUMULATIONS

This is an increasingly critical subject for industrialized nations as the level of pollutants in air, earth, and water increase. It is also affected by the level of additives in our foods. These can be either intentional additives such as preservatives, flavorings, and colors, or unintentional additives such as pesticides and fertilizers left on the skin of vegetables and fruits and ingested by animals into meat, fish, and dairy products. Also, yeast infections release toxins into the bloodstream. Our filtering processes must deal with all these toxins, plus partially digested foods leaking from our perforated stomachs. The immune system, the liver, and the skin all play important roles in filtering out toxins. Toxins can also exit the body through bowel movements, urine, sweat, and breath. Any of these organs and processes can become overwhelmed by their filtering responsibilities.

The liver has an especially tough time. Like the pancreas and adrenal gland, the liver neglects certain functions while it deals with problems arising from refined carbohydrates. It meets requests for glycogen and for filtering out additives, toxins, and polypeptides. Other essential functions like regulating cholesterol and making peptides are neglected. Heart disease stemming from unregulated cholesterol is one of the by-products of refined carbohydrate consumption.

Even when all is not well, our bodies perform heroics to the best of their abilities. Our bodies are miracles of functioning and endurance. It is positively amazing how long our organs can continue to protect us with inadequate nutrition. Resilience and stamina have been bred into us over the millennia. We have survived for good reason. Humans are tough critters. So how is

---

[26] Pert, Candace B., Ph.D. *Molecules of Emotion.* 161.
[27] *Ibid.* 171.

it that as a nation, we are so sick?  The next section holds the answers as we cut the information another way to see how benefits are generated by abstinence from refined carbohydrates.

# THE THEORY AND THE BENEFITS:
## UNITED AT LAST

The consequences of refined carbohydrate usage are so numerous and appear in so many parts of the body that I am reminded of the way that horrid aliens pop out of everywhere on the spaceships in the *Alien* movie series. The number of different ways that this disease renders its illnesses is almost frightening. The image of a giant parasite buried in its human host begins to appear as the lists of sources of disease grow longer and longer. When I mentioned this image to a recovering friend, she said she would see alien monsters popping from pop-overs from then on. So, let's take one more deep breath and move to take a final look at why recovery from eliminating sugars and flours is so powerful and so multidimensional.

## DEPRESSION, ANXIETY, ANGER, CONFUSION, AND LOW SELF-ESTEEM
## TURN TO
## OPTIMISM, CONFIDENCE, SERENITY, AND CLEAR MENTAL ACUITY

- Blood glucose levels are steady, ensuring a steady supply of glucose fuel to the brain. Mood swings disappear.
- Levels of adrenaline and corticosterone are reduced because the need to correct low blood glucose levels is reduced. The sensation of panic and thoughts of suicide are reduced. Life is no longer perceived to be dangerous, overwhelming, and bleak.
- Brain chemistry is balanced as all amino acids are present and available to be converted into a complete range of neuropeptides and neurotransmitters. Self-confidence and mental clarity are restored while depression and confusion are banished:

    - Adequate proteins, fats, vitamins and minerals are consumed.
    - The stomach is functioning to break down proteins and fats into usable amino acids and fatty acids.
    - A correct alkaline/acid ratio creates the environment for conversion of proteins to amino acids.
    - The absence of insulin keeps all amino acids available for conversion to a complete range of brain chemicals.
    - Serotonin levels stabilize because insulin and tryptophan levels stabilize.
    - Beta-endorphin function with the correct level of receptors.

- Readily available neuropeptides make emotional responses more appropriate.[28]
- Healthy peptide receptors receive messages more clearly.[29] Mental fog lifts.
- The stomach, pancreas, adrenal gland, and immune system are again able to manufacture information substances that regulate mood and emotion.[30] Emotional responses appropriately match stimuli from the environment.
- Polypeptides (partially digested proteins) leaking from the stomach are reduced. Irritability diminishes.

---

[28] Smith, Lendon H., M.D., *Feed Your Body Right*, 181.
[29] Pert, Candace, Ph.D., *Molecules of Emotion*, 298.
[30] *Ibid*, 183.

- Polypeptides, toxins, and food additives in the bloodstream no longer irritate brain tissues.
- Polypeptides which mimic the endorphins naturally produced during panic attacks are gone.[31]
- Polypeptides no longer trigger attacks from the immune system on brain proteins.

- Improved blood circulation brings more oxygen and information substances to the brain and instructions from the brain are more accurately carried to organs.
- The adrenal gland is freed up to produce the hormone DHEA which is thought to have anti-depressive effects.[32]
- The liver is freed up to produce the enzyme GGT. Low GGT levels correlate with high anxiety.[33]

## WEIGHT RETURNS TO NORMAL

- Insulin levels decline allowing stored glycogen to be released.
- Serotonin levels stabilize removing the urge to 'get high' on food. (For anorexics, abnormally high serotonin levels may drop, restoring normal appetite.) Hunger signals return to normal, instead of being induced by addictive needs.
- Blood glucose levels stabilize eliminating the need for panic eating to avoid crashes. Ceaseless cravings finally cease.
- Nutrition improves removing the urge to eat that would otherwise be caused by vitamin and mineral deficiencies.[34]
- Positive feelings prevail due to balanced brain chemistry, decreasing the inclination to numb painful feelings with food.
- Fear is reduced because adrenaline levels are reduced. Two fears are especially applicable: the fear that being thin will invite unwanted sexual attention, and the fear of offending people (Mom and other emotional providers) by refusing their offers of harmful foods.
- Fatigue is reduced because the adrenal gland is repaired, creating energy for exercise.
- Fat consumption is reduced because many high-fat foods such as commercial baked goods that also contain sugar and flour are no longer in the diet.[35]
- Messages about hunger and satiety carried by peptides and produced by the pancreas are restored. CCK peptides produced by the stomach are also more available and accurate. Appetite is tied to actual nutritional needs.

## CHRONIC INFECTIONS, ALLERGIES, AND SWELLINGS IMPROVE
### (Including Headaches, Joint Aches, Eczema, Sore Throats, Sinus Pain, and Congestion)

- The immune system ceases to be called upon constantly to attack partially digested foods, food additives, and yeast infections. Triggering of white blood cells production by the

---

[31] Null, Gary, Ph.D., *Nutrition and the Mind*, 26.

[32] *Ibid*, 3.

[33] Smith, Lendon H., M.D., *Feed Your Body Right*, 174.

[34] Hoffer, Abram, M.D., *Hoffer's Laws of Natural Nutrition*, 66.

[35] Crayhon, Robert, M.S., *Nutrition Made Simple*, 52.

thymus and lymph nodes due to chemically-induced stress in the brain is also reduced. The immune system can rest and rejuvenate.

- Because processed foods are not used, a broad range of common food ingredients and additives are no longer repeated throughout every day. Food allergic reactions are reduced because the number of frequently eaten foods is reduced. The immune system has less to do and can focus on more efficiently handling the allergens that still come along. This means removing allergens without noticeable reactions such as swollen, itchy eyes, asthma, sore throats, coughing, sneezing, congestion, etc.[36]

- The immune system immunopeptides are reinforced by an ample supply of amino acids. Immunopeptides, white blood cells, (macrophages, etc.) are readily manufactured as needed, including those that control swelling.

- Favorable conditions for infections are diminished, including swelling, absence of friendly bacteria, vitamin and mineral deficiencies, sluggish food in intestines, inhibited blood supply, and well-fed yeast organisms.

- Healthy peptides are available to occupy receptors on molecules. These receptors would otherwise be available for viruses, resulting in viral infections.[37] DHEA, an anti-viral hormone, is also more available.

- A healthy immune system is able to generate the appropriate immunopeptides to control swelling from allergic irritants and environmental toxins without causing an allergic reaction.[38]

## OTHER

- Heart disease is reduced because the heart is no longer stimulated by high adrenaline levels. Unhealthy fat consumption is reduced. and the blood supply to the heart is improved. High cholesterol is lowered because the liver is free to regulate cholesterol instead of spending its attention on releasing glycogen stores. Liver receptors are repaired so the liver can read cholesterol levels accurately and respond appropriately. Lower insulin levels also mean that tryglycerides and low density lipoproteins are broken down reducing arterial blocking.

- High blood pressure is controlled because the adrenal gland is free to manufacture aldosterone which promotes sodium reabsorption. The adrenal gland is free to do this because it no longer has to spend its energy controlling unstable blood glucose.

- Pre-menstrual syndrome is improved because adequate hormones in the right amounts are available from glands due to an improved supply of vitamins, minerals and essential fatty acids.

- The risk of cancer is reduced because the immune system is strong enough to kill emerging cancer tumors. The immune system is also not taxed by having to remove toxic food additives from the system. Adequate fiber is consumed to move waste effectively through the digestive system reducing chronic bacterial infestations which would attract macrophages with the potential to mutate into cancerous cells.[39]

- Fatigue is reduced as adrenal glands return to normal.[40]

---

[36] Hoffer, Abram, M.D., *Putting It All Together*, 8.

[37] Pert, Candace B., Ph.D., *Molecules of Emotion*, 190.

[38] Rapp, Doris, M.D., *Is This Your Child?*, 314.

[39] Pert, Candace B., Ph.D., *Molecules of Emotion*, 171.

[40] Crayhon, Robert, M.S., *Nutrition Made Simple*, 40.

- Acne is reduced and the skin glows because it is no longer processing toxins. The liver is clear so toxins are cleaned through it rather than the skin.[41]
- Stomachaches and bloating go away because the stomach is no longer irritated.
- Nails and hair are healthier because they are receiving adequate proteins.[42]
- Snoring is diminished because the adenoids, located in the back of the nose, are no longer swollen.[43]
- Almost every chemical ratio is restored in the body. See *Lick the Sugar Habit*[44] for detailed discussions of how this clears up dozens of other conditions.

OK, so by now you have the picture of the theory and how its related to the benefits. However, if you skipped reading this chapter then here are the . . .

---

[41] *Ibid*, 174.

[42] *Ibid*, 176.

[43] Rapp, Doris, M.D., *Is this Your Child?*, 49.

[44] Appleton, Nancy, *Lick the Sugar Habit*.

# TOP TEN POINTS TO KNOW ABOUT THE RESEARCH

1. Consumption of all sugars and flours, i.e. refined carbohydrates produces elevated insulin levels in the bloodstream.

2. Refined carbohydrates produce unstable brain chemicals, including beta-endorphins, serotonin, epinephrine, and dopamine which when combined with unstable blood glucose create emotional disorders such as depression, anxiety, and irritability.

3. Refined carbohydrates create a leaky gut so partially digested proteins escape into the bloodstream. This provokes an immune response and wears out the immune system so allergies and infections run out of control.

4. Refined carbohydrates interfere with the formation of amino acids, the building blocks of molecules.

5. Repeated glucose stabilization directly wears out the pancreas, stomach, pituitary gland, adrenal gland, and liver. These organs and glands have many other functions which cannot be carried out such as swelling control, hormone regulation, filtering, cholesterol regulation, neurotransmitter formation, and peptide formation.

6. High insulin levels interfere with the breakdown of triglycerides and low density lipoproteins which clog heart arteries.

7. Unstable glucose levels combined with unstable brain chemicals create powerful addictive forces which may encourage the formation of other compulsive habits. Sugar addiction in children may lead to alcohol, nicotine, and drug usage in teenagers and adults.

8. The need for high blood pressure and diabetes medications may drop rapidly after eliminating sugars and flours from the diet.

9. Refined carbohydrates leech vitamins and minerals from the body for processing leaving critical chemical ratios out of balance and creating vitamin and mineral deficiencies.

10. Carbohydrates which are unrefined will not trigger an insulin release when eaten with a protein.

# Chapter 4
## PATTERNS OF CONSUMPTION AND CONSEQUENCE

The per capita increase in American consumption of refined carbohydrates has been rising steadily and relentlessly over the last twenty years. Total caloric consumption has been mounting and the percentage of refined carbohydrates within that total has been growing. We are consuming more specialty breads, more breakfast cereals, more pasta, more candy, and more sweetened drinks. Potatoes in the form of French fries and chips are included in these consumption trends because they are cooked at such high temperatures that the starch in them turns into a form close to glucose. Consequently, they can have the same effect on many people that flours and sugars do.

**While consumers were focused on fats, they were blind-sided by the increase in consumption of refined carbohydrates. Today, we Americans consume about**

## A POUND PER DAY OF REFINED CARBOHYDRATES!

U.S. Consumption of Sugars and Flours

| (Pounds Per Capita) | 1970 | 1994 |
|---|---|---|
| Cane and beet sugar, corn sweeteners | 121 | 146 |
| Syrups and honey | 2 | 1 |
| White and whole wheat flour | 104 | 130 |
| Durum flour | 7 | 14 |
| Rye flour | 1 | 1 |
| Corn Flour, Meal, and Starch | 9 | 20 |
| TOTAL SUGARS AND FLOURS | 244 | 312 |
| French Fries | 13 | 29 |
| Potato Chips and Shoestrings | 4 | 4 |
| TOTAL SUGARS, FLOURS AND "REFINED POTATOES"** | 261 | 345 |

Source: Economic Research Service/United States Department of Agriculture

*The decrease in consumption of cane and beet sugars is the result of a shift to corn sugars, which are cheaper and more stable.** Total consumption does not include oat and barley flour. Also not included is alcohol consumption of 21 gallons in 1970 and 25 gallons per capita in 1994. All amounts are based on deliveries to stores and restaurants. They therefore include waste and spoilage that occur after that point.

The United States Department of Agriculture attributes the increase in consumption of flour to appreciation for variety breads, fast-food sales of hamburger buns, and in-store bakeries. It also notes that breakfast cereal consumption has grown in spite of sharp price increases because of aggressive advertising and health claims by food processors and because of the convenience of ready-to-eat breakfast cereals. Consumption of sugars in sodas has benefited from heavy advertising. Consider just the following three statistics:

| Annual Per Capita Consumption | 1970 | 1994 | % increase |
|---|---|---|---|
| Ready-to-eat breakfast cereals | 9 lbs. | 16 lbs. | 77% |
| Pasta flour | 7 lbs. | 14 lbs. | 100% |
| Regular (non-diet) soft drinks | 235 cans | 460 cans | 95% |

It's easy to understand why half of our country is overweight. Given that refined carbohydrates stimulate hunger and cravings, it is not surprising that our country is in constant grazing mode. The trends may reflect the use of heavy advertising by soft drink companies, food manufacturers, and fast-food restaurants. However, I believe that the trends also reflect the progressive nature of the disease of refined-carbohydrate addiction. It takes more and more of the substances to produce the same effect on brain chemicals, in a manner similar to that of addictive drugs.

The USDA also tells us that older Americans buy the most bread and cereal products. I believe this also can be attributed to the progressive nature of refined-carbohydrate craving.

| AGE | ANNUAL EXPENDITURE ON BREAD AND CEREAL PRODUCTS | % INCREASE OVER THE PRIOR AGE |
|---|---|---|
| 25-34 | $140 | |
| 35-44 | 154 | 10% |
| 45-54 | 174 | 13% |
| 55-64 | 200 | 15% |

Does the progressive nature of the disease of refined-carbohydrate addiction explain why older people in our society suffer from so many diseases? I don't know. However, if you know senior citizens who are depressed, suffer from arthritis, or are unusually fatigued, they may benefit from knowing about the effects of refined carbohydrates. Please tell them.

How did this trend get started? Perhaps it was a combination of several factors, one being the need for convenience foods to meet the needs of dual-career families. Convenience foods are loaded with refined carbohydrates at the expense of the proteins that balance the creation of serotonin. Advertising convinced us that convenience foods were easier and quicker to prepare than homemade foods. I don't think this is true because homemade food is very quick to prepare. People rely on convenience foods because the art of simple, quick preparation of fresh foods is not promoted through the media. This book contains dozens of recipes that can be put together in less time than it takes to heat a TV dinner.

I think that lifestyle stress made the numbing effects of refined-carbohydrate consumption more attractive. Also, availability has mushroomed. There are bagel shops, pizzerias, bakeries, sandwich (mostly bread) shops, and yogurt or ice cream shops on almost every corner.

Within the context of America's total diet, refined carbohydrates play a very large role. In combination with fats, they make up about half of the calories we eat. In contrast to the plan advocated in this book, fruits, vegetables, and proteins represent only half of the American caloric intake. The plan advocated in this book uses very little fat and no refined carbohydrates.

Consider the following breakdown of calories consumed daily by the average American versus those consumed by a practitioner of the ideas advocated in this book:

|  | CALORIES CONSUMED BY THE AVERAGE AMERICAN | NO SUGARS AND FLOURS PLAN[45] |
|---|---|---|
| Refined carbohydrates | 1,410 calories | 0 calories |
| Whole carbohydrates | 110 | 400 |
| Fats | 700 | 110 |
| Fruits and vegetables | 370 | 320 |
| Meat, poultry, fish, eggs dairy and legumes | 1110 | 780 |
| TOTAL | 3,700 calories | 1,600 calories |

When I did this analysis, I was surprised to find that alongside the fats and refined carbohydrates, the average American consumes enough fruits, vegetables, and proteins to meet basic daily requirements. Of course we know that the presence of refined carbohydrates so unbalances our body chemistry that we cannot use the minerals available to us in otherwise nourishing foods. Nonetheless, it is reassuring to know that there are adequate supplies of the whole foods that we need in the American food supply.

Now for the grand finale of *Part I Situation Assessment*: The consequences of this incredible consumption of refined carbohydrates. We will first consider the opinions of leading experts and then take a look at cause-of-death statistics.

- 33% of Americans had allergies in 1985. Clinical ecologists estimate that this number is low. 75% may be more accurate.[46]
- 80% of juvenile delinquents appear to be hypoglycemic and 90% have food and environmental allergies.[47]
- At least half of the population has blood sugar instability.[48]
- 40 million Americans suffer from some kind of mental illness.[49]
- 30% of the population has candida.[50]
- Perhaps close to a majority of the population has relative hypoglycemia. 100% of alcoholics have hypoglycemia. 66% of neurotics and depressed people have hypoglycemia.[51]

---

[45] Calories shown are at a weight-loss level. Weight maintenance levels are at approximately 2,100 calories per day. For information on maintenance levels, see *Food Addiction: The Body Knows* by Kay Sheppard, (Deerfield Beach, Fla.:1993) Health Communications, Inc.,101.

[46] Rapp, Doris, M.D., Is This Your Child? 33.

[47] *Ibid.* 412.

[48] Null, Gary, Ph.D., *Nutrition and the Mind.* 146.

[49] *Ibid.* vii.

[50] *Ibid.* 92.

[51] Hoffer, Abram, M.D., *Putting It All Together: The New Orthomolecular Medicine.* 20.

- 33% of Americans are obese (more than 20% overweight) and 75% of Americans are heavier than optimal.[52]
- 22% of children and adolescents are overweight. The percentage is increasing at the rate of about one point per year.[53]

Given this evidence of the widespread nature of the damage caused by sugars and flours, the following leading causes-of-death statistics[54] and their link to refined carbohydrates should come as no surprise. Obviously refined carbohydrates are not the only contributing factor to these diseases, but it is interesting to see that they play a significant role in every one.

Remember that the primary organs regulating glucose are the pancreas, the brain, the adrenal gland, and the liver. The chemicals released in the process are insulin and adrenaline. The restabilization of glucose may take place as many as eight times per day.

## REFINED CARBOHYDRATES IN THE TOP TEN CAUSES OF DEATH

1. **Heart Disease**: Arteries are clogged from triglycerides because insulin interferes with their breakdown. The heart wears out from stimulation by constantly high levels of adrenaline.
2. **Cancer**: The immune system is worn out from removing debris from refined carbohydrate usage and from fighting infections, both bacteria and yeast.
3. **Stroke**: High blood pressure is aggravated by the fact that the adrenal gland is not available to regulate sodium (salt). The adrenal gland is diverted into glucose balancing functions.
4. **Chronic Obstructive Pulmonary Disease (Emphysema)**: Food may play a role insofar as the pain of food chaos creates a need for numbing from other substances such as nicotine. A worn out immune system cannot fight the ravages of tobacco use.
5. **Accidents**: Mental fogginess and fatigue create poor judgement and lack of attention. Rage is an allergic reaction that can be triggered by some foods and can lead to inappropriate actions.
6. **Pneumonia/Influenza**: The corrupt immune system cannot handle infection. Tired glands cannot generate the "information substances" necessary to regulate swelling and fluid accumulation.
7. **Diabetes**: The pancreas is worn out from regulating fluctuating glucose levels. The pancreas can no longer generate adequate or accurate amounts of insulin.
8. **HIV/AIDS**: The condition is made worse by a worn-out immune system.
9. **Suicide**: Depression is caused by poor neuropeptide and neurotransmitter formation and reception, fluctuating serotonin levels, fatigued adrenal gland, inappropriate immune responses, irritating polypeptides, and fluctuating glucose levels.
10. **Chronic Liver Disease and Cirrhosis**: The liver wears out from constantly stabilizing glucose levels. The liver is also clogged from filtering the debris (polypeptides and toxins) left by heavy refined carbohydrate usage.

---

[52]  Fumento, Michael. *Land of the Fat*. Wall Street Journal. September 29, 1997.

[53]  Canedy, Dana. *Letting Out the Seams for Chubby Children*. The New York Times. May 30, 1997. B1.

[54]  National Center for Health Statistics, Center for Disease Control. *Deaths/Mortality*. Monthly Vital Statistics Report, Vol. 46, No. 1 Updated 9/29/98.

## SITUATION ASSESSMENT

So, what is the situation? Well, it's simple. And it's scary. No horror movie script ever came close to imagining the reality of destruction of these proportions. You might say it goes like this:

- Substances called 'sugars and flours' look benign, even fun, but are actually quite devastating.
- They're consumed by the most powerful nations in the world at lethal rates.
- Very few health professionals are trained to diagnose the many illnesses that sugars and flours create.
- Even fewer health professionals know how to help people escape the addictive powers of sugars and flours to achieve huge life-changing benefits.

*UNTIL NOW . . .*

# PART II

## WHAT CAN I DO ABOUT IT?

# Chapter 5
## THE DAILY PLAN[55]

| Breakfast | Lunch | Dinner | Bedtime |
|---|---|---|---|
| Protein | Protein | Protein | Half Protein |
| Half Protein | Whole Starch | Whole Starch | Fruit |
| Whole Starch | Raw vegetable | Raw vegetable | |
| Fruit | Cooked/raw vegetable | Cooked/raw vegetable | |

The system of eating outlined above was adapted from a plan developed by Kay Sheppard, LMHC, CEDS, for an eating disorders clinic in Florida. The plan was developed to help people recover from eating disorders rising from carbohydrate addiction. As such it is not a weight loss diet; it is a lifetime means of keeping carbohydrate addiction and other food addictions in remission by abstaining from refined carbohydrates, just like alcoholics keep alcoholism in remission by abstaining from alcohol. Kay Sheppard noticed that wheat triggered cravings so it is also part of abstinence. I have modified the plan to take into account food allergy concerns, especially concerns about dairy usage. Thanks to the allergists such as Dr. Doris Rapp and Dr. Theron Randolph, and the nutritionist Dr. Nancy Appleton, I now understand why Kay Sheppard's plan heals so many behavioral, emotional, and physical problems in addition to keeping eating disorders in remission.

The concept is extremely simple: eat fourteen glorious, highly nutritious items per day. The items are simple: protein, vegetables, starch, and fruit. The system eliminates all the reactive substances of sugars, flours, wheat, and *de facto* most food additives. In the ensuing physical calm, the structure of the food plan makes identifying additional food allergies easier.

> Initially, making the plan work seemed difficult to me because I wanted to learn everything at once. I also wanted to know the parameters of what I could get away with. Gradually, I gave up focusing on the parameters settled on the four core food categories and came to appreciate how simple this system is.

The substances specifically excluded are more complicated. (See the chapter *Reactive Foods* for a complete list of the names for sugars and flours.) Refined carbohydrates are all forms of sugars and flours, including honey and alcohol. Sugars and flours appear in almost all processed foods, so *de facto,* processed foods are rarely OK to use. Therefore, the food additives that are used in processed foods are automatically eliminated. For the same reason, two other troublesome substances, chocolate and yeast, are also automatically removed from our diet, since they almost always appear with sugars or flour. So any allergic reaction to food additives, chocolate, or yeast which we may unknowingly be experiencing will be alleviated.

Of the other commonly allergic foods, allergists recommend testing for them by eliminating them from the diet for four days (but no more than 14 days), then reintroducing them and monitoring the results. Effects may appear in the form of a mood, behavior, or physical change

---

55  Kay Sheppard, LMHC, CEDS. *Food Addiction: The Body Knows.* 92.

and can vary vastly from person to person. Some of the many kinds of food reactions are listed in the chapter *Falling Off the Wagon*.

Wheat as a reactive food belongs in a category all by itself. Americans consumed an average of 195 pounds of wheat per person in 1994. According to the food allergists, this makes wheat the king of frequently eaten foods. This means that we all must ask ourselves if we are allergic to wheat. Almost every big wheat-eater who eliminates wheat from his or her diet for four days has a reaction when it is reintroduced. Reactions range from a feeling of being overwhelmed to a headache to cravings. Wheat is definitely eliminated from all recipes and food lists in this book.

Dairy is next on the list of common allergic foods. As Kay Sheppard initially conceived the food plan, it allowed two servings of dairy products per day for breakfast and bedtime snack. In addition, dairy could also be used as any of the protein servings at breakfast, lunch, or dinner. She has since rescinded this guideline because dairy does not contain enough protein to counter the effects of carbohydrates. Kay Sheppard clearly encourages using a variety of foods and permits a half portion of protein to be used in place of dairy. So, do not make the mistake of overusing dairy in this food plan.

Food allergists and clinical ecologist object to overuse of diary on many grounds: (1) dairy is already a very common allergic food, (2) any food eaten frequently is a good candidate to become a new food allergy, (3) dairy products contain the pesticides, herbicides, and fertilizers spread on the grass that cows eat, (4) diary products contain hormones that are suspect in some forms of cancers, (5) fat particles are altered during the homogenizing process, making them more difficult for the body to use, and (6) dairy products trigger extra secretions of acids in the stomach.

Dr. Abram Hoffer is an expert in dairy reactions. Dr. Hoffer himself has a fixed dairy allergy meaning it will not go away even if he eliminates dairy for months. He observes that between 25% and 40% of his patients have dairy allergies.[56] As many as 7.5% of babies may have dairy allergies, particularly those babies who are started early on milk. Dr.

> Right along with sugars, flours, and wheat, dairy must be examined as a potential source of food-related illness.

Rapp states, "The food that causes more chronic and acute illness in all of society to my mind, is, unquestionably, milk and dairy products."[57] Of additional concern for us here is the fact that a food allergy can trigger a hypoglycemic attack. Dr. Rapp feels that since any organ can be the object of an allergic attack, why not the pancreas in the form of an inappropriate insulin release? Dr. Lendon Smith backs her up, "We know that if people are sensitive to dairy products, for instance, the blood sugar will rise and get up to maybe 180 mg after eating a diary food and then drop precipitously down to 60 mg. Then they crave these same dairy products again. They go up and down, up and down."[58] So we see that diary can cause the same addictive response that refined carbohydrates do.

The category I have labeled as 'Half Protein' was originally conceived by Kay Sheppard as a dairy category. Kay Sheppard herself no longer uses dairy. She replaces dairy with a cup of soy milk or 2 oz of protein. So, I renamed her dairy category 'Half Protein'. It actually simplifies the food plan, making breakfast three items (one and one half protein, fruit, and starch) instead of four (dairy, protein, fruit, and starch).

---

[56] Hoffer, Abram, M.D. *Hoffer's Laws of Natural Nutrition.* 46.
[57] Null, Gary, Ph.D. *Nutrition and the Mind.* 216.
[58] *Ibid.* 224.

Some readers may raise questions about the amount of protein in the plan. Kay Sheppard's levels are the highest I have seen in mainstream diet literature, but they are comparable to other plans that address carbohydrate addiction: six ounces at breakfast, four each at lunch and dinner, and two at bedtime. (For men the amounts are seven, five and two, respectively.) However, for the recovering carbohydrate addict, protein is essential to balance the absorption of carbohydrates. You may recall that protein provides a range of amino acids as precursors to a variety of brain chemicals. As such, protein is the basis for stable brain chemistry. Starches, on the other hand are capable of triggering an insulin release which suppresses all amino acids except tryptophan, thus allowing only tryptophan to enter the brain and be converted to serotonin. The resulting serotonin "high" is what every active carbohydrate addict seeks. This "high" is what every recovering addict tries to avoid lest the inevitable accompanying "low" trigger relapse.

Most concerns about protein levels revolve around the development of protein allergies. Indeed, beef, pork, dairy, soy, and eggs appear frequently on food allergy lists. Dr. Hoffer throws up his hands on this issue declaring that everyone should eat the amount that makes them feel best.[59] Robert Crayhon feels that for recovery from hypoglycemia, protein should be eaten in small quantities throughout the day.[60] He also points out that different cultures evolved and adapted to the availability of food. For example, the Chinese get a lot of mileage out of a small amount of protein and would not fare well on a high-protein diet.[61]

For the purpose of this book, the most important point about protein to bear in mind is that the book's intention is to help a specific readership recover from refined carbohydrate addiction/allergy and the accompanying hypoglycemia. The recovering carbohydrate addict/allergic often has an underlying tendency to reduce protein portions in favor of increasing starches in order to get the serotonin high. Kay

> Protein is the key to off-setting carbohydrate absorption.

Sheppard's plan is based on extensive observations made under clinical conditions. Many followers of her plan in 12-step recovery groups such as Food Addicts Anonymous and Food Addicts in Recovery are in fact very successfully in remission from carbohydrate induced diseases even while they eat the amounts of carbohydrate advocated in the plan.

The most successful recovering carbohydrate addicts religiously eat the amount of protein specified in the plan. Wise recovering carbohydrate addicts are suspicious of thoughts of reducing protein amounts. Their experience tells them that such thoughts may be the result of the ever-present, relentless internal addict trying another devious route to relapse. Bottom line: Protein sources should be carefully varied to avoid developing protein allergies. Kay Sheppard's protein amounts from all observations support recovery from refined carbohydrate addiction/allergy.

Fruit is another food that some addicts can use to get high. Although experts tend to agree that the sugar in fruit (fructose) is handled differently than sucrose (processed by the liver rather than by the pancreas), most also agree that the pancreas can nonetheless be triggered by the presence of fructose. Hypoglycemics have been shown to tire if they eat more than two servings of fruit per day.[62] Nancy Appleton has discovered that fruit can cause many of the same harmful

---

[59] Hoffer, Abram, M.D. *Putting It All Together*. 74.

[60] Crayhon, Robert, M.S. *Nutrition Made Simple*. 197.

[61] *Ibid*. 31.

[62] *Ibid*. 41.

effects that sugars can and one of her food plans does in fact eliminate fruit.[63]  Kay Sheppard says never to eat a fruit without a protein.

The food allergists suggest testing for fruit reactions by eliminating them and then reintroducing them in four days.  When I tried this, I was astonished to find that I had a headache about twenty-four hours after ingesting the last piece of fruit, *and* that the headache went away when I ate a plum.  These are sure signs of withdrawal from an addictive/allergic relationship.  I eliminated fruit for about six months, and only now am I adding it back once every four days.  (I find that I am still more prone to sneezing on fruit days.  Some fruit families affect me more than others.)  I substituted vegetables for the fruit servings which simplified the food plan again since dinner leftovers could be used for breakfast with the addition of a half serving of protein.

Many readers may be surprised to see starch in the food plan.  The permitted starches are unrefined, slow absorption, and were not observed to trigger cravings.  I am baffled by the lengths some people go to calculate and count their ingestion of carbohydrate grams.  This seems like a large amount of unnecessary effort.  I am also baffled by "addict diets" that allow no carbohydrates at all.  Among my support network, we eat *whole* carbohydrates several times per day

> Recovering carbohydrate addicts can eat a large variety of whole carbohydrates throughout the day as long as the carbohydrate is eaten with a protein and it is not refined.

(always with a protein) with no ill effect such as weight gain or brain fog, in other words, without triggering an insulin release.  Starches do need to be measured to make sure that we are not using them to get high.  I prefer to eat them after eating a few bites of protein and vegetable so that absorption is slowed even further.  I definitely do not eat them first in the meal.

We will revisit the topic of carbohydrates and what constitutes refinement in the chapter, *Marginal Foods.*  We will discuss the fact that cooking at high temperatures, such as in the case of baked potatoes, or even flattening a grain such as in the case of rolled oats can make certain whole carbohydrates too readily absorbed to be comfortable for recovering carbohydrate addicts/allergics.

Although I did not eliminate corn from this book, I would ask every reader to test for a corn allergy by eliminating it for four days and then reintroducing it.  Corn has invaded the American food supply in the form of sweeteners.  It's hard to find a processed food product that does not have corn in it.  This makes corn another frequently eaten food.  Some people are more allergic to fresh corn than to dried corn (as in polenta and grits).  Test this out for yourself through elimination and isolated reintroduction.

Caffeine is another reactive food that belongs in a category all by itself.   It is tough to withdraw from, usually causing fatigue and headaches lasting as long as three weeks.  It can be brutal upon reintroduction, causing excruciating headaches.  I gave it up when I tied it to raging and insomnia.  It almost makes me crazy when I see parents giving it to their children in the form of soft drinks.   It is hard to distinguish its effects while we are reacting to the refined carbohydrates that cause big swings in our systems.  But once those swings no longer occur, the effects of caffeine are surprisingly pronounced.  It does not belong in the daily plan, especially since it can also trigger a release of glucose from glycogen stores.

Fortunately, I no longer need the stimulation of coffee, since my energy  is steady all day.  As long as I get enough sleep and eat well, I do not experience the slumps or sluggishness that would make me think about using caffeine as a stimulant.  I realize that I used to need coffee in the morning because I was in withdrawal from caffeine, not because I needed help waking up.

---

[63] Appleton, Nancy, Ph.D. *Lick the Sugar Habit*. 163.

One last item of controversy about the plan is the guideline of eating all items at one meal. Kay Sheppard was concerned with eating disorders and therefore with breaking obsessive patterns. She wanted her clients to be absolutely free from thinking about food between meals. For most people on the plan, this freedom is a great gift. However, some people with more severe hypoglycemia cannot last four to five hours between meals. Their sugar levels fall too low, they become exhausted from fighting cravings, and they relapse.

These people are better off dividing their meals into two equal parts of all components. For example, one half serving of protein, one half of starch, one half of fruit and one half of a half protein (one ounce) would be eaten for breakfast. And then the same thing would be eaten a few hours later. This would follow the recommendations of many hypoglycemia experts for stabilizing blood sugar levels by limiting the amount of sugar entering the blood stream at any one time.

The plan is a safe haven for the food addict/allergic. I have often heard recovering food addicts describe straying from the plan and the difficulties that result. Their next sentence is usually one of gratitude for the knowledge that no matter what the transgression, they can always go back to the plan and find peace. They say that they must do it as written, not as their internal addict would like it. This may sound rigid, but people recovering from food addiction/allergies have trouble thinking clearly about food. The food plan parameters do the thinking for the addicted/allergic sufferer. As you will see in the next chapter, there is *huge* flexibility and variety within the food lists for each category. There is plenty of room for adaptation to cultural and lifestyle preferences. So the food plan combines the safety of limits with the pleasure of variety.

The title of this chapter is taken from the inevitable reply to the simple statement, "I don't eat sugars and flours." The expression on the face of the speaker is one ranging from shocked disbelief to horror. The often repeated question instigated my drive to write this book.

The answer to the question is, 'only about a zillion things.' My household eats a much greater variety of foods now than before we eliminated sugars, flours, and other reactive foods. I relied on bread for starch so much that I don't know how long it had been since we'd had sweet potatoes or squash. The only substance I ever served under tomato sauce was pasta. My children had never tasted barley and only rarely brown rice. We have since included many grains and seeds in our daily repasts, some that I had never heard of!

The pages following show the number of choices in each category for each meal. I laid the choices out this way so that my family could express their preferences, and also so that they could figure out what to eat at different times of the day. I copied these pages, one for each member of the family, and asked them to cross off anything they did not like. This done, I honored these choices when I went to the grocery. This consideration gave my household the sense that I still cared about them, even though I was planning significant changes in the food that I would be willing to buy and keep in the house. It also gave them the chance to see that they would still be eating a variety of foods.

The second thing I did with these sheets was to put a copy on the refrigerator. The family referred to them often when they could not figure out what to eat. It helped ease the transition from automatically reaching for junk food to automatically reaching for fruits, vegetables, or leftovers.

## USING THE CHART FOR ALLERGIES

No matter how many food allergies you have, there are still so many foods in the world that you can easily find fourteen items to eat per day and maintain your sense of well-being and balance. Use these charts to keep track of whether you are properly nourishing yourself even if you have to avoid many foods. Simply cross off the foods that you cannot eat, and then focus with joy on the remaining variety. Avoid high fat vegetables such as avocado and high sugar foods such as tropical fruits.

**Rotating Foods** Rotating foods is a very good idea. When we rotate our foods, we get a good range of vitamins and minerals. We are able to detect food allergies. We avoid developing new food allergies through frequently eaten foods.

However, please wait until you have gone through withdrawal from sugars and flours before you try to vary your foods. Rotating will become second nature as you get used to shopping for variety. But if you try to rotate at the same time that you start replacing reactive foods with the fourteen items in Kay Sheppard's plan, you could make yourself crazy chasing after details. Always remember it's progress, not perfection that we strive for. First get used to eating a lot of great food, then start trying to vary the food, then try rotating.

> First: Replace reactive foods.
> Second: Vary foods.
> Third: Rotate foods.
> Always: Be patient with yourself.

On the other hand, if you already know you already have a number of food allergies and need to vary your diet promptly to avoid creating new food allergies, I would suggest the following technique. Make copies of the food list. Put a check mark next to a food each time you eat it. The food lists are organized by food families, so you will soon see if you are eating out of one family too often. Take the lists with you to the grocery store and purchase foods from groups that you eat less often. This will get you through the challenge of broadening the variety of foods you eat. Progressing from eating a good variety to actually rotating takes only a little more awareness.

Rotating means that you eat from any one family no more often than once every four days. For the day that you are eating from that family, you may eat it all day as many times as you like. (But obviously not if you have an allergy to that family.) So, if I had a beef steak on Sunday, I would avoid all foods from the bovine family (lamb, goat, and dairy) until Thursday when I might have mutton stew. On the other hand, on the Sunday that I had steak for dinner, I could also have dairy for my Half Protein at breakfast and bedtime snack and lamb chops for lunch. (Actually, I probably would not do this since that's a lot of high-fat meat, but you get the point.) On a chicken day, I might have eggs for breakfast and leftover chicken from dinner for lunch. I can use leftovers from dinner for lunch because I am eating both meals in the same 24-hour period. If you eat two different families in the same 24-hours, that's fine, but just avoid both of them for the next four days.

Some families appear in more than one column. These are noted by the name of the family in parenthesis after the name of the food. If you eat cantaloupe (fruit from the gourd family) for breakfast, it's fine to have cucumbers (vegetable from the gourd family) for lunch and squash (starch from the gourd family) for dinner because they are all from the gourd family. But you would want to wait for four days to have watermelon or zucchini or pumpkin because they are all also from the gourd family.

Some columns will be easier to rotate than others. The protein column has 46 families while there are only eight families in the starches column. Please see the chapter *It's Not Working* for more ideas about rotating foods. See also Theron Randolph's *Alternative Approach to Allergies*[64] for complete lists of members of each food family.

These lists also easily lend themselves to adaptation to food plans that advocate eating according to blood type. You could star the items that are highly beneficial to you and cross off those which are to be avoided.

You may wonder about foods which are not on these lists, nor on the lists of names for sugars, flours, or wheat. These are marginal foods and they are quite treacherous in terms of their tendency to lead to relapse. I devote a whole chapter to marginal foods in Part II.

Carefully add foods to these lists by haunting your local ethnic grocery stores, as they may carry exotic vegetables and plant proteins that could be sufficiently different from your allergic foods to avoid reactions. If you have trouble deciding which category the food belongs in, try looking it up in a reference book such as *Good Food* by Margaret M. Wittenberg. (The Crossing Press: Freedom, CA. 1995). Match carbohydrate and protein content with other foods already on the lists. In any event, do not include any foods from the marginal food lists in the chapter *Marginal Foods*. Check out any ideas with someone who has experience in the food plan.

At first glance, these lists may look like the gateway to a life-time of confinement. I think they are the gateway to liberation. When I was eating breakfast cereal, muffins, bagels, pasta, pizza, bread, cake, and candy as my daily staples, it didn't even cross my mind to ask if I was eating a good variety of foods. My carbohydrate addict had full control so a meal of pasta with

---

[64] Randolph, Theron. *An Alternative Approach to Allergies.* 289-307.

bread, followed by a dessert looked like three different foods. Compared with a narrow range of false variations on combinations of sugars and flours, the following food lists are honestly rich in variety. There has never been a better one page road map to a joyful, healthy life!

## PICK-ONE-FROM-EACH-COLUMN[65]

Notes to PICK-ONE-FROM-EACH-COLUMN Chart

BREAKFAST: One and a half servings from Column A, one from B or C, and one from D. One cup of dairy may be substituted for a half serving of protein.

LUNCH: One serving from Column A (not dairy) and two from C (at least one raw). One from D is optional.

DINNER: One serving from Column A (not dairy), two from C (at least one raw), and one from D.

BEDTIME OR TEATIME: One half serving from A or a dairy, and one serving from B or C.

---

[65] Adapted from Sheppard, Kay, LMAC, CEDS. *Food Addiction: The Body Knows.* 93-99.

| COLUMN A: PROTEIN (4 oz for women, 5 oz for men) | COLUMN B: FRUIT servings as specified | COLUMN C: VEGETABLES (1 cup) | COLUMN D: STARCH (1 cup) |
|---|---|---|---|
| beef | 1 apple | asparagus | Grass family: |
| veal | ½ cup apple juice | onions | amaranth |
| goat | ½ cup applesauce | - | (rolled) barley |
| lamb | 1 pear | beets | brown rice |
| mutton | - | chard | cream of brown rice |
| - | 3 apricots | spinach | corn, grits |
| pork | 1 nectarine | - | millet |
| - | 1 peach | beans: yellow/green/wax (beans) | oat bran (1/3 c raw) |
| game meats (2 families) | 3 medium plums | snow peas (beans) | oat groats |
| - | 1 cup prune juice | sprouts (beans) | oatmeal |
| chicken | - | - | rye |
| 2 eggs | 1 cup berries | artichoke | cream of rye |
| - | - | bok choy | - |
| turkey | ½ cantaloupe (gourd) | broccoli | buckwheat |
| - | 1/4 honeydew (gourd) | brussel sprouts | - |
| duck | 1 cup watermelon (gourd) | cabbage – Chinese – | beans (beans) |
| - | - | coleslaw | soy products (beans) |
| game birds (4 families) | 1 cup cranberry juice | cauliflower | peas (beans) |
| - | 1 cup blueberries | collards | chickpea (beans) |
| mollusks (clams, etc) | - | radishes | jicama (beans) |
| - | 3 kiwi | rutabaga | - |
| crustaceans (shrimp, etc.) | - | turnips | white potato (nightshade) |
| - | 1 cup pineapple | watercress | - |
| saltwater fish (19 families) | 1 cup pineapple juice | - | sweet potato |
| - | - | carrots | - |
| freshwater fish (13 families) | 1 cup rhubarb | celery | tapioca |
| - | - | parsley | - |
| 1 cup of beans (beans) | ½ cup grapefruit | - | winter squash (gourd) |
| - | 1 cup grapefruit juice | chicory | pumpkin (gourd) |
| 1 cup of quinoa | 2 tangerines | endive | - |
| - | 1 orange | escarole | quinoa |
| 1 cup of buckwheat | 1 cup orange juice | lettuce | quinoa flakes, rolled |
| | 3 lemons or limes | romaine | |
| Men can have 6 oz of fish. | | - | |
| | | mushrooms | |
| DAIRY (may be substituted at breakfast for 1/2 serving of protein) | | - | |
| 1 cup of milk | | eggplant (nightshade) | |
| 1/2 cup of cottage cheese | | peppers (nightshade) | |
| 1 cup of yogurt | | pimento (nightshade) | |
| 1 cup of buttermilk | | tomato (nightshade) | |
| 1 cup of goat milk | | - | |
| 1 cup of soy milk | | water chestnuts | |
| | | - | |
| | | cucumber/pickles(gourd) | |
| | | yellow squash (gourd) | |
| | | zucchini (gourd) | |
| | | - | |
| | | bamboo shoots (grass) | |
| | | - | |
| | | okra | |

I wrote some of this material while traveling in Costa Rica. On a hike through the jungle, I realized that I was quite safe as long as I looked carefully before I put my hand anywhere. The grocery store is the same way. Most processed foods are not safe for us. I look carefully at everything before I reach out to put it in my basket.

A successful change in eating habits starts with the shopping. Having only the right food in the house is a good defense against relapse. If an inappropriate craving appears, and an inappropriate food is in the house, there is not much time for a second thought. If even a short drive can be inserted between the craving and the bite, a second thought has time to come to the rescue. It is truly amazing how those few minutes can serve to restore reason to a driven brain.

## THE BASIC SHOPPING FOR ONE PERSON FOR ONE WEEK

If you are using vegetables in place of fruit, adjust your purchases accordingly.

> 21 servings of protein: eggs, meat, poultry, fish, beans combined with grains, quinoa and buckwheat (7 for breakfast, 7 for lunch, and 7 for dinner)
>
> 14 servings of dairy or an additional 7 servings of protein (1 dairy or 1/2 protein at breakfast and teatime or bedtime)
>
> 14 pieces of fruit (7 for breakfast and 7 for teatime or bedtime)
>
> 28 1-cup servings of vegetables, at least half raw (14 for lunch, 14 for dinner)
>
> 14 1-cup servings of starch: grain, beans, potato, sweet potato, squash, buckwheat, quinoa and tapioca (7 for breakfast and 7 for dinner)
>
> (7 additional servings of starch if you are eating a starch at lunch.) Oils, condiments, flavorings, spices, vitamins, and mineral supplements

Quantities are simply the number of times that the category appears in a week. Quantities shown are for one person, for four meals per day. For more than one person, multiply the amounts by the number of people that you are buying for. Variety in each category ensures that you will have enough different foods so you won't have to eat any one item more often than once very four days. Even if you must eat out for business purposes, consider the option of taking your lunch to work, and then eating a plain salad at the restaurant. This will ensure that you get variety, and a good quantity in all elements of the lunch.

The weekly shopping trip becomes the only shopping trip of the week. Because the thirteen or fourteen daily items are simple and quantities are known, we can buy enough with ease and clarity to feed us and our dependents for a week. The chaos and stress of running out of food and having to run to the store are gone.

As my sister points out, she and I mostly shop the walls of the grocery store where fresh whole foods are kept. There are not a lot of processed foods in this book, because most of them are sweetened or thickened with substances that we need to eliminate. So we generally avoid the aisles where canned, frozen, or packaged goods are kept. Many aisles have only two or three items that do not contain sugars, flours, or wheat.

The first shopping trip after committing to a food plan free of reactive foods can take a long time if you need to convince yourself that most processed foods contain reactive substances. Most people *do* need to see for themselves. They come back to me with shock on their faces. It *is* hard to believe. Even in health food stores, most products have been thickened or sweetened with reactive substances. Health food stores try to stock items that contain rice syrup or concentrated fruit juice as sweetener, but these products wreak the same havoc in our bodies as more refined products. Fortunately, I am now seeing new products in the health food stores that are unsweetened (catsup, mayonnaise, and canned chili, for example) where there were none when I started eliminating reactive foods from my diet.

> The first shopping trip without sugars and flours is a shock.

Why do food manufacturers add so much sugar to products? It is quite simple. Whenever a corporate food researcher puts two products in front of a consumer and asks the consumer to taste them and indicate a preference, the consumer will inevitably choose the one with the most sugar. The addictive voice in us has become so strong that we can perceive sugar even in trace quantities. So don't get mad at the manufacturers. They are only responding to market demand. When market demand shifts to unsweetened products, the manufacturers are sure to take notice and make their own shifts. I am grateful that I live in a market-driven economic system for that reason.

One moment that stands out in my memory was the time I was in a convenience store and realized that the only thing I could safely buy was a bottle of water. Every other product was loaded with sugars, flours, wheat, or fat. Convenience stores are islands of food addiction/allergy. They are to the food addict what a bar is to an alcoholic. Avoid them.

In my commercial grocery store, 100% of the following products have sugars, flours, wheat, or caffeine in them: bread, crackers, cookies, corn chips, baked potato chips, pretzels, doodles, soft drinks, catsup, mayonnaise, liquid smoke, ice cream, frozen desserts, frozen juice, frozen TV dinners, frozen pizza, pasta, gelatin, "sugar-free" gelatin, pudding mixes, cake mixes, muffin mixes, corn muffin mixes, iodized salt, canned fruits, canned chili, canned stews, canned meat spreads, flavored milk, bottled tea, wine, and beer.

More than 90% of the following have sugars, flours, or wheat in them: Salad dressing, mustard, potato chips, canned soups, jams, fruit spreads, tomato sauce, peanut butter, cold cereal, spaghetti sauce, processed meats, yogurt, and low-fat dairy products.

More than 50% of the following have sugars, flours, or wheat in them: Applesauce, mustard, and cooked cereals.

Less than 25% of the following contain reactive substances: Pickles, canned beans, canned fish, canned chicken, fresh produce, fresh fish, fresh meats and poultry, fresh milk, powdered milk, teas, seasonings, bottled water, vinegar.

Another way to see how simple the situation has become is to list the aisles I visit only briefly, or not at all. I never need to go down the bakery or the snacks aisles. I slip into the end of the canned aisle for a few select salad dressings and beans. In the drink aisle I only get bottled water. The baking aisle is good for herbs, non-iodized salt, and powdered and canned milk only. I pick up plain vegetables in the frozen aisle. I hit the end of the cereal aisle for oatmeal, cream of rice, oat bran, and puffed rice cereal. I skip the pasta aisle except for salsa and canned fish and chicken. Otherwise all shopping is

> Shopping is vastly simplified. Instead of looking at all 50,000 items in the store, I may be looking at only a few hundred.

58

done around the periphery of the store, i.e., in the produce, fresh fish, fresh meat and poultry, and dairy departments. My shopping is over much more quickly than in pre-plan days. People who are worried about whether they have the time to do this program can look to a shorter shopping for reassurance that the time will be there.

At the health food store, I focus on bulk products that most commercial grocery stores do not carry. A broad variety of beans and grains are available. I am particularly grateful to find products such as quinoa and buckwheat, both in dry bulk and in boxed breakfast cereal. These are seeds with high protein content that can be used like grains. However, unlike the grains that I have various reactions to, I have no negative reaction at all to quinoa and buckwheat. Health food stores carry rice cakes, stevia, truly plain yogurt, goat milk products, unsweetened soy milk, unsweetened catsup, unsweetened mayonnaise, puffed millet, etc. If you have no health food store nearby, write for a Natural Foods Catalog from Jaffe Bros., P.O. Box 636, Valley Center, CA 92082- 0636. Or find Whole Foods Markets on the internet and use their on-line shopping service.

Health food stores also carry a greater variety of **organic products**. Although the organic issue is not the focus of this book, it makes a great deal of sense for recovering hypoglycemics, food addicts, and suffers of food allergies to try to use as much organic produce as possible. The toxins found in non-organic products are a drain on the immune system. Most of us have already beaten up our immune systems quite badly in the course of using refined carbohydrates. It is time to give the immune system a chance to rebuild itself by relieving it of the job of processing the chemicals used in growing commercial produce.

You may recall that use of refined carbohydrates also creates vitamin and mineral deficiencies. Organic produce, which is higher in vitamins and minerals, addresses this problem.

Since I am always pressed for time when fixing meals, I look for produce which has already been prepared to some degree. Here is the sublime trade-off for the modern industrialized consumer. How much nutrition am I willing to trade off for shortened preparation time? For myself, obviously I am unwilling to trade off anything for a product that contains sugars, flours, or wheat. This is my absolute bottom line. I don't care how quickly I could prepare that product. I know what it would do to me and I am decidedly not interested! Beyond that, the shades of gray come drifting in.

For example, although I know that vegetables that have been cleaned and cut up by the grocery store have probably lost some of their nutritional value, I still buy them. I am much more likely to eat them if preparation is limited to opening the bag, dropping the vegetables into a bowl, and dribbling on the salad dressing. This means I can produce a raw vegetable salad in less than one minute. This is very worthwhile. On an evening with no time or energy left to prepare a meal, having a pre-cut-up vegetable on hand might mean the difference between having a vegetable or skipping it altogether.

I have noticed an increasing number of prepared vegetable items in the fresh produce section. Shredded broccoli, cabbage, and carrots make great quick slaws. Cherry tomatoes, cleaned baby carrots, and celery sticks go into lunches with only the briefest of effort. Sweet peppers and cucumbers are two other frequent lunch raw vegetables. Lettuce and baby spinach are now available in cellophane bags. I always get large quantities of these 'minimal preparation' vegetables.

Where I draw the line personally is with canned (beans excepted) and frozen vegetables. Frozen vegetables take a long time to prepare. Canned vegetables are just not appealing. But if you need these products in order to make your program work, then do not hesitate to put them in your basket. While you're at it, give thanks that they are available.

Initially, I had a hard time believing I needed to buy so much food! I worried about the **expense**. However, because I am no longer buying costly snacks and prepared food, I can afford better quality produce and meats while keeping expense about even with what I spent before I started replacing reactive foods. I also find that because I have enough food in the house, I am not spending so much money in restaurants.

---

## READ EVERY *LIST OF INGREDIENTS* EVERY TIME.

---

Even if the sweetener is the last item on a minor condiment, put it back. Do *not* look at the sugar content in the nutrition analysis box; look at the LIST OF INGREDIENTS. Some foods have natural sugars in them that are OK. For example, a cup of milk has seven grams of sugar known as lactose. An apple has 18 grams of fructose. Lactose and fructose are OK for some people, because other substances in the meal such as fat and fiber slow down the absorption of the sugar. However, a very sensitive pancreas might react to lactose and fructose, so test these foods out for yourself by eliminating them for four days, reintroducing and watching for reactions.

Generally if I pick up a can and it has more than about eight ingredients, I can assume that one of them is a taboo substance, and I do not even have to read the list of ingredients to know it is not for me.

'**Low-fat**' on a label is a dead give-away that lots of sugar in the form of maltodextrose lurks therein. It is such a ironic turn of events that an addictive, fattening substance would be put in products purporting to help people lose weight.

Every **"sugarless"** product I have ever looked at has sugars under other names in it. A famous frozen yogurt store advertises a "sugarless" frozen yogurt. However, this product has forms of sugar as the first and third ingredients. Also, avoid "sugarless" gelatin and gum.

**Polenta or grits** is a very coarsely ground dried corn. Do not substitute corn meal. If you see a package marked "Polenta," but it says that it can also be used for corn bread, then it is too finely ground and should be avoided. Instant grits cannot be used to make Polenta.

**Oatmeal** comes in degrees of fineness. I have seen the most coarsely cut labeled as "Ranch Style." I suppose this is the healthiest, but it has an after-taste that I am not fond of. Regular and minute oatmeal do not contain added sugar, but they need to be checked out carefully because they are more refined. Test them especially to see if they make you drowsy. The instant oatmeal in individual packets has sugar added to it, even in the "regular flavor."

**Oils** are an essential element of recovery from refined carbohydrate use. They carry many essential components of a well functioning body. Try to buy oils in dark glass bottles. It's better if they are refrigerated, but good luck finding any even in the health food store. Open yourself to flaxseed oil, canola oil, and extra virgin olive oil, first cold pressing. Use a variety of oils just as you would any other food group. I think it would be better to avoid the nut oils like walnut and peanut on the chance that they could trigger cravings for nuts. Please choose butter over margarine. Margarine and other hydrogenated oils are very hard for the body to process.

**Alternatives to Dairy.** Some researchers are beginning to estimate that as many as half of all children are allergic to cows' milk. **I would strongly suggest that, even if you are not lactose intolerant, you should not use dairy products more often than once every four days.** You run the risk of developing an allergy to milk and milk products if cow dairy is a "frequently eaten" food. The quick menus in 'Top Ten Favorite Breakfasts' in the chapter *MECHANICS:THINK THREE PLUS ONE* offer breakfast alternatives that do not depend on daily dairy consumption. "Milk" made from soy is a good substitute.

Read the list of ingredients on soy milk products very carefully, because most contain sweeteners, especially brown rice syrup. If you have had congestion from dairy items in the past, try them again after you have been off reactive foods for a few weeks. You may find that they no longer produce a bad result. Rice milk is not a good dairy substitute because it contains little if any protein. Oat milk is only slightly better. Consider alternating with goat milk. My local health food store carries skim, powdered, and canned goat milk. Powdered goat milk gives baked goods a delicious tangy flavor. Please read the list of ingredients on all dairy products. I have even found sweetener added to milk in a wholesome-looking glass bottle.

Low-fat and non-fat **yogurt** comes in many flavors. However, they contain modified food starch which is a refined carbohydrate and aspartame, which gives many people headaches. Even plain yogurt can contain pectin, a fruit extract. The plainest yogurt contains nothing but milk and cultures. If you eat yogurt often, try to develop a taste for the plainest. Flavoring and spices such as vanilla and cinnamon make a dent in the tartness.

Be careful when buying **drinks**. Most sodas contain caramel coloring, caffeine, or concentrated fruit juice. Steer clear of these substances. Diet 7-Up, diet Sprite, and some of the flavored sparkling waters don't have caffeine or caramel coloring, but do contain aspartame. Many tea bags contain roasted barley malt, which is a sweetener that must be avoided. Carbonated drinks contain phosphorus which increases calcium excretion. Buy just enough to drink every four days.

> Manufacturers will go to any length to get sweeteners into their products.

The best drinks are **herbal teas**. Once through withdrawal from artificial sweeteners and caffeine, the sense of taste returns. The subtle variety of herbal teas is delightful. Vary these teas as you would any food. Do not drink any particular one more often than once every four days unless more frequent use has been recommended by a health care professional. Learn about herbal teas' various medicinal properties. Use them to augment your program. I am fortunate to live in a house with a "hot box" on the sink. This appliance keeps water at boiling. It makes the preparation of teas quick and easy.

**Fruit juice** is not used in this food plan. Because the fiber has been removed, it is absorbed quickly and can trigger an insulin release. Fruit juice has also been shown to suppress the immune system. As if these were not enough reasons to drop fruit juice, remember that fruit is heavily treated with pesticides and these pesticides are concentrated in the manufacture of juice.

Many people in recovery from caffeine addiction turn to decaffeinated **coffee**. This seemed like a very good idea to me until I learned what is in it: hexane, methylene chloride, pesticide residues, trichloroethylene, and hydrocarbons if roasted over a gas flame. It also has trace quantities of caffeine in it. I find that I am thinking about caffeine the day after I drink a cup of decaffeinated, so guess what? I try to avoid it, but at least limit my intake to no more than once every four days.

**Aspartame is a food additive that causes problems for a lot of people. Aspartame in the little packets is mixed with a form of sugar called dextrose, so it is to be avoided.** The only **other sweetener** that Food Addicts in Recovery does not specifically prohibit is saccharin, which can be bought as *Sweet 10,* and Saccharine tablets, which early laboratory tests linked to cancer. New research has cleared saccharine for human use, but I would still use it only in sheer desperation and definitely no more often that once every four days. An herbal sweetener that does not seem to have any adverse health consequences is stevia. Although it appears to be acceptable from a health standpoint, I would still not use it any more often than once every four days and watch for allergic reactions of cravings. With cereal, try applesauce or cut-up fruit as your sweetener.

My supermarket carries a wonderful **salad** mix of greens. I use this because of its variety of greens. However, lettuce is not the most nutritious raw vegetable, so do not over-rely on it.

**Meat and fish** lose weight in cooking. The amounts shown in the PICK-ONE-FROM-EACH-COLUMN LIST are the amounts that you should eat. For example, 6 oz of raw salmon weighs only 4 oz after cooking. I have to buy 6 oz raw in order to end up with 4 oz cooked for a woman's serving. In order to end up with a man's fish serving of 6 oz, I would buy 9 oz. Men's servings of meat are 5 oz, so I buy a little more than 7 oz. of meat for a man.

Pay particular attention to **ground chicken and ground turkey** to make sure that high-fat skin has not been ground into them. Ground meats in general are more prone to bacterial growth because more surface is exposed to the air. Nonetheless, ground meats cut down substantially on preparation time so just cook them thoroughly.

**Beef** is a food that you must use very carefully in a weight loss program because it is high in fat compared with other protein sources. Combine this drawback with the use of hormones and antibiotics in commercial beef, and the fact that pesticides are concentrated in beef fat, and it is easy to see why beef needs a critical look. As the chart below shows, top sirloin and bottom round are the lowest fat choices. When having beef, I often substitute ½ cup of beans for 2 oz of steak to cut down on the amount of beef I am consuming. Buying low fat meats for grilling has another important advantage: the smoke created by fat dropping on hot coals has been implicated in cancer.

|  | % of weight from fat | % of calories from fat |
|---|---|---|
| hot dog | 28% | 83% |
| bottom round | 9 | 36 |
| brisket | 31 | 72 |
| chuck blade roast | 14 | 50 |
| ground extra lean | 15 | 52 |
| ground lean | 17 | 54 |
| ground regular | 20 | 60 |
| short ribs, lean | 17 | 56 |
| tenderloin steak | 10 | 44 |
| top sirloin steak | 7 | 35 |

I stood in front of my supermarket **deli meat** counter one slow day and got a delightful, curious clerk to check every list of ingredients in the case. Out of the thirty or so deli meats, only two showed no sugars. One was a peppered beef, the other a spicy turkey breast. Buyer, beware! Outside of the deli case, almost all processed meats contain sweeteners. The only ones worth even checking are kosher products. Even if the processed meat is free of sugars and flours, preservatives and a high fat content make processed meat undesirable.

**Eggs** have made a nice comeback in recent months. The initial studies have been refined,

Be extremely cautious of Lite and low-fat products. Generally the fat has been replaced with sugar products.

and now eggs in moderation are considered OK. I have heard several stories of dramatically lowered cholesterol from replacing reactive foods. Theoretically the liver functions better to filter and produce optimal cholesterol when it is not overloaded from filtering other substances created by reactive foods.

Hint: Make your produce stop the last stop of your shopping. The produce will be on top, and the heavier protein and dairy items will not squash it.

I would also urge you to buy extras for stockpiling. Ground meat patties, chicken breasts, chops, hard-boiled eggs, and the like can be kept in the freezer or refrigerator for quick meals. Other good emergency items are canned fish (shrimp, crab, tuna, salmon, sardines, oysters, and clams), canned chicken, and beans. Packages of frozen fruit are a good idea. Frozen vegetables take longer than most fresh vegetables to microwave. Freezing also reduces the nutritional value of foods. But if canned and frozen foods make your program possible, go for it!

Never shop on an empty stomach. Stick with a shopping trip until you have bought everything on the list. This will keep you out of the stores and away from temptation for a week at a time. Buy whatever produce is in season and substitute it into recipes as it makes sense. Think global, buy local; i.e., save the use of energy for transport by buying produce that is locally grown. Buy domestic because unregulated pesticides may be used on foreign produce. This is especially the case with fruit which is more heavily treated with pesticides than vegetables. Your recovering immune system does not need the extra burden of expelling toxic pesticides. Buying local also means that the essential fatty acid content of the produce is likely to match your needs.

Dr. Abram Hoffer sums up the crux of the issue about foods manufactured in industrial countries.

> **There is no way to process a food into as nutritious a product as the original food.**

This just means the less processing the better. I ask myself if the food is as safe and nourishing as the food from which it is fashioned? Could I find this food in a less processed form? I also have to remember the reality of a busy life. Unprocessed food is a trade off with time. Sometimes "processed" means I can just open a can of beans, wash a vegetable and sit down and eat. This is less than 60 seconds of preparation. Although the food program described in this book is primarily aimed at less processed carbohydrates, all foods serve us better in their less processed forms. But like all aspects of this food program, principle is not meant to be practiced to perfection. Just do the best you can.

Enjoy the simplicity of your shopping. Take time to see the colors and texture of produce. Express gratitude for the good food that comes your way.

Use the pick-one-from-each-column list as your shopping list. Buy items from as many different groups as possible. Recipes are designed to ease substituting fruits, vegetables, starches, and proteins. So buy the items that are in season, or on sale, or just look good!

In addition to the basic foods, you may want these condiments:

# OTHER SHOPPING ITEMS

salad dressing (Newman's Own and some of the Cardini)
Bragg's Amino Acid Sauce (substitute for soy sauce, which has wheat in it)
spray olive oil
unsweetened mayonnaise (at your health food store)
unsweetened salt (generally iodized salt contains dextrose)
vinegar
tomato sauce
seasonings
vanilla and other flavorings
sweetener
mustard
decaffeinated coffee (with caution)
decaffeinated tea
water
sparkling water
poultry seasonings
extra cans of beans
extra cans of soup
unsweetened evaporated skim milk
sweet peppers (optional for flavoring)
vitamins

Please don't think that you are going to cook 14 items per day. I basically make three items per day: a starch, a protein, and a vegetable. I serve the same items for twenty-four hours with plus a raw vegetable for lunch and dinner or fruit for breakfast and the bedtime snack. Try to

| |
|---|
| Once a day, think **THREE PLUS ONE** |

picture that once per day, you are going to move three items from counter, cabinet, or refrigerator to a bowl, roaster, pot, crock pot, grill, skillet, or oven. Along the way, you may have to wash and cut up the items. Or, if you already got the grocery store to do this by buying semi-prepared foods, you are just tossing the ingredients into the container and adding seasonings. This is the point at which ground or cubed meats, pre-shredded vegetables, canned beans, etc. are handy.

Multiply the servings by the number of meals you need to make for the twenty-four hours. If you have a few hours on a day off, you can fix meals for the whole week and freeze them. This may cut down on their nutritional value, but if it makes your program work, go for it. Baking or grilling meats, poultry, and fish right out of the grocery bag before freezing can also cut down tremendously on preparation time during the week. While preparing meat, boil grains or beans and put them in airtight containers while still hot. They will keep for many days in the refrigerator.

All the Basic Recipes and Favorite Recipes in this book are based on these principles. Preparation times are about ten minutes. Since cook times can be long, up to an hour, I sometimes cook after dinner. I put out anything I need to thaw in the morning so it's ready to cook in the evening. Since my oven has a timer on it, I can put a roast, chicken, or beans in a roaster pan with potato and onion, set the timer and go to bed. As long as the food gets hot enough to kill bacteria and it is covered tightly, it can cool in the oven overnight. A crockpot works the same way. Just make sure it's covered tightly.

If you buy a variety of foods, you will automatically cook a variety of dishes. Keeping the dishes to three ingredients saves on preparation and creative thinking. It makes tracking food allergies easier. For breakfast, I add some extra protein. If I really don't want a vegetable for breakfast, I add fruit instead. For lunch and dinner, I add a raw vegetable. This is totally complete. Bedtime or teatime snacks are leftovers.

While preparing dinner each night, also look at the ingredients required for the next day. Make sure that you take meats out of the freezer to thaw. Boil time-consuming grains the night before and refrigerate. Do the entire Oven Roast the night before so that it is ready when you come through the door on the evening when you are going to eat it. Do not try to cook on an empty stomach. When you get home, you should just be throwing together food that is already cooked. So cook tonight for tomorrow night. I find that dinner preparation time is my most likely over-eating hour, so I do everything I can to make it short.

## TECHNIQUES

The cooking techniques that I am about to describe are simple ones that I use every night. **Which technique you choose is _not important_.** It makes absolutely no difference whether you make a soup every night or an oven roast. It does make a difference whether vegetables are cooked or raw. Make sure you have at least one raw vegetable per meal. (If you have two raw vegetables at lunch, it's OK to have two cooked at dinner.) Raw vegetables are listed last on each dinner menu. Steam vegetables until they are warm, but still crisp. Use the microwave to do this, or a steamer over boiling water.

Grains should be stirred into plenty of boiling salted water. Cooking times are stated on the package. Water should remain freely boiling around the grain until it is done. Taste for doneness. Do not depend solely on the cooking time to determine doneness. Drain off the water and serve. If storing the grain for later use, drain off the water, rinse, and refrigerate immediately in a plastic container.

## VARIETY

One of the most important features of the weekly plan is that it does not repeat any food more than twice. Varying foods is *very* important for the following reasons: it avoids creating new allergies from frequently eaten foods, it avoids triggering existing allergies from over-exposure to any one food, and it ensures complete availability of vitamins and minerals, some of which are found only in a few plants or animals.

I gave the lists of food choices to some friends without emphasizing the importance of variety. Since baked potatoes were their favorite thing, they ate them twice a day. However, they also developed aching joints.

Using the same plant in two different forms does not achieve

> Over-dependence on any one food substance can unbalance your system. Eating a variety means that our nutrition is complete. We also avoid setting ourselves up for new food allergies.

variety. For example, oat bran, oatmeal, and oat groats are all oats. If you ate oatmeal on Monday, you would want to wait until Friday to eat the oat bran muffin. However, the food allergists say that we can eat as much as we want of a food in the same 24- hour period. So I could eat polenta (corn grits) for breakfast and fresh corn for dinner and still meet my goal of variety, providing that I did not eat corn again for four days.

I myself did not vary dairy foods for the first ten months that I was on this program. As a result, I developed an allergy to milk and yogurt. For "dairy," the sample menus in this book use soy milk, goat milk, oat milk (only with quinoa, which is high in protein and calcium), fish with bones (such as sardines, anchovies, and salmon), and spinach instead of cows' milk. Other foods that can be used to boost calcium intake in place of cows' milk follow in the next chart.

## FOODS HIGH IN CALCIUM

| Proteins | Fruits & Vegetables | Starch |
|---|---|---|
| garbanzo beans | bok choy | acorn squash |
| navy beans | broccoli | garbanzo beans |
| sardines with bones | butternut squash | navy beans |
| salmon with bones | collard greens | parsnips |
| shrimp | kale | quinoa |
| soy milk | mustard greens | rutabagas |
| tofu | okra | soy milk |
| | orange | sweet potato |
| | spinach | |
| | turnip greens | |

So don't depend on any one food. The objective is to eat no one food more than twice a week. It's OK to eat the same food more than once in a twenty-four-hour period. It's OK to have leftovers from dinner for lunch the next day. But then wait four days before having that food again. This includes drinks such as decaffeinated coffee and tea.

Varying protein is especially important. I schedule red meat one or two days per week, poultry twice, fish twice, and vegetarian once or twice, but you can alter these choices to suit your preferences. Vegetarians have a four-day rotation of eggs, grain combined with beans, buckwheat, and quinoa. Use the suggested variations at the end of each menu in the chapter of basic recipes section. Also, refer back to the pick-one-from-each-column page for foods that you might not normally eat.

Eat everything. Skipping items means that some essential nutrient or fiber is not getting into your body. Leaving out an item means that you will be out of fuel by the next time you eat. An undernourished body is an anxious body. An anxious body will be thinking about food and will set the mind up for a binge or for eating something reactive. Whether it's a minimal bowel movement and eventually cancer, or just weak fingernails, skipping items means that something will not happen in your body that needs to. It also means that carbohydrate and protein balance may not take place which means that brain chemistry will be awry.

Eat on time. Try to eat at regular intervals, such as 8 am, 12 noon, 5 pm, and 10 pm. Take dinner to the office with you if you need to. Eat the bedtime snack with your family if you regularly come home late. My husband eats a snack at 5 pm and then dinner later. I would only try this very carefully. If you are tempted to binge or are thinking about food, then just take your dinner to work along with your lunch. If you get invited out to lunch, eat your home-made lunch and then just have a house salad at the restaurant

There is very little fat in the menu. You have to be careful to get a tablespoon per day, usually in salad dressing or in an oil drizzled on grilled meat. Adding more than 1 tablespoon of fat will bring any weight loss to a rapid halt. If you are reading this book to lose weight then, when you have finished losing weight, add oil very slowly to ensure that you do not start gaining again. See Sheppard, Kay, LMHC, CEDS. *Food Addiction: The Body Knows.* 1993. Health Communications, Inc. Deerfield Beach, Florida. p. 101, for more information on maintenance.

Breakfast is 1 ½ protein, starch, and fruit or vegetable. The dinners are shown with protein followed by starch, cooked vegetable, and raw vegetable. Initially, it may be difficult to remember what to include in each meal. Use the pocket chart in the back of this book to help you remember.

The following "Top Ten" lists will show you how easy this food plan really is. The lists are the 'Top Ten Easiest *Think Three* Combinations,' 'Top Ten Favorite Breakfasts,' and 'Top Ten Emergency Meals.' These three sheets will take you a long way down the road. But I recommend pausing here and working the work sheet at the end of this chapter to develop your own list of 'Top Ten Favorite *Think Three* Combinations'.

## TOP TEN EASIEST THINK *THREE PLUS ONE* COMBINATIONS

Prepare these three items once every twenty-four hours. *Add raw vegetable for lunch or dinner. Add one half extra serving of protein for breakfast.* Substitute fruit for vegetable for breakfast if you can tolerate fruit. Refer to the notes to the Pick-One-From-Each-Column for help with quantities and the elements of each meal. The pocket guide at the end of the book also summarizes the element of each meal.

1. <u>Sweet Potato Bake</u>  Sweet potatoes, turkey breast, and onions. Bake in an oven. (Vegetarians: Yogurt with protein powder and cinnamon for dessert replace turkey.)

2. <u>White Potato Bake</u>  White potatoes, an eye of round roast, and big carrots. Bake in an oven. (Vegetarians: Sautéed buckwheat replaces roast)

3. <u>Shrimp Stir Fry</u>  Rice, shrimp, and snow peas. Sauté in a saucepan. (Vegetarians: Firm tofu replaces shrimp.)

4. <u>Quinoa Salad</u>  Quinoa, fish, cilantro, and chopped tomatoes. Steam fish, boil quinoa, toss with vegetables. (Vegetarians: Eliminate fish and double quinoa.)

5. <u>Polenta Grill</u>  Polenta, lamb or pork chops, and mushrooms. Grill. (Vegetarians: Beans or sliced grilled tofu replaces chops.)

6. <u>Potato Salad</u>  Boiled new potatoes, hard-boiled eggs, and celery. Boil potatoes and eggs. Toss with celery and mayonnaise.

7. <u>Mexican Rice</u>  Beans, rice, and salsa. Toss.

8. <u>Pea Soup</u>  Split pea, rice, and baby carrots. Cover with double water mix and simmer.

9. <u>Egg Bake</u>  Spinach and eggs. Mix and bake. Serve with chilled garbanzo beans which have been tossed with salad dressing.

10. <u>Chicken Soup</u>  Chicken breasts, rice, and zucchini. Chop, cover with enough water to cook rice. Boil until done. (Vegetarians: Buckwheat replaces both chicken and rice.)

# TOP TEN FAVORITE BREAKFASTS

These breakfasts use starches and proteins that you've already prepared in your THINK THREE PLUS ONE combinations. Vegetarians use eggs, beans with grain, buckwheat, or quinoa.

| Quantities are for one person. | Starch | Fruit or vegetable | Protein |
|---|---|---|---|
| Bowl of cooked cereal  Prepare cereal according to manufacturers' directions. Top with yogurt and fruit | Rolled oats or cream of rice | 1 c sliced kiwi | 1 cup of yogurt and 1 serving of protein powder |
| Smoothie  Blend all ingredients in a blender. | Raw cream of buckwheat | Peach, nectarine, or apricot | 1 cup of soy milk and 4 oz tofu |
| Sauté | Sliced white potatoes | Peppers and onions | 6 oz turkey |
| Sweet Potato Whip  Blend potato and pineapple. Heat through, serve shrimp on the side. | Baked sweet potato | Pineapple | 6 oz cooked shrimp |
| Tapioca Pudding  Mix all ingredients except fruit, let stand five minutes. Cook, stirring constantly until boiling. Let cool, add fruit. | 3 tablespoons of pre-cooked tapioca | Strawberries, raspberries, blackberries or boysenberries | 2 eggs 1 cup milk or soy milk |
| Pumpkin Bake  Blend canned pumpkin pack with pork. Heat through. | 1 cup pumpkin pack | One orange on side | 6 oz cooked pork |
| Oat Bran Muffin (See Recipes.) | ½ cup dry oat bran | Mashed blueberries | 3 eggs |
| Squash Bake (Substitute squash into Oat Bran Muffin Recipe.) | Mashed cooked butternut squash | Applesauce | 3 eggs |
| Rice and Bean Omelette | 1 cup rice and 1 cup beans | Cantaloupe on side | 2 eggs |
| Smoothie Blend all ingredients in a blender. | ¼ cup quinoa | apple, pear, peach, or berry | 1 cup soy milk 4 oz tofu |

# TOP TEN EMERGENCY MEALS

1. Cup of beans, cup of instant grits, and a carton of cherry tomatoes. Top grits with beans and tomatoes.

2. Cup of beans, cup of canned corn, cup of salsa, cup of baby carrots. Toss.

3. 2 micro waved or scrambled eggs, top with a cup of beans, cup of tomato sauce, cup of chopped lettuce.

4. Cup of cottage cheese, blend with 2 cups raw vegetables, spread on 2 rice cakes.

5. 4 oz canned chicken, 1 cup canned green beans, 2 rice cakes. Serve with any raw vegetable on hand.

6. 4 oz canned tuna, toss with 1 tablespoon of mayonnaise, spread on 2 rice cakes, serve with 2 cups raw vegetables on hand.

7. 4 oz canned clams, 1 cup tomato juice, 1/3 cup rice, and 1 cup water. Combine and simmer until rice is done. Serve with 1 cup of raw vegetable on hand.

8. Cup of plain yogurt, mix with 1 tablespoon of curry and a serving of protein powder, use as dip with 2 cups of raw vegetables or toss with shredded vegetables. A cup of oatmeal with cinnamon for dessert.

9. 4 oz canned chicken, two cups any raw vegetable on hand. Microwave little new potatoes until a fork just pierces them. Toss all ingredients with one tablespoon of salad dressing.

10. 1 cup canned pumpkin (plain packed pumpkin, not pie filling), two eggs, cinnamon, and vanilla. Blend well and bake or microwave until firm. Serve as dessert after two cups of raw vegetables tossed with salad dressing.

> Do you get the impression you should stockpile cans of beans, corn, salsa, instant grits, pumpkin, clams, tuna, chicken, and raw vegetables? "I don't want to cook!" is not a reason to lose your food program.

*Notebook:*

## YOUR OWN TOP TEN THINK THREE PLUS ONE COMBINATIONS

Dear Reader:  Most American families only make about ten different dinners.  Think through your favorite ten meals and how you will adapt them to the *THINK-THREE-PLUS-ONE* combinations.  List them here.  Check for variety.  Remember that dinner is a protein, a starch, a raw vegetable, and another vegetable that can be either cooked or raw.  Refer to the pick-one-from-each-column sheet for inspiration.

*Notebook:*

## YOUR OWN TOP TEN FAVORITE BREAKFASTS

The very first moments of the day can be a difficult time to think up breakfast combinations. So, take a few minutes here and write down your own favorite combinations. Remember breakfast consists of a protein, a dairy or another half protein, a fruit and a starch.

I have tried to keep the menus as simple as possible. Each one has the four items called for by complete nutrition. Each lunch and dinner has lots of substitutions. I have designed them this way so that you will get a sense of a system of eating. The four elements can be combined and cooked in an endless variety of ways. You just add your preference for food and technique and make the menus fit you. I am happy to recommend *Recovery Cookbook* by Kay Sheppard, LMHC, CEDS and Barbara Caravella (Palm Bay, FL) Kay Sheppard publisher 1998. She is a master at the art of sane cooking.

**Quantities are for four meals, i.e., enough for two people for dinner and leftovers for lunch the next day.** Breakfasts are all for one person for one meal.

I microwave cereals, meats, and vegetables. Microwave cereals in a wide flat container to prevent them from boiling over the edge. Microwave meats for a minute or two before putting them on the grill to reduce the amount of time you are standing over the grill or in front of the broiler. The meat should be steaming and slightly gray when you take it from the microwave. This also reduces drying, leaving the meats moist and tender. Slightly microwave vegetables to keep your kitchen from heating up in the summer. Always try to cook vegetables as little as possible to retain their nutrients. Fresh vegetables should only take a minute or two. Eat them as crunchy as you can stand without feeling like a rabbit.

Adapt the variations to your own tastes. If some combination does not sound good to you, don't use it. Beans can be either protein or starch.

Tofu literally disappears into a scrambled egg and so is a good source of low-fat, cholesterol-free protein. Feel free to substitute 4oz tofu for one egg if cholesterol is your issue. Please choose any other protein from the lists in the chapter, *What Else Is There To Eat?*. Vary them as much as you can. Do not repeat any item more often than once every four days if you suspect that you are sensitive to eggs or dairy.

In the POTATO-TOPPED menu you will see a combination of steak and beans. This is in an attempt to reduce the amount of red meat in the menu. If you do not have an aversion to red meat, please use a full 4 ounces. A cup of beans may be substituted for any protein.

The design of these menus depends on leftovers for lunch to reduce the amount of meal preparation. During the course of preparing dinner, put a plastic container on the counter and put a serving of each item in the container. Cut up large items such as a potato into cubes. Thin slice meats. The idea is to have the four basic items in the plastic container ready to be eaten with a fork. Put greens on top and salad dressing on the bottom to prevent the greens from wilting. Refrigerate overnight. Shake the container just before eating. You can also try making soup from some of these ingredients by putting them in a food processor with a little broth. The splendor of your honest satisfying dinners is thus spread simply to lunch.

These recipes generally take less than 10 minutes. They are so easy that two meals can be made in one evening. The two which require longer cook times are the Oven Roast and the Pot Toss, but they also have the shortest preparation times. So, make them the night before. Also boil brown rice and bake potatoes the night before. (Don't forget, you can microwave potatoes for five minutes if you have forgotten to bake them.)

## TOFU AND EGGS

2 oz tofu
2 eggs
Salt and pepper
Spray oil

Weigh 2 oz tofu and slice into bowl.

Smash tofu with the back of a fork.

Break eggs onto tofu and mix well.

Spray sauté pan with oil.

Put pan over medium heat.

Pour tofu and egg mixture into pan.

Stirring occasional, cook until mixture is firm.

Or, place mixture in an oiled microwave dish.  Microwave for 2-3 minutes stirring frequently until firm.

This is one and one half protein.  Eat it with a starch and fruit for a complete breakfast.

(As a variation for a travel breakfast, I let this mixture sit in the pan, covered, without stirring until it is firm.  I slide it out of the pan, cut it into strips, mix it with left-over rice and sprinkle with Bragg's.  I only need fruit  to complete the meal.)

## TOFU, EGGS, AND LOX

1 oz tofu
1 oz lox
2 eggs
Pepper

Follow directions for TOFU AND EGGS, substituting 1 oz of salmon for 1 oz of tofu. Since lox is very salty, only add salt after you have tasted.

This is one and a half proteins.  Eat it with a starch and fruit.

## TOFU, EGGS, AND POTATO

1 c cut-up leftover baked potato
2 oz tofu
Salt and pepper
1 egg
Spray oil

Spray frying pan with oil and place over medium burner.  Place potatoes in pan, stirring occasionally until brown.

Make egg mixture and pour over potatoes.

Stirring occasional, cook until eggs are firm.

Micro Waving is an option, but potatoes will not be brown or crisp.

This is protein and starch.  Eat it with fruit and dairy.  I would not eat this very often as potatoes are a source of starch frequently available in restaurants.  Brown rice works well as a substitute for the potato.

## YOGURT MIX

1 c yogurt
1 c any cooked or cold cereal
One cut-up fruit
1 serving of protein powder  mixed with spice of choice.
Mix yogurt, cereal, fruit, and flavorings together.  This is a complete breakfast.

## POLENTA

5 c water
bouillon cubes for 5 c water
3 c grits or Polenta
Spray oil
Put water on a high burner.
Add bouillon cubes according to package directions.
Heat broth until it is boiling.
Add Polenta slowly, stirring constantly.
Lower heat.
Stir Polenta until it is thick, scraping the bottom often.
Spray oil into any kind of casserole dish or bread pan.
Pack Polenta into the casserole dish, pressing down with spatula or cutting board.
Makes 5, 1 c servings.
This is a starch.  Serve with protein, fruit, and dairy or one half protein for a complete breakfast.

## EGGS AND POLENTA

1 serving of prepared Polenta
3 eggs
Salt and pepper
Spray frying pan with oil and set over medium burner.
Slice Polenta into 2 slices and place into frying pan.
(If Polenta is coming directly from the refrigerator, heat it first in the microwave.)
Make a very deep depression in the Polenta slice with the back of a spoon.
Break one egg onto each slice of Polenta.
Cover the pan until the film over the yolk has turned opaque.  Serve.
This is starch and one and one half protein.  Eat with fruit for a complete meal.

## INSTANT GRITS

Empty 2 packets into a bowl.
Add 1 c very hot water.
Let stand until thick.
Or, empty grits and cold water into a large, flat bowl and microwave 1 minute.
This is a starch. Eat with protein, fruit and dairy or another half protein.
A quick option is to place 2 packets of instant grits in a large, flat microwave dish.  Add 1 c water. Gently break 3 eggs into the grits and microwave for four minutes.  Eggs will not be done when you remove the dish from the oven.  Stir eggs and hot grits together thoroughly.  The hot grits finish cooking the eggs. Add salt and pepper to taste.  Eat with fruit.

## OATMEAL
½ c oatmeal
1 c water
Mix ingredients and place in microwave for 2 minutes.
Let stand to thicken if necessary.
Or, boil water, stir oats in gradually, reduce heat, cook until thickened stirring occasionally.
Serve with one and a half protein ( or one protein and one diary), and fruit.

## BREAKFAST MUFFIN
Spray oil
1 egg
4 oz tofu or another egg
½ c oat bran
½ c applesauce or  1 chopped apple
1/3 c non-fat dried milk or another egg
1 t baking soda or powder
1 t vanilla
2 t cinnamon
10 drops liquid sweetener (optional)
Preheat oven to 350'. Oil a casserole dish.
Smash tofu into egg very thoroughly
Mix all ingredients together and pour into casserole dish.
Bake for 20 minutes.
This is a complete meal.

## BREAKFAST ICE CREAM
4 oz tofu
1 egg
1 c milk or soy milk
1 c cut up fruit
½ c toasted oatmeal
Place tofu, egg, and milk in blender or food processor.  Blend until very smooth.
Cook on high in the microwave for 3 minutes, whisking after each minute.
Return mixture to blender, add fruit, and blend again until smooth.
Place in freezer until extremely cold but not frozen, about 3 hours.  Prevent ice crystals from forming by stirring occasionally, more frequently toward the end.
Process in an ice cream maker according to manufacturer's directions.
Serve topped with toasted oatmeal. (Recipe follows.)  With the oatmeal, this is a complete breakfast.

## TOASTED OATMEAL
½ c raw oatmeal.
1 T oil
Preheat broiler to high.
Mix oatmeal and oil.
Spread evenly on jelly roll pan.
Place under broiler until brown.  Stir and brown again. Store in airtight container.

# BASIC

# LUNCH AND DINNER

# MENUS

# SALAD TOSS
### (4 servings)

| | |
|---|---|
| 1½ lb salmon steaks or fillet* | 4c Garbanzo beans or chick peas |
| Juice of one lemon | 4c Lettuce mix |
| Olive oil spray | 4c Celery |
| Salt and pepper | 4T Salad dressing |

    1. Heat grill.  Prepare salmon by squeezing lemon juice over it.  Sprinkle with salt and pepper and brush with olive oil.

    2. Place salmon in microwave until it is hot and edges have started to turn opaque.

    3. Grill salmon on a medium hot grill until it flakes.

    4. Allow salmon to cool until it can be handled.  Flake and toss with other ingredients in a large salad bowl.  Dress and serve.

For lunch the next day:

While preparing dinner, place salad dressing, salmon, Garbanzo beans, celery, and lettuce (in that order) in a plastic container.  Refrigerate.  Toss just before eating.

## VARIATIONS

| Protein | Starch | Vegetables | |
|---|---|---|---|
| 16 oz cooked | barley | artichoke | okra |
| (20 oz for men) | brown rice | asparagus | onions |
| beef | millet | bamboo    shoots | parsley |
| veal | beans | yellow/green beans | peppers |
| pork | corn | Belgian endives | pickles, dill |
| lamb | parsnips | bok choy | pimentos |
| chicken | potato (sweet, white) | broccoli | radishes |
| turkey | peas | Brussels sprouts | romaine |
| deli sliced turkey | | cabbage | radicchio |
| deli sliced beef | | carrots | sauerkraut |
| fish | | cauliflower | snow peas |
| shellfish | | celery | spinach |
| tofu | | chicory | sprouts |
| 8   eggs   (hard boiled) | | Chinese cabbage | summer squash |
| | | cucumber | tomato |
| 2c cottage cheese (low-fat) | | eggplant | turnip |
| | | endive | water chestnuts |
| | | escarole | watercress |
| | | greens | zucchini |
| | | lettuce | |
| | | mushrooms | |

*28 oz for men

# POTATO TOPPED
## (4 servings)

| | |
|---|---|
| 4c Boiled potatoes | 8c Total of mushrooms, onions, |
| 2c Beans | or sweet peppers |
| 8oz Steak | Salt and pepper |

1.  Boil potatoes by dropping into salted, room temperature water. When water comes to a boil, reduce heat to a simmer for 20 minutes. Potatoes are done when they are still slightly resistant to being pierced by a fork.

2.  Heat grill. Prepare steak by sprinkling with red wine vinegar, salt, and pepper and brushing with olive oil. Place steak in microwave until it is hot and edges have started to turn slightly brown. Grill or broil steak on a medium hot grill until it is firm.

3.  Chop the vegetables. Sauté slightly in a pan sprayed with olive oil. (if using greens as a substitute, do not sauté. Just chop and pile on.)

4. Thin slice steak. Pile on top of potato with beans and sautéed vegetables.

For lunch the next day: Chop potato, and put in a plastic container with steak, beans vegetables, salt, and pepper. If using chopped greens, put them in last, after potato has cooled. Toss just before eating.

## VARIATIONS

| Protein | Starch | Vegetables | |
|---|---|---|---|
| 16 oz cooked | potato (sweet or white) | artichoke | okra |
| (20 oz for | winter squash | asparagus | onions |
| men) | acorn squash | yellow/green beans | parsley |
| beef | hubbard squash | Belgian endives | peppers |
| ground beef | spaghetti squash | bok choy | pickles, dill |
| veal | butternut squash | broccoli | pimentos |
| pork | | Brussels sprouts | radishes |
| lamb | | cabbage | romaine |
| chicken | | carrots | rutabaga |
| turkey | | cauliflower | sauerkraut |
| ground | | celery | snow peas |
| turkey/sausage | | chicory | spinach |
| deli sliced | | Chinese cabbage | sprouts |
| turkey | | eggplant | tomato |
| deli sliced beef | | endive | turnip |
| 4 c beans | | escarole | water |
| tofu | | greens | chestnuts |
| | | lettuce | watercress |
| | | mushrooms | zucchini |

# SKILLET TOSS
## (4 servings)

| | |
|---|---|
| 1½ lb (Uncooked weight) Shrimp | Salt and pepper |
| 4c Rice cooked | 2T Ginger root |
| 4 large Onions | 2T Tamari sauce |
| 4c Snow peas | |

1. Boil rice for 40 minutes, drain. (Hopefully, you have remembered to do this beforehand. If not, substitute a quick grain such as quinoa.)

2. Sauté onion in a large skillet until onion is translucent. Add peeled shrimp until it is solid pink. Add snow peas just for a few minutes when shrimp is almost done.

3. Peel ginger root, chop fine, and add to onions and peas.

3. Toss rice into onion, shrimp, and snow peas. Serve.

For lunch the next day: Put tossed ingredients into a plastic container.

## VARIATIONS

| Protein | Starch | Vegetables | |
|---|---|---|---|
| 16 oz cooked | barley | artichoke | okra |
| (20 oz for men) | brown rice | asparagus | onions |
| beef, ground or cubed | millet | bamboo shoots | parsley |
| veal, ground or cubed | beans | yellow/green beans | peppers |
| pork, ground or cubed | corn | bok choy | pimentos |
| lamb, ground or cubed | potato, | broccoli | radicchio |
| ground chicken or chopped breast | cubed | Brussels sprouts | sauerkraut |
| ground turkey or chopped breast | peas | cabbage | snow peas |
| fish | | carrots | spinach |
| shellfish | | cauliflower | summer squash |
| tofu | | celery | tomato |
| 4 eggs (mix, pour into pan, | | Chinese cabbage | turnip |
| let set, cut into strips) | | eggplant | water chestnuts |
| 4 c beans | | escarole | zucchini |
| deli sliced turkey | | greens | |
| deli sliced beef | | mushrooms | |

For a second vegetable in place of snow peas, a salad could be served on the side.

# OVEN ROAST
## (4 servings)

1 Turkey breast        2c Chopped cabbage
2 Sweet potatoes      4c Baby carrots
Salt and pepper        4T Unsweetened mayonnaise
Poultry seasoning

   1. Preheat oven to 400'.  Wash and dry turkey breast, sweet potatoes, and carrots.
   2. Arrange meat and vegetables in a casserole dish.  Heavily sprinkle seasonings on turkey. Place turkey in middle with vegetables around it.
   3. Place meat and vegetables in oven and lower heat to 350' for one hour.
   4. Dress cabbage with mayonnaise, salt, and pepper.

   For lunch the next day, place sliced turkey and sliced vegetables in a container.  Place dressed cabbage on top, or in a separate container according to your preference.

# VARIATIONS

| Protein | Starch | Vegetable | |
|---|---|---|---|
| 16 oz cooked | barley* | Raw on the side | Roasted |
| (20 oz for men) | brown rice* | bamboo shoots | carrots |
| tougher cuts of beef | beans | Belgian endives | celery |
| veal roast | potato (sweet or white) | bokchoy | onions |
| pork roast | winter squash | broccoli | peppers |
| leg of lamb | acorn squash | cauliflower | eggplant |
| whole chicken | hubbard squash | celery | turnip |
| turkey breast | spaghetti squash | chicory | zucchini |
| hearty fish | butternut squash | Chinese cabbage | |
| | | cucumber | |
| | | endive | |
| | | greens | |
| | | lettuce | |
| | | mushrooms | |
| | | parsley | |
| | | peppers | |
| | | pickles, dill | |
| | | pimentos | |
| | | radishes | |
| | | romaine | |
| | | snow peas | |
| | | spinach | |
| | | sprouts | |
| | | summer squash | |
| | | tomato | |
| | | water chestnuts | |
| | | watercress | |

   Place grain and lightly salted water in casserole dish, then meat and vegetables.  See package for quantity of water.

# MIXED GRILL
## (4 servings)

| | |
|---|---|
| 1½ lb (Uncooked weight) Butterflied leg of lamb | Spray olive oil |
| 4T Red Vinegar | 4 Slices of Polenta |
| Salt and pepper to taste | 4c Summer squash |
| 2t Oregano | 4c Sliced cucumber |
| 2t Garlic (powdered or sliced) | ½c Yogurt (dill optional) |

1. When unpacking groceries, prepare lamb by sprinkling vinegar, salt, pepper, oregano, and garlic on it. Freeze in marinate. Remove from freezer and leave in refrigerator before using.

2. Spray summer squash with oil and sprinkle with salt and pepper. Place in microwave until hot and slightly steamed.

3. Place lamb in microwave until it is hot and edges have started to turn gray.

4. Spray Polenta with oil.

5. Grill lamb and squash on a medium hot grill until lamb is crisp on the outside, about 20 minutes on a side. Place squash and Polenta around the cooler edge of the grill.

6. Thin slice lamb. If it is underdone, return it to the microwave. Serve with cucumber dressed in yogurt, salt, and pepper.

For lunch the next day: While preparing dinner, place lamb and sliced squash in a plastic container. Polenta goes in one plastic bag, and the dressed cucumbers in another.

## VARIATIONS

| Protein | Starch | | | Grilled Vegetables |
|---|---|---|---|---|
| 16 oz cooked | potato*** | | | mushrooms |
| (20 oz for men) | | | | onions*** |
| beef steak | | | | peppers*** |
| veal chop | | | | eggplant*** |
| pork chop | | | | tomato |
| chicken breast* | | | | zucchini*** |
| turkey** | | | | |
| fish* | | | | |
| Vegetable: Raw on the side | | | | |
| bamboo shoots | | | | |
| Belgian endives | cucumber | pickles, dill | | sprouts |
| bokchoy | endive | pimentos | | summer squash |
| broccoli | greens | radicchio | | tomato |
| cauliflower | lettuce | radishes | | water chestnuts |
| celery | mushrooms | romaine | | watercress |
| chicory | parsley | snow peas | | |
| Chinese cabbage | peppers | spinach | | |

*Marinate in lemon juice, salt, and pepper. **Do not marinate. ***Microwave until hot before grilling.

# POT TOSS
## (4 servings)

4 Cubed raw chicken breasts     Poultry seasoning
2c Uncooked barley     4c Sliced tomatoes
4c Carrots     4T Salad dressing
Salt and pepper

1. Drop all ingredients into a pot except tomatoes and dressing, cover with water.
2. Allow liquid to come to a boil, then turn down to a simmer for about 1 hour.
3. Serve with tomatoes on the side.

For lunch the next day, either leave the chicken on the bone, or if you prefer, remove it. Place leftovers in a plastic container or a thermos. Heat before leaving the house in the morning and place in a small cooler. Place sliced tomatoes in a separate container.

## VARIATIONS

| Protein | Starch | Vegetable | |
|---|---|---|---|
| 16 oz cooked | barley | Raw on the side | Boiled |
| (20 oz for men) | brown rice | bamboo shoots | carrots |
| any cubed meat | whole grain rye | Belgian endives | celery |
| pork chop | quinoa (drop in for the last 15 | bokchoy | escarole |
| turkey breast | minutes of cooking only) | broccoli | mustard or |
| hearty fish | beans | cauliflower | collard greens |
|  | cubed potato | celery | mushrooms |
|  | peas | chicory | onions |
|  |  | Chinese cabbage | peppers |
|  |  | cucumber | eggplant |
|  |  | endive | turnip |
|  |  | greens | |
|  |  | lettuce | |
|  |  | mushrooms | |
|  |  | parsley | |
|  |  | peppers | |
|  |  | pickles, dill | |
|  |  | pimentos | |
|  |  | radishes | |
|  |  | romaine | |
|  |  | snow peas | |
|  |  | spinach | |
|  |  | sprouts | |
|  |  | summer squash | |
|  |  | tomato | |
|  |  | water chestnuts | |
|  |  | watercress | |

For barley or brown rice, place grain and lightly salted water in casserole dish, then meat and vegetables.

# BEANS TOPPED
## (4 servings)

4 c Refried beans, or any other kind of beans
4 c Salsa
4 c Spinach

1. Spread beans on a plate and heat for 1-2 minutes in the microwave

2. Top with 1 cup per serving of salsa and 1 cup per serving of chopped spinach. Serve.

For lunch the next day: It would be better to use a bean such as a pinto, Garbanzo or great northern. Put salad dressing in first, then beans, then salsa and spinach last. Toss just before eating.

## VARIATIONS

| Protein | Starch | Vegetables | |
|---|---|---|---|
| 16 oz cooked | potato (sweet or white) | artichoke | okra |
| (20 oz for men) | winter squash | asparagus | onions |
| beef | acorn squash | yellow/green beans | parsley |
| ground beef | hubbard squash | Belgian endives | peppers |
| veal | spaghetti squash | bokchoy | pickles, dill |
| pork | butternut squash | broccoli | pimentos |
| lamb | | cabbage | radishes |
| chicken | | carrots | romaine |
| turkey | | chicory | sauerkraut |
| ground | | Chinese cabbage | sprouts |
| turkey/sausage | | steamed eggplant | tomato |
| deli sliced turkey | | endive | water chestnuts |
| deli sliced beef | | steamed escarole | watercress |
| tofu | | steamed greens | zucchini |
| | | lettuce | |
| | | mushrooms | |

Note: The beans serve as both protein and starch in the meal. Any of the proteins listed above are necessary to provide a complete set of enzymes for digestion.

# FAVORITE LUNCH AND DINNER MENUS

When I started putting together these recipes, it really came clear to me that refined carbohydrate sensitivity is the disease of industrialized nations. As I thought about the most dramatic and memorable meals that I have eaten, many were so because of their setting, but also because of the clear, honest flavors of food which had not been weighed down or muted by refined carbohydrates. And many of them took place away from the highly populated centers where processed foods proliferate. What I really hope to portray with these recipes is that honest, life-sustaining food has deep character, mood, and texture.

Food can be romantic, sensual, and at the same time balanced. In fact, I would go so far as to say that food which is not wholly contributing to the well being of my body is neither romantic or sensual because it is robbing the body of the grounding it needs to make heart-to-heart, soul-to-soul connections. Food which numbs us robs us of precious memories. Food which makes us tired or irritable robs us of the chance to end an evening on romantic terms with our partner.

Through every triumph and disaster, we need never lose the foundation that comes from eating soundly. So I have placed these recipes in the context of life, both good and bad, relaxed and stressed, joyous and routine, simple and complex. Somewhere on these pages, I hope you will find the inspiration to support yourself well under all circumstances.

To emphasize the importance of balance in food planning, I have listed the ingredients according to their role as protein, vegetable, and starch. All dishes are complete meals.

There are weight gain options for people who are using this program to recover from underweight eating disorders and for parents who want their thin children to stop eating refined carbohydrates without losing weight. These weight gain options would include using higher-fat grades of diary products (milk and yogurt) in place of non-fat or low-fat diary products. Extra olive oil can be added to many dishes, either mixed into stews or added to salad dressing. I would advise against using nuts as they often cause unforeseeable reactions.

All quantities are for four servings. Even if you are cooking for one, I encourage you to make and refrigerate or freeze extra servings.

Bon appetite!

# FIVE FAVORITE SALAD TOSSES

The word salad is used very loosely here. The basic idea is to take any ingredients from the lunch and dinner food groups, chop them as big as you like and toss together with dressing. I first realized the simple power of unprocessed food when I began grabbing leftovers willy nilly from the refrigerator and tossing them together in plastic containers for quick take-away lunches. No matter which vegetables, protein, and starch I used, the clean, clear flavor of the ingredients worked wonderfully together.

## THANKSGIVING REINVENTED
### (4 servings)

This is one of the quickest salads in the book. Be careful when choosing the spicy deli turkey. Only one brand does not contain a form of sugar.

| | |
|---|---|
| Protein: | 1 lb. Spicy sliced deli turkey, cut into strips |
| Raw vegetable: | 4c Chopped cabbage |
| Raw vegetable: | 4c Whole baby carrots |
| Starch: | 4c Cubed boiled sweet potato |
| Dressing: | 4T Unsweetened mayonnaise |
| Seasonings: | Salt and pepper to taste |

Cabbage can be tossed into the food processor, but I vastly prefer to chop it coarsely on the chopping board. Remember to boil the sweet potato the night before. If you have forgotten, you can microwave the sweet potato for five minutes and serve it on the side. Otherwise, just chop all ingredients and toss together.

## VERY GREEN SALAD
### (4 servings)

This is a variation on a oft-made childhood potato salad. In fact, it was one of the first dishes I ever learned to make. My thoughts turn in this direction whenever the summer temperatures climb.

| | |
|---|---|
| Protein: | 8 Hard boiled eggs, chopped or 1 lb cubed firm tofu |
| Raw vegetable: | 4c Chopped green pepper |
| Raw vegetable: | 4c Chopped green onion |
| Starch: | 4c Green peas (or 2c peas and 2c boiled potatoes, *al dente*) |
| Dressing: | 4T Unsweetened mayonnaise |
| Seasonings: | Salt and pepper to taste |

Toss all ingredients together. Chill thoroughly.

# TEXMEX SALAD
## (4 servings)

This refreshing combination uses the unusual ingredient of quinoa. I was first introduced to quinoa in a leadership training conducted by my beloved women's healing group, *Woman Within*. I sat next to a woman from the plains states who had brought this salad. She had such hardy, clean, lean pioneer looks that it was easy to picture her stepping right out of a sod hut. During the course of the training I came to appreciate her honesty, energy, humor, and eagerness for spiritual progress. I suppose that is why I associate quinoa with these qualities as well. (Yes, quinoa is humorous. Each grain has a little tail that appears when it is done cooking.) If you learn only one new food from this book, let it be quinoa.

Because quinoa has a relatively short cook time, it is a good candidate for a last minute meal. The salad turns out a little like tabbouleh with quinoa taking the place of bulgur wheat. To make this more like tabbouleh, substitute parsley for the cilantro.

| | |
|---|---|
| Protein: | 4 Chopped cooked chicken breasts |
| Raw vegetable: | 4c Chopped tomato (or bottled salsa) |
| Raw vegetable: | 2c Chopped purple onion and 2c cilantro |
| Starch: | 4c Quinoa |
| Dressing: | 4T Balsamic vinegar (4T olive oil optional) or lime juice |
| Seasonings: | 1t Garlic salt, pepper to taste |

Rinse quinoa in a fine strainer and swirl into boiling, salted water. Boil it just until its tails appear, about 12-15 minutes. Chicken breasts can be grilled, or even just cooked in the microwave. Chop all ingredients and toss with dressing of choice.

# SUMMER SEAFOOD SALAD
## 4 servings

This salad will grace your table in just a few minutes if you buy greens that are already washed and shrimp that are already boiled and peeled. If you are really pressed for time, just open a can of corn instead of shucking and boiling corn on the cob. The asparagus needs only a few minutes in a steamer or the microwave. Don't hesitate to serve it on the side uncut to shorten preparation time. The pastel pink, green, and yellow of the ingredients in this salad are soothing to the eye.

| | |
|---|---|
| Protein: | 1 lb Cooked chilled boiled shrimp (or any cooked seafood) |
| Raw vegetable: | 4c Field greens |
| Raw vegetable: | 4c Slightly steamed asparagus, cut into 1" lengths |
| Starch: | 4c Fresh corn cut off the cob, or served on the side, or canned corn |
| Dressing: | 4T Vinaigrette |
| Seasonings: | Salt and pepper to taste |

Toss all ingredients together.

# JAW BREAKER SALAD
## (4 servings)

I invented this salad for people who yearn for something "crunchy" after they've been on the program for a few weeks. I offer this salad as a way to absolutely wear out the jaw and banish all further thoughts of chewing. The more wild rice you add in place of the raw jicama, the greater the chewing challenge. Like the spicy deli turkey, there is only one peppered deli beef that does not have a kind of sugar added. The colors of the bright and white vegetables against the nearly black rice make this dish visually stunning.

| | |
|---|---|
| Protein: | 1 lb Peppered deli beef, cut into strips |
| Raw vegetable: | 4c Whole baby carrots |
| Raw vegetable: | 4c Chunky sliced celery |
| Starch: | 4c Raw jicama cut into strips, or 2c jicama and 2c wild rice |
| Dressing: | 4T Vinaigrette |
| Seasonings: | Salt and pepper to taste |

Toss all ingredients together.

# FIVE FAVORITE POT TOSSES

As you might imagine, pot tosses find their way to the table more often in winter than in summer, but they make a welcome relief from salads at any time of year. They can take a while to cook, but also require perhaps the least preparation. Investing in a crock pot is advisable since many pot tosses can be assembled on our way out the door in the morning and left to simmer while we're away. A crock pot is especially useful if you have forgotten to thaw meat. Just throw the meat still frozen into the crock pot with all other ingredients. For ground meat, break it up and stir it in when you get home. For something like a chicken breast, just serve the pot toss in a shallow dish and cut up the chicken breast as you eat. Pot tosses are excellent dishes in which to use the hearty "greens" such as mustard, collard, and beet. These greens are rich in calcium as well as other elusive minerals. Be creative.

## CURRY
### (4 servings)

This recipe holds a very special place in my memories because my mother made lamb curry for the parties she gave for the men under my father's command in the Navel Reserves. I looked forward to being fed before the guests arrived and to having the leftovers for days. It is still a favorite among guests to my home today.

| | |
|---|---|
| Protein: | 1½ lb (Uncooked weight) Cubed meat or 1 lb cubed firm tofu |
| Cooked vegetable: | 2c Onion, 2c eggplant |
| Starch: | 4c Green peas, potatoes or brown rice |
| Seasonings: | 1/2t Cumin, 1t turmeric, 1/4t cayenne pepper, 1/2t mustard seed, 1/4t coriander, ½t cinnamon, zest of ½ lemon or orange |
| Side raw vegetable: | 4c Total of cucumber, tomato, green pepper, onion, all coarsely chopped |

Brown meat, onion, eggplant in a skillet, sprinkle with seasonings, cover with water, and simmer until meat is tender. Cook rice separately by boiling salted water, swirling rice into the water and cooking until rice is just edible, about 35 minutes. Turn rice onto a platter and spoon curry over it. Chop raw vegetables and serve each vegetable in its own small cup around the curry.

Quick version: Toss meat, onion, eggplant, peas, potatoes, and/or rice into a crock pot set at low heat, cover with water, (use 2 ½ times water if using raw rice) sprinkle with 2T of prepared curry powder, set on low, and take off for work. Serve with any of the side vegetables.

# CLAM CHOWDER
## (4 servings)

This is one of the easiest yet most satisfying dishes in the book. My children, who are not crazy about fish, are always happy to see this chowder on the stove.

| | |
|---|---|
| Protein: | 1 lb Canned clams (or 1½ lbs. of any hearty raw white fish fillet) |
| Cooked vegetable: | 4c Chopped celery |
| Starch: | 4c Cubed potato |
| Seasonings: | 1 8 oz Bottle of clam juice, 1t oregano, salt, and pepper |
| Side raw vegetable: | 4c Cauliflower |
| Dressing: | 4T Curried mayonnaise |

Toss clams, celery, potato, clam juice, and seasonings into the pot, cover with water and walk away. Cook until potatoes are tender, about 35 minutes. If you would like this to be creamy, just run it through the food processor before serving.

To make curried mayonnaise, add 1T curry to 1c unsweetened mayonnaise. Toss cauliflower in 1T of mayonnaise and refrigerate the remainder in an air- tight jar.

# MARY'S ZUCCHINI SOUP
## (4 servings)

This recipe comes from the woman behind the deli counter in my neighborhood health food store. She believes that it is her personal responsibility to make everyone smile who comes into the store. I unconsciously head toward her counter when I need a lift. She especially made me smile one day when I was late for lunch and needed something quick. As she ticked off the list of ingredients in this soup and I realized that it was an honest, clean, balanced dish, I *really* smiled.

It seems odd to think of hot soup in the summer, but because zucchini plays such a big role in this recipe, it makes sense to make this dish in the summer. You won't regret it. For vegetarians, any kind of bean will substitute for the chicken.

| | |
|---|---|
| Protein: | 1½ lb Cubed raw chicken breast |
| Cooked vegetable: | 4c Zucchini, cut into chunks |
| Starch: | 4c Brown rice |
| Seasonings: | 1t Oregano, 1t thyme, salt, and pepper to taste |
| Side raw vegetable: | 4c Broccoli |
| Dressing: | 4T Herbed mayonnaise |

Put chicken, zucchini, rice, and seasonings in a pot. Cover with twice the amount of water as ingredients. It takes about 30 minutes from when the water starts to boil. So, throw it together and let it cook while you're making dinner the night before.

To make herbed mayonnaise, mix 1t of herb of choice into 1c mayonnaise. Good candidates for herbs would be oregano, thyme, tarragon or dill. I like little jars of each in the refrigerator. They perk up raw vegetables incredibly.

# NESTED VEAL
## (4 servings)

I learned how to make this from a summer *au pair* I hired over the phone from Ohio. It was a rough summer for her because her parents were getting a divorce and she was quite homesick. I suspect that the homey feeling of this dish comforted her, as it did all of us whether we needed it or not. We ate it happily each of the many times she made it.

| | |
|---|---|
| Protein: | 1½ lb (Uncooked weight) Cubed veal (or chicken), plus milk for the potatoes |
| Cooked vegetable: | 4c Pearl onions |
| Starch: | 4c Mashed potatoes |
| Seasonings: | 1T Rosemary, salt and pepper to taste |
| Side raw vegetable: | 4c Shredded carrots |
| Dressing: | 4T Unsweetened mayonnaise |

Simmer meat, onions, and seasonings together until done. (Sauté meat and onions in spray olive oil first if you would like a little color on them.) Frozen pearl onions will save the labor of peeling all of those onions.

Make a nest of the potatoes on each plate and fill with the veal mixture. The shredded carrots will complete the image of a nest.

# COLD WATERCRESS SPREAD
## (4 servings)

This recipe was given to me by Thea, whose story appears in the *Personal Triumphs* chapter in the back of the book. She stands out in my mind as one of the most elegant transformations wrought by the food plan. When she eliminated refined carbohydrates from her food, not only did she develop a slender figure, but her self-confidence came up and her tremendous intellect and spirituality emerged through her vision and words. She got herself a very chic haircut and began wearing bias cut dresses which flowed with her smooth gait. Her posture changed and she held her head high. You would never imagine that she had ever been anyone but a cherished princess. Whenever I eat this dish, I thank God for giving me the gift of knowing Thea.

| | |
|---|---|
| Protein: | 1 lb soft tofu |
| Vegetable: | 4c Watercress |
| Vegetable: | 4c Chopped tomatoes |
| Starch: | 8 Ricecakes |
| Seasonings: | Salt and pepper to taste |

This technically does not require a pot, but as it is a beautiful spread, I include it here. All you do is put the ingredients (except ricecakes) in a food processor, swirl, spread and enjoy.

## FIVE FAVORITE SKILLET TOSSES

Making skillet tosses is fun for company since they can see what's going into the skillet. If you wish to include guests in preparations, they can chop ingredients for you. Skillet tosses are also quite lovely since the minimal cook times leave vegetables with their bright colors.

## CHINESE CORNUCOPIA

The kids and I wander down Mulberry Street, cross Canal, and enter Chinatown in lower Manhattan. I am a little intimidated by the abrupt change from Little Italy to a sea of undecipherable signs and voices. Somewhere we will need to eat lunch. How will we order if the waiter doesn't speak English? I had always known that Chinatown was insulated, but I wasn't prepared for the degree of cultural cohesion. Within a few doors, a smiling restauranteur motions us to descend a steep flight of stairs. We find ourselves in a very plain, low-ceiling room chock full of Chinese families conversing and eating at full tilt. At the table next to ours, a family feasts from platters of fragrant vegetables, fish, meat, and rice. All I have to do for the waiter is smile, point to the neighboring table, say "No soy sauce, please," and wait. Here is what he brought.

## SPRING BEEF
(4 servings)

| | |
|---|---|
| Protein: | 1½ lb (uncooked weight) Beef cut into strips (or pork, fish, seafood, firm tofu, etc.) |
| Cooked vegetable: | 4c Asparagus |
| Starch: | 4c Brown rice |
| Seasonings: | 3 Cloves of garlic, 4T vinegar, 4T Bragg's, 4T Sesame oil, and/or hot chili oil |
| Raw vegetable: | 1c scallions and 3c sliced cucumber |

If you haven't cooked the rice beforehand, start the water now. When water is boiling, stir in rice and check after 35 minutes. Drain when done and turn into a platter. Chop chicken breasts into chunks. Brown chicken breasts and garlic in hot skillet with oils. Slice asparagus into 1"diagonal pieces and add it to chicken mixture. Add vinegar and Bragg's and stir continually until asparagus is bright green. Turn onto rice. Slice cucumbers and scallions. Sprinkle liberally over servings of the chicken.

# BROCCOLI AND CHICKEN
## (4 servings)

Protein:              4 Chicken breasts
Cooked vegetable:     4c Broccoli
Starch:               4c Brown rice
Seasonings:           2 Cloves of garlic, juice of one lemon, salt and pepper to taste
Raw vegetable:        4c Sprouts

Make rice if you have not already done so. Marinate chicken breasts in lemon juice, salt, and pepper. Grill and cut into chunks. Brown garlic in a skillet which has been sprayed with olive oil. Slightly steam broccoli and add to skillet with garlic. Add chicken chunks and toss. Place rice on platter, cover with the chicken mixture, sprinkle on sprouts, and serve.

# PICK-UP STICKS SCALLOPS
## (4 servings)

Protein:              1½ lb (Uncooked weight) Scallops
Cooked vegetable:     4c Total of red, green, yellow, and purple peppers, scallions
Starch:               4c Brown rice
Seasonings:           4T Bragg's
Side raw vegetable:   4c Chopped cabbage
Dressing              4T Oil and vinegar

When you are serving this dish, you will see where it got its name! Make rice if you have not already done so. Toss scallops in Bragg's and sauté in pan which has been sprayed with olive oil. Slice peppers and scallions into strips and sprinkle over scallops. Cover skillet and let peppers cook slightly. The golden color of the scallops with the bright peppers is very pleasing to the eye. Chop cabbage coarsely. Toss with oil and vinegar.

# VERY ELEGANT CAMP STEW
## (4 servings)

Taking advantage of the kids being in camp, my husband and I went hiking in the Ozarks north of Little Rock. We knew that on the third day, there was the likelihood of rain. So after hiking beautiful, absolutely deserted woods for two days, we decided to push 14 miles in order to arrive at a camping area near to the store where we had left our car. I don't know if I have ever been so completely empty and exhausted as I was when we arrived at camp. Fortunately, all I had to do to make the ultimate fabulous simple dinner was the following:

| | |
|---|---|
| Protein: | 4 Sliced chicken breasts |
| Cooked vegetable: | 1c Total of dried onion and dried Porcini mushrooms |
| Cooked vegetable: | 1c Dried tomatoes |
| Starch: | 4c Dried brown rice |
| Seasonings: | 1/4t Saffron, salt and pepper to taste |

Drop all ingredients into a skillet. Cover with water. Simmer until all ingredients are reconstituted and heated through, adding water as needed. I used chicken breasts which I had grilled, sliced thinly, and then dried in my dehydrator. I also used instant rice, and dried onion and mushrooms which I purchased already dried at the store. At home, of course, you would use all fresh ingredients, serving the tomatoes fresh on the side.

# VEAL AU CHATEAU
## (4 servings)

Imagine yourself pulling into a French chateau late at night along the banks of the Loire River. Fortunately, you have called ahead so the hostess has prepared a late supper for you. In a softly lit room which has been sheltering travelers for centuries, you sit down to this meal.

| | |
|---|---|
| Protein: | 4 Thick cut veal or pork chops, appx. 8oz each (please weigh after cooked and deboned to make sure you have 4oz) |
| Starch: | 4c New potatoes |
| Seasonings: | 4T Rosemary, 4 cloves of garlic, salt and pepper to taste |
| Side raw vegetable: | 4c Sliced Rome tomatoes |
| Side raw vegetable: | 4c Boston lettuce (also known as butter lettuce) |
| Dressing: | 4T Watercress, blended with 4Toil and 4T vinegar, salt and pepper to taste |

Boil potatoes in their jackets *al dente*. Spray oil in a sauté pan, sprinkle with rosemary and sliced garlic, add potatoes, and sauté until brown. Remove potatoes and without cleaning pan, respray with olive oil and add veal chops which have been slightly microwaved. Sprinkle with rosemary, salt, and pepper to taste. Brown chops slowly until cooked through. Remove any slices of garlic and serve with potatoes and salad.

# FIVE FAVORITE OVEN ROASTS

Like the pot tosses, you might tend to make the oven roasts in the winter. Don't forget, because they are the easiest to make, but have the longest cook times, oven roasts should be assembled and baked during dinner the night before you intend to eat them.

## SPAGHETTI SQUASH
### (4 servings)
If your family is yearning for something that looks a little like spaghetti, this is it.

| | |
|---|---|
| Protein: | 4 oz Non-fat mozzarella cheese |
| Cooked vegetable: | 4c Tomato sauce and optional onion |
| Starch: | 4c Spaghetti squash |
| Seasonings: | Garlic (optional) |
| Side raw vegetable: | 4c Endive |
| Dressing: | 4T Italian |

Bake the spaghetti squash at 350' for one hour. If you have an oven with an automatic shut off, you can put the squash in the oven when you leave in the morning. Otherwise, you can bake it the night before. Scoop out the squash into a large casserole dish. Brown onion and garlic in spray olive oil. (Or just use prepared garlic powder.) Pour tomato sauce into skillet, heat, and then pour over squash. Top with cheese. Put under broiler until cheese is melted. Serve with salad.

Quick version. Scoop out baked squash and mix with tomato sauce, seasonings, and cheese. Microwave until heated through. Serve with salad.

## POLENTA PIZZA
### (4 servings)
This dish filled the gap in our hearts for pizza. Of course, polenta pizza is vastly improved over the cardboard version available from pizza shops. It is the hands-down favorite of my daughter for her birthday dinner.

| | |
|---|---|
| Protein: | 1½ lb Unsweetened Kielbasa, or Italian sausage (or any ground meat) |
| Cooked vegetable: | 4c Mushrooms |
| Starch: | 4c Polenta |
| Seasonings: | 4t oregano, 4t garlic salt |
| Side raw vegetable: | 4c Celery sticks |

Make polenta by boiling water then swirling in corn grits, and simmering gently until a spoon stands up in the pan. (Ratio of water to corn grits is 4c water to 2c corn grits.) Spread the hot polenta onto a jelly roll pan which has been sprayed with olive oil. Sauté meat and mushrooms with oregano and garlic salt and spread over polenta.

Make 1 serving of polenta by boiling 1c broth, adding ½ c corn grits, and stirring until a spoon stands up in it. If you are only making one serving, you could use a small soufflé dish rather than the jelly roll pan.

## STUFFED PUMPKIN
### (4 servings)

Actually, any squash will do, especially acorn squash. Learning to eat a variety of squashes has been a great gift of eliminating sugars and flours from my diet. This is quick to do but takes a long time to cook, so make it the night before.

| | |
|---|---|
| Protein: | 1½ lb Ground turkey |
| Cooked vegetable: | 4c Chopped onions |
| Starch: | 2 Small pumpkins |
| Seasonings: | ½t Sage, 1T rosemary |
| Side raw vegetable: | 4c Carrot sticks |

Cut pumpkins in half, scoop out seeds. Mix turkey, onions, and seasoning and stuff loosely into pumpkin halves. Bake one hour at 350'.

## CHICKEN POT PIE
### (4 servings)

I appreciated this dish wholly after dusk on a freezing night in Vermont. My husband and I skied a long trail that led from one town to the next. We had lingered at one too many charming spots and still had a long ways to go when the light began to fail. As the sun dropped so did the temperature. The trail began to freeze up which in combination with tired, quivering legs made for very dangerous conditions. Finally the inn we were heading for came into view at the bottom of one last short, steep curve. I knew I couldn't make the slope and yet I had absolutely no choice. Down I flew and sprawled every which way into the back yard of the inn. After collecting my possessions and stumbling into the dining room, I was very happy to be seated before the fire and served this life-restoring dish.

| | |
|---|---|
| Protein: | 1½ lb (Uncooked weight) Cubed chicken breasts, plus ½ c milk for potatoes |
| Cooked vegetable: | 2c Carrots, 2c celery |
| Starch: | 2c Mashed potatoes, 1c frozen peas and 1c canned, drained corn |
| Seasonings: | 1t Oregano, 1t thyme, salt and pepper to taste |
| Side raw vegetable: | 4c Total of Arugula and Boston lettuce |
| Dressing: | 4T Oil and vinegar |

This is a little more complicated than most of the recipes in this section. You might wait until a week-end to make this since it's nice to be at home to enjoy the aroma of this dish as it bakes. A time management tip is to bake the casserole up to the point of adding mashed potatoes the night before you intend to eat it. Refrigerate and finish the next night. You could also add extra peas and corn and skip the mashed potatoes altogether.

Place all ingredients except potatoes in a large casserole dish. Cover with water. Cover tightly with foil and bake at 350' for 45 minutes.

Make mashed potatoes by dropping red potatoes in cold, salted water, cook *al dente*, 15-20 minutes from when the water boils. The potatoes should yield with resistance to a piercing fork. Do not let them get mushy. (If you overcook the potatoes and then process them, their glucose content could be high enough to make you sleepy, or trigger you in some other way. So cook them as little as you can stand. If they are lumpy because they undercooked, this just adds to the homey, honest feel of the dish.)

Heat milk in the microwave while potatoes are draining. Cut up potatoes, place them in a food processor with salt and pepper, and pulse process until they are uniformly chopped. Drizzle in hot milk just until potatoes are somewhat smooth.

Spread potatoes over casserole. Briefly return to 450' oven until potatoes are brown.

Quick version. Skip the potatoes. Double the amount of peas and heat in microwave. Cube and toss with canned chicken, double the amount of canned corn, baby carrots, and chopped celery. Reheat in microwave if desired, or eat at room temperature. Serve salad on side.

## GOOD OLD MEAT LOAF
### (4 servings)

If you cook for someone who fears that his "meat and potatoes" are going to disappear on this new food plan, then reassure him with this meat loaf.

| | |
|---|---|
| Protein: | 1 lb and 2 oz Ground meat, mixed with 4T raw oatmeal and 2 eggs |
| Seasonings: | 1/4c Chopped parsley, 1/4c unsweetened catsup, salt and pepper to taste |
| Cooked vegetables: | 4c Green beans and 4c onions (tossed with 2T olive oil, 2t salt, and 2t pepper) |
| Starch: | 4c Boiled potatoes tossed with with 2T chopped parsley and 2T butter |

Mix meat with oatmeal, eggs, and seasonings. Form meat into an oval, or pack into a loaf pan. Bake along with potatoes at 350' until done. Remove meat loaf from oven. Turn oven up to highest setting. Toss green beans and sliced onions together with olive oil, salt, and pepper. Spread on a cookie sheet and put in very hot oven until the beans and onions begin to brown. The vegetables will still be a little on the raw side, but the crispiness is part of the pleasure of the dish.

# FIVE FAVORITE GRILLS

Grilling is associated with summer all over the world. When I moved south five years ago, I found to my delight that my local gas company would install a gas pipe to my outdoor grill for next to nothing. Now I grill year 'round. To shorten grilling time and retain moisture in the food, I microwave all items, both meats and vegetables, until they are slightly opaque around the edge and steaming. Always grill extra items to put in the freezer. When you pull them out at odd times, you will savor the aroma of the grill as if you had just come from its side. Use a hot broiler if you don't have access to a grill.

## FAJITAS BUFFET
### (4 servings)

When I think of this menu, I see hungry teen-agers crowded around the long counter of my kitchen. I express thanks to my Higher Power for bringing me the food plan which allows me to stay calm during parties and be on good terms with teen-agers in general. I used to have temper tantrums before parties, out of feelings of being overwhelmed and unsupported. I used to embarrass my own teen-aged children when they had guests because I made critical remarks in front of them. The ability to shift away from this behavior to warm, accepting behavior is a gift of the food plan that I especially treasure.

This summer, a friend of my daughter's asked to stay at our house because her alcoholic mother was verbally abusing her. Another friend asked to stay with us for a few weeks while her parents were traveling. I am filled with awe that teen-agers would see my house as a safe, inviting environment because I am the product of a household that my own high school friends thought was crazy and scary.

The popularity of this buffet with teen-agers is a symbol to me of the triumph of the food plan in healing personal relations.

| | |
|---|---|
| Protein: | 1 ½ lbs. (Uncooked weight) Chicken breasts or steak (preferably a mixture of both) |
| Cooked vegetable: | 4c Total of green and red peppers, and onions |
| Starch: | ½ c Non-fat refried beans |
| Seasonings: | 4T Lantana or other red pepper based seasoning mix |
| Side raw vegetable: | 4c Total of lettuce, tomatoes, onions, salsa, and cilantro |
| Dressing: | 4T Sour cream |

Coat chicken or steak with Lantana seasoning. Microwave meat until it is steaming and slightly opaque around the edges. Grill until firm. Cut peppers and onions in quarters, spray with olive oil, microwave until just steaming, turn into a grilling basket, and put on a very hot grill, turning once, just until edges turn brown. Coarsely chop lettuce and tomatoes. Finely chop onions and cilantro. Serve all items in separate bowls so guests can pile up their plates according to their own preferences.

Quick version: Open cans of refried beans, chicken, and tomatoes. Mix together and microwave until hot. Serve with any raw vegetable you happen to have.

# SUMMER CLASSIC GRILL
(4 servings)

This is a menu to prepare close to the beginning of changing your family's food. The simple glory of the items speak for themselves and your household will see that their favorites will still be on the table. When I think of this menu, I see family and friends standing on the edge of Long Island Sound on the Fourth of July. Kids are climbing on the rocks and adults are enjoying the breeze and the company of old friends. What bliss.

| | |
|---|---|
| Protein: | 1½ lbs. (Uncooked weight) Meat patties (turkey, chicken, beef) or unsweetened hot dogs |
| Cooked vegetable: | 4c Whole mushrooms |
| Starch: | 4 Ears corn, unshucked |
| Seasonings: | 1T Garlic powder, salt and pepper to taste |
| Side raw vegetable: | 4c Total dill pickles, chopped onions, relish, sauerkraut, carrot, and celery sticks |
| Dressing: | 4T Unsweetened mayonnaise. Unsweetened catsup and mustard to taste. |

Mix ground meat with garlic powder, salt, and pepper to taste. Form patties and microwave until steaming and opaque around the edges. Spray with olive oil and grill on a hot grill 2-3 minutes on a side until firm. Put mushrooms on a wooden skewer, sprinkle with salt and pepper to taste, and microwave until steaming. Spray with olive oil, place on hot grill only until browned.

Soak corn in salted water. Microwave 30 seconds each. Place around edge of grill until steaming. Shuck and serve.

# SLOW GRILL
(4 servings)

I had never had roasted or smoked turkey before I moved to Texas. It is one of the many delights of the "Third Coast" cuisine that has put Houston on the culinary map.

| | |
|---|---|
| Protein: | 1½ lbs. (uncooked weight) Turkey breast or sliced turkey breast |
| Cooked vegetable: | 4c Grilled zucchini |
| Starch: | 4c Grilled sweet potato |
| Seasonings: | 4T butter, salt and pepper to taste |
| Side raw vegetable: | 4c Carrot sticks |

This turkey breast requires indirect heat. If you have a double grill, put the breast on the unlit side with an aluminum tin of water underneath it. Leave it until the timer button pops up.

If you don't have time to wait for the whole turkey breast, then slice it, microwave until steaming and slightly opaque around the edges. Spray with olive oil, sprinkle with an unsweetened red pepper based seasoning mix. Grill slices briefly, 1-2 minutes on a side depending on how thin they are, until firm.

Cut zucchini in half lengthwise, sprinkle with salt, pepper, and garlic salt, microwave until steaming slightly, brush with melted butter or spray with olive oil. Grill on a very hot grill 2-3 minutes on a side until browned.

Cut sweet potatoes in cubes.  Microwave or steam until slightly steaming.  Toss in melted butter. Turn into a grill basket and grill until edges are crisp and brown.

## BAJA BEAUTY
### (4 servings)

We had this meal after a long trek into the jungles, deserts, and mountains of Baja.  We were searching for cathedrals and cave paintings.  We found both to be absolutely breath-taking and well worth the treacherous driving on rock-strewn "roads".  We ended the trip by camping on a beautiful beach at a little fishing village on the west coast.  Our hosts prepared this incredible meal for us over a fire at sunset.  It doesn't get any better.

| | |
|---|---|
| Protein: | 1½ lb (uncooked weight) Fresh tuna |
| Cooked vegetable: | 4 Large tomatoes |
| Starch: | 4c Yucca |
| Seasonings: | 4t Dill, juice of one lime, 4T olive oil, salt and pepper to taste |
| Side raw vegetable: | 4c Total of cucumber and celery |
| Dressing: | Snipped dill to taste |

Marinate fresh tuna in lime juice, dill, salt, and pepper.  Microwave until edges are opaque.  Spray with olive oil and grill until firm, 2 minutes on a side, depending on how thick the fillets are.

Tomatoes are best if they are firm.  Cut in half, sprinkle with salt and pepper, and microwave until just steaming.  Spray with olive oil and place cut side down on the grill.  Grill just until grid marks appear on the tomatoes.

Slice yucca into 1" slices.  Spray with olive oil.  Microwave slightly and grill until brown.

Slice cucumbers and sprinkle with dill.  If you prefer fresh tomatoes, serve them sliced with the cucumbers.  Quick version.  Boil 1c new potatoes and cube.  Toss with canned tuna, chopped tomatoes, cucumber, dill, olive oil, and vinegar.

## SEAFOOD BROCHETTES
### (4 servings)

The first meal I ever ate in Paris was a seafood brochette served over rice.  I will never forget the excitement of that night, full of exotic smells on the Left Bank.  I have eaten numerous other meals in Paris, but the first was, in some ways, the best.

| | |
|---|---|
| Protein: | 1½ lb (Uncooked weight) Shrimp (or any other seafood such as scallops, squid, octopus) |
| Cooked vegetable: | 4c Onion (quartered, tossed in oil, microwaved, and put in grill basket) |
| Starch: | 4c Basmati Brown Rice |
| Seasonings: | 4T Butter melted with garlic and oregano |
| Side raw vegetable: | 4c Cucumber |
| Dressing: | Snipped dill, salt and pepper to taste |

If you have not made rice the night before, start it now.  Swirl rice into plenty of boiling, salted water.  Taste for doneness after about 35 minutes.

Put shrimp on wooden skewers, slightly microwave until just steaming, brush with butter which has been melted with garlic and oregano.

Toss onions in olive oil, microwave until just steaming, turn into grill basket. Grill until edges are brown, then flip basket, and repeat.

Turn rice onto a platter, top with onions, and place brochettes on top.

Slice cucumbers and sprinkle with dill, salt and pepper to taste.  Serve on the side.

# FIVE FAVORITE TOPPED POTATOES

This is where we trot out all the gorgeous toppings that we used to put on pasta.  Don't use a baked potato for these recipes; baked potatoes are very high in carbohydrates.  Boiled potatoes are preferable, as are any of the grains.  Boil potatoes *al dente* to reduce the conversion of starch to glucose.

## NORTHERN ITALY REVISITED
### (4 servings)

This dish calls for a ham cured in the Prociutto province of northern Italy.  As made in Italy, it does not contain the sugars found almost universally in American cured ham.  Prociutto is very expensive and very strong tasting, so use non-fat mozzarella with it to make 4 oz of protein.

| | |
|---|---|
| Protein: | ½ lb Prociutto and ½ lb non-fat mozzarella |
| Starch: | 4c Sautéed potatoes |
| Seasonings: | Garlic, sage, salt and pepper to taste |
| Side raw vegetable: | 4c Field greens |
| Side raw vegetable: | 4c Green peppers, cut into spears |
| Dressing: | 4T Oil and vinegar |

Roast potatoes by microwaving slightly, then sautéing on high heat in olive oil spray with garlic and sage until brown and crisp.  Add cut-up prociutto to sauté pan and heat through.  Top with shredded mozzarella. Serve with green peppers which have been tossed with dressing.  If you are trying to reduce oil, just serve the peppers with salt and pepper.

## POTATOES PESTO
### (4 servings)

The first time I made this, it was so good that I must confess that I ate more than I should have.  This recipe uses all the basil you can get from your neighbor's garden.  Pesto sauce also freezes well.

| | |
|---|---|
| Protein: | 4 Grilled chicken breasts, chopped |
| Cooked vegetable: | 4c Young green beans, cut into 1' lengths |
| Starch: | 4c Boiled little new potatoes (or rice or millet) |
| Seasonings: | Juice of one lemon, salt and pepper to taste |
| Side raw vegetable: | 4c Cherry tomatoes |
| Dressing: | 4T Pesto: 2c basil, 4 cloves garlic, 1/4c olive oil, salt and pepper to taste |

Grill chicken breasts by sprinkling with lemon juice, salt and pepper to taste.  Microwave 1 minute per pound.  Grill until firm, about 2-3 minutes.  Steam green beans slightly.  Chop into 1" lengths.  Boil potatoes by dropping into cold water, bringing to boil, then simmering 20 minutes until firm but just edible.

Make pesto by blending olive oil, basil, garlic, salt, and pepper together.  Toss all ingredients in a large bowl and enjoy.

# TRADITIONAL TOMATO SAUCE
## (4 servings)

This recipe almost needs no introduction since its use must be almost universal in the western world.  My family is glad to see this dish almost no matter how often it appears.

| | |
|---|---|
| Protein: | 1½ lb. (Uncooked weight) Unsweetened Italian sausage or ground beef or pork |
| Cooked vegetable: | 2c Tomato sauce and 2c chopped onions |
| Starch: | 4c Boiled potatoes (or Polenta, rice or cannellini beans) |
| Seasonings: | 1T Parsley, 2t oregano |
| Side raw vegetable: | 4c Escarole |
| Dressing: | 4T Hot oil and vinegar |

If you have not boiled potatoes already, start heating salted water.  When water is boiling, drop in potatoes and cook until firm and just edible, approximately 20 minutes.

To make sauce, brown meat and onions in a skillet. Add seasonings and cover with tomato sauce.  If potatoes are coming from the refrigerator, add them to the sauté pan.  If they are hot, arrange them in a shallow bowl and cover with tomato sauce.

To make escarole, heat olive oil in the a sauté pan, add escarole, and wilt slightly.  Remove to serving plate and sprinkle with vinegar.

# ANCHOVY SAUCE
## (4 servings)

This sauce reveals the secret of many great restaurant chefs, i.e. adding anchovies to sauces. It is so prevalent that if you have an allergy to anchovies, it is wise to ask the waiter if anchovies have been used in the dish you're ordering.

| | |
|---|---|
| Protein: | ½ lb Anchovy fillets (plus 4 eggs on top of the asparagus) |
| Cooked vegetable: | 4c Canned plum tomatoes |
| Starch: | 4c Boiled potatoes (or polenta or brown rice or cannellini beans) |
| Seasonings: | Capers, garlic, salt, pepper, 4T olive oil |
| Side raw vegetable: | 4c Slightly steamed asparagus, topped with chopped, hard-boiled eggs |

Drain anchovy fillets and place in food processor with tomatoes and seasonings. Blend and transfer to saucepan.  Heat thoroughly, adding potatoes if you are taking them from the refrigerator.  If you are boiling potatoes on the spot, arrange them in shallow bowls while still hot from being drained. Cover with sauce.

To prepare asparagus, snap off ends, wash, and place in a steamer. (Or microwave until just steaming).  Arrange on side plates and sprinkle with chopped egg, one egg per person.  The egg is necessary to provide enough protein in the meal since the anchovies are too strong to use as the sole protein.

# SALUTE TO SILVER PALATE
## (4 servings)

I must here give credit to Julee Rosso and Sheila Lufkins for their brilliant work in the Silver Palate Cookbook series. They bring a freshness and distinction to American home cooking that is so clear, that I can tell when my hostess has been cooking from one of their books. This recipe is loosely adapted from their *The New Basics Cookbook*.

| | |
|---|---|
| Protein: | 1½ lb (Uncooked weight) lamb, julienned |
| Cooked vegetable: | 4c Sautéed onions |
| Starch: | 4c Sautéed boiled new potatoes (or Polenta or brown rice or millet or barley) |
| Seasonings: | Garlic, salt and pepper to taste |
| Side raw vegetable: | 4c Sliced tomatoes |
| Dressing: | 4T Oil and vinegar |

If you have not boiled potatoes the night before, start heating salted water or microwave a baking potato for five minutes. When water is boiling, drop in potatoes and cook until firm and just edible, approximately 20 minutes. Sauté coarsely garlic, herbs, chopped onions and julienne lamb in spray olive. Drop in potatoes just to heat. Serve with tomatoes drizzled with dressing.

# FIVE FAVORITE BEAN TOSSES

The statement that 'beans are versatile' would make any experienced cook reach for the understatement award of the decade. Beans work for emergency meals, as well as the most elegant company spreads. Should I arrive home with no meal plans whatsoever, I grab two vegetables from the refrigerator, open almost any can of beans, toss, heat, and sit down to eat. A tablespoon of sour cream completes the satisfying experience of this very quick meal. On the other hand, one of the most fashionable meals I ever ate was in a Manhattan bistro in Murray Hill in the east 30's. It consisted of savory beans topped with sliced roasted quail. The perfectly complimentary flavors created a memory I still enjoy twenty years later. I am sorry I had no idea what was in it, but here are other fabulous bean dishes.

## CHILI
(4 servings)

This recipe takes me to the other side of Manhattan to the Empire Diner in Chelsea. They serve chili in glass sundae cups with sour cream to mimic whipped cream and a cherry tomato to imitate the maraschino cherry. A mandatory stop on many trips to the Big Apple.

| | |
|---|---|
| Protein: | 1½ lb Ground sirloin |
| Cooked vegetable: | 2c Chopped onion and 2c chopped tomato |
| Starch: | 4c Kidney beans |
| Seasonings: | Chili powder, garlic powder, salt and pepper to taste. |
| Side raw vegetable: | 4c Chopped cabbage |
| Dressing: | 4T Unsweetened mayonnaise |

You can throw this in the crock pot all day. It will be savory and inviting when you return. If you are going to cook it all day, you should use dry kidney beans, or any other beans that you have stashed in the kitchen. Make sure you put in at least 2 ½ time the amount of water as beans.

Quick version: Brown the onions and beef, add seasonings, tomatoes, and canned beans to make this a quick meal. Substitute ground turkey if you are not a beef eater. To make this vegetarian, you could drop the beef and serve the chili over polenta.

Very quick version: Toss deli beef with a cup of canned kidney beans. Add and toss cabbage and chopped tomatoes. Season to taste. Replace mayonnaise with 1T of sour cream.

# RED, WHITE, AND GREEN CHILI
## (4 servings)

Who said chili had to be red? This is a beautiful combination of distinct colors that just occurred to me one night when I was figuring out which vegetables would complete a meal that began with white chili. This makes a good "big party" dish.

| | |
|---|---|
| Protein: | 1½ lb (Uncooked weight) Cubed chicken breasts |
| Cooked vegetable: | 2c onions and 2c spinach |
| Starch: | 4c Great northern beans (a.k.a. Cannellini beans) |
| Seasonings: | Garlic, cumin, Cayenne pepper, jalapeno peppers |
| Side raw vegetable: | 4c Chopped tomatoes |
| Dressing: | Salt and pepper to taste |

Soak beans overnight. Drain and cover twice over with water. Place over high heat and drop in cubed chicken breasts and quartered onion. Add more water if necessary to cover chicken. When boiling, reduce to a simmer and add spices. When beans are done (approximately 2-3 hours), swirl in spinach at the last minute, serve with chopped tomatoes on top.

Quick version: Open and drain cans of beans and chicken. Toss with heated frozen spinach and heat again if necessary. Top with chopped tomatoes.

# SOOTHING CONCILIATION SALAD
## (4 servings)

When the kids were just past toddler-hood, I took them and my poor overwhelmed and aching heart to the Caribbean over spring break, trying to forget that my husband traveled constantly and then took his precious vacation with the boys helicopter skiing in the Canadian Rockies. The effort of being a corporate executive and handling two little children without my husband made me feel deserted, abandoned, unloved and unlovable. Then, late one morning, he just showed up. Decided spur of the moment to join us. Came down the lawn from the main dining room to the little cabin on the beach like an apparition. In that moment, it was easy to see that he loved me. Pride made me hide my tears of joy and relief. He changed and we went to the dining room to eat this salad.

| | |
|---|---|
| Protein: | 4c Black beans |
| Raw vegetable: | 4c Chopped tomatoes |
| Raw vegetable: | 4c Chopped green and yellow peppers |
| Starch: | 4c Jicama, peeled and julienned |
| Seasonings: | Juice of 1 lime, 4 dashes of Tabasco sauce, salt and pepper to taste |

Toss all ingredients together.

# ULTIMATE TUNA CONVERSION
## (4 servings)
This is the ultimate in drastic shift from quick version to best company interpretation.

| | |
|---|---|
| Protein: | 1½ lb (Uncooked weight) Tuna, marinated in 4T tarragon vinegar |
| Raw vegetable: | 4c Total of capers, red onion, and green beans |
| Starch: | 4c Cannellini beans (great northern) |
| Seasonings: | For boiling water, 1 clove garlic, 1t oregano, ½t thyme, salt and pepper to taste |
| | For bean toss, 1 clove garlic, 1t oregano, ½t thyme, salt and pepper to taste, 4T tarragon vinegar, 2T olive oil, and lemon quarters |
| Side raw vegetable: | 4c Romaine and spinach, torn and tossed |
| Dressing: | 2T of best olive oil, blended with 4 black olives |

Company version. Soak, boil, drain, and rinse Cannellini beans, using fresh garlic and herbs in the boiling water. Toss with capers, red onion, green beans, more finely chopped garlic, chopped fresh herbs and 2T of olive oil.

Marinate fresh tuna in tarragon vinegar. Microwave until edges are opaque. Spray with olive oil spray and grill until firm. Arrange beans in shallow dishes and place a tuna fillet on each plate. Garnish with lemon quarters and serve with Romaine and spinach greens which have been tossed in 2T of the blended olive oil and black olives.

Quick version: Toss together 1 lb of drained, canned tuna; 4c drained Cannellini beans; canned, drained green beans; dried herbs; garlic powder; salt and pepper to taste. Serve with salad.

# BEAN AND GAZPACHO SOUP
## (4 servings)
This is the product of creative ordering at my favorite Houston restaurant, Cafe Express. The restaurant's ingredients are fresh and the staff are willing to add, subtract, and substitute items on all their dishes. My kind of joint.

| | |
|---|---|
| Protein: | 4c sour cream (plus the protein in the beans) |
| Starch: | 4c Pinto beans |
| Seasonings: | Juice of one lime, salt and pepper to taste |
| Side raw vegetable: | 4c Total of tomato, onion, green pepper, cilantro |
| Dressing: | 4T Olive oil (optional) |

Blend sour cream, tofu and beans with seasonings in a food processor and microwave thoroughly. Cut vegetables in large pieces with optional olive oil and process until fairly fine. Spread beans in a shallow bowl and top with vegetable mixture.

# Chapter 10
## RESTAURANTS

I have had many lovely experiences in restaurants while avoiding reactive foods. Once waiters and waitresses know that I have a special situation, they generally rise to the occasion. They usually know the obvious sugar and flours and they never know the subtle ones. If you doubt that the wait staff understands what you are saying, ask them to write on the check that you are allergic to sugars and flours so the chef sees it too. Do not depend on either of them to know that there is sugar in mayonnaise, tomato sauce, and salad dressing, or even that there is flour in pasta. Avoid ordering these things.

> You can eat at almost any restaurant, including fast food chains.

**If you do not see something on the menu that works, ask for a plain, grilled chicken breast or piece of fish, a baked potato (or beans or rice), and a large salad with cruets of oil and vinegar on the side.**

I evaluate restaurants based on how much negotiating I will have to do with the wait staff, how many choices I will have, and how many side dishes I will have to order to get a complete meal. I also prefer restaurants that carry a variety of fresh vegetables.

In general, I have done better at some restaurants than others:

| GO FOR | NOT SO EASY |
|---|---|
| Steakhouse | Mexican (marinades) |
| Fish/seafood | French (sauces made from flour) |
| Indian | Chinese (wheat based soy sauce, rice flour wrappers, sweet sauces, corn |
| Grills | starch, and MSG) |
| Southwest | Italian (sweetened tomato sauce, pasta) |
| Middle east | Home style (gravy, breaded, Ranch, deep fried, BBQ) |
| Cajun | Hot Dog Stands |
| | Bar-b-que |
| | Deli |
| | Pizza |

I also look for certain words in the menu descriptions. I have good luck with grilled, skewered, fajitas, salads, broiled, steamed, fresh fruit, eggs, garden, roasted, baked, burgers (hold the bread), sautéed, pico de gallo, mushroom, peppered, and Chicken Caesar.

Descriptions which indicate the probable presence of a sweetener or thickener are: ranch style, Bar-b-que, tortilla, sauces, pasta, wrapped in, breaded, battered, fried, soups (especially cream), croutons, honey Dijon, salad dressing, cheese, sausage/charro, meat loaf, casserole, gravy, smothered, marinara, cinnamon-apple, Hawaiian, glazed, Teriyaki. I know that many marinades have sugars in them. I have now and then been triggered by a marinated item. Tread carefully here.

> Qualify a number of solid restaurants in your price range and use them repeatedly. Do this for both sit-down and carry out.

A good strategy for handling this food program in restaurants is to stake out a few and use them regularly. "Vetting" a new restaurant takes some effort. Studying the menu and asking questions is an effort. So, after I have satisfied myself that certain dishes are clean, I tend to return to that restaurant and order those dishes. If I'm lucky, I may get the same waiter who already knows my story.  Using a small number of restaurants repeatedly also decreases the possibility that I will inadvertently eat a reactive food because I am trying a dish for the first time.

As an example, I ranked five Houston restaurants as follows:

| | # OF ENTREE CHOICES | % OF ENTREES THAT NEED A SIDE DISH | SIDE DISH REQUIRED |
|---|---|---|---|
| Empire Cafe (Italian) | 5 | 100% | Salad or Polenta |
| La Mora (Italian) | 14 | 40% | Various |
| Bombay Palace (Indian) | 44 | 100% | Salad |
| Hunan (Chinese) | 0 | 100% | Salad |

Salad bars are excellent, but avoid any mixed salads such as potato salad or bean salad as these usually contain sugars.  Always ask for oil and vinegar on the side for salad dressing.  If you have trouble with binging at All-You-Can eat buffet bars, then this idea is not for you.

Eastern Indian and Middle East buffets are also a favorite because of the availability of a large variety of steamed vegetables, savory stews made without thickeners, light yogurt dressings, and the choice of rice or potato for starch.  The bread made from lentil flour in Indian restaurants in *not* OK for us since it is still made from a carbohydrate which has been ground into a powder.  Even though lentils are not a grain, they are a carbohydrate.

> The number of times that waiters and chefs have risen to the occasion to produce a lovely dish far outweighs the number of times that we have had to struggle with uncooperative staff.  Our tips and words of appreciation are always generous in return.

Therefore, in powder form, our bodies absorb them too quickly and our bio chemistry is tipped out of balance.

Oriental restaurants can be tricky because of soy sauces which contain wheat, sweet and sour dishes, rice paper, noodles, and overcooked white rice.  However, they have the advantage of using unusual ingredients which are very fresh.  I usually just ask for stir-fried vegetables and fish over brown rice without soy sauce.

Really **fancy restaurants** present the greatest challenge to ordering straight off the menu. They justify their prices in part because of the complexity of their dishes.  As a general rule, the more ingredients in a dish, the more likely it is that one of these ingredients will be something I do not want.  However, fancy restaurants usually have more highly trained wait staff who may be able to work with the chef to prepare a wonderful dish.  I am always humbled by the experience of a chef doing something special for my family and me.

Sometimes in an elegant restaurant, especially in front of my husband's important clients, I feel a tinge of embarrassment as I describe my needs to a waiter.  At that moment, I just remind myself that anyone at the table could unknowingly be suffering from refined carbohydrate sensitivities. If not them, then someone they know. (I think carbohydrate sensitivity is extremely common and widely unrecognized.) Therefore, I might be saving a life or relieving suffering by modeling my adherence to my food program.  With these thoughts, I return to a sense of grace and confidence.

In **fast food restaurants,** I order two large beef patties on paper, no cheese, no sauce, no catsup, no bun.  The largest patties weigh 2 or 2 1/4 oz, so I need to get two of them.  An example would be a double quarter pounder.  I get a side order of deluxe salad, no dressing, with lemon wedges.  Absolutely everything else (except mustard and pickles) in a fast food restaurant

110

has sugar or flour in it. The chicken has been soaked in sugar. The fish has been drowned in breading. (One serving of fish I tested weighed a total of 4 oz: the breading and oil was 2.5 oz and the fish itself was 1.5 oz.) The French fries have been dipped in dextrose to make them crispy. Even without the dextrose, French fries are cooked at such a high temperature that their starch is too close to glucose for me. Add in the fact that they are soaked in fat and they are off my list as a starch.

I am nonetheless grateful. I eat those beef patties whenever I need to and I am glad that I can work this program anywhere in this country. However, the 'no more often than once every four days' rule applies especially here. Those hamburger patties may be free of sugars and flours, but you can be sure that they are high in fat and contain added hormones and antibiotics.

Best bet for fast food is Wendy's which has a nice salad bar. It includes oil and vinegar. Even at the drive-through window, you can order the deluxe salad which actually comes with a variety of vegetables. Wendy's also has the only clean starch (i.e. containing no dextrose) and it has a choice of three kinds: baked potato, green peas, or kidney beans at the salad bar! Not all salad bars have all choices but thank you Wendy's, anyway!

I must explain why I don't simply order a hamburger and then take the bun off. First, my mission is to educate. Many, many fast food workers need this program. Every time I order a sandwich without a bun, I know they hear it. I explain that I am allergic to sugars and flours. The seed is planted. If they hear it enough, it might occur to them that eliminating flours and sugars could be their doorway to a life free of suffering.

Secondly, I don't want to deal with the extra trash. Third, I don't want to have to mess up my fingers by removing the patties from the bread. And fourth, the bread sticks to the patties. Patties come wrapped in paper. I just peel down the paper like I would a banana and go about my business. I'm not going to claim that this procedure is not messy. It is. Swathing my healthy body in paper napkins takes care of the problem.

Please develop a sense of humor about how fast-food workers respond to a request for a double hamburger with no bun. It usually takes all of the supervisors to understand what is needed. The cook usually gets very confused and asks for clarification and further direction a dozen times. I overhear really funny comments like, "If she don't want this on a bun, what does she want it on?" Once I said that I was allergic to wheat and the clerk told me indignantly that their buns were OK because they had no whole wheat in them. Keep smiling. If you hear any really good comments, send them to me.

Please enjoy your restaurant experiences. Be confident about asking for what you need. If you get a really nasty waiter, just tell him or her that you are allergic to sugars and flours and that you will have a wild, uncontrollable fit right in the middle of the restaurant if you ingest even a small trace! I've never had to do this, but I am prepared to defend my food program at all costs. Smile, make that wait staff feel like a hero, develop routines, have fun, tune into the love and grace that accompany this food program.

*Notebook:*

## TOP TEN FAVORITE RESTAURANTS

Dear Reader,

List your favorite restaurants here and keep notes about how well they serve you in your recovery efforts. Call them during off hours and ask their chefs about the dishes that have no sugars, flours, or wheat. Ask especially about salad dressings.

# Chapter 11
## TRAVEL

Our family is famous for its long car trips. We have logged thousands of miles back and forth across the country. (When the next Ice Age comes, I plan to drive across the Bering Strait and tour China.) I have devised methods for packing enough food for three days at a time. After that, I need an evening in a kitchen to replenish my stores. If we do not have a friend to stay with, we try to rent an efficiency with a kitchen.

I get a sense of safety, like being in a cocoon going down the road with a supply of glorious food. It saves time because we do not have to wait in restaurants. We sometimes eat outside which gives us a nice break from being in the car.

Please replenish the ice in your cooler regularly to keep bacteria from growing.

**Protein:** I microwave and grill meats as usual. Right off the grill, I put them in zip lock bags and put them in the freezer. This vastly minimizes the potential for spoilage from bacterial growth. They stay in a well iced cooler for several days. Hard boiled eggs are a good alternative for breakfast.

**Starch**: Likewise, I put hot potatoes (sweet and white) and Polenta in zip lock bags. I chill them thoroughly in the refrigerator but I do not freeze them. They get very wet from condensation as they cool, but I feel it is the safest method. They also stay in the cooler. For breakfast, packets of instant grits will soften enough to eat with hot tap water.

**Fresh produce** also stays well in the cooler for several days. Just steam the stringier vegetables before putting them hot into zip lock bags. Chill thoroughly in the refrigerator before putting them in the cooler.

**Dairy**: Small cartons of yogurt also keep several days in a well chilled cooler.

# TRAVEL SHOPPING LIST
## 3 Days, 1 person

**BREAKFAST**

6 small cartons of yogurt or skim milk

6 hard boiled eggs

6 pieces of fruit

6 packets of instant grits (2 packets make one serving)

OR

3 recipes of Breakfast Muffins.  Use a different fruit in each one for variety.

**LUNCH AND DINNER**

6 servings of raw vegetables (carrots, celery, sweet pepper strips, cucumber, whole mushrooms, etc)

6 servings of lunch and dinner protein (grilled chicken breast, sliced steak, leg of lamb, Boar's Head hot dogs, pork chops)

6 servings of lunch and dinner starch (baked potato, baked sweet potato, Polenta cubes, rice cakes).

A good cooked vegetable is tomato juice.

Hint: Use baked potato halves as you would bread to make a sandwich.  Sweet potato with hot dogs is a good combination.

## VISITING ANOTHER HOUSEHOLD

When you are traveling to visit a family, you must make a decision as to whether to trust the food shopper in that family to do your shopping properly.  You can try to dictate a list, but frankly, shopping is a learned skill in this program and if your hosts are not trained, then I would assume that they are probably going to buy items which you are going to have to reject.  This is going to set a tense edge to your visit, so...

I would handle the household shoppers in the following manner.  I would tell them in advance that I follow a diet which is difficult to shop for.  I would offer to take them to lunch or dinner on the day that I arrived and then go shopping afterwards.  With list in hand, I would be confident that I could complete a shopping and keep myself and my own family safe.  If I were arriving too late in the day to shop, I would consider carrying enough breakfast cereal and fruit to get through breakfast and make sure that a shopping was scheduled as the first activity for the next day.

I would also offer to cook for my host household.  I figure this makes the visit balance out in terms of how much work each of us is doing to make the visit a success.  It also gives me a chance to model the program.  Of course, I would NEVER comment on what my hosts were eating, unless they asked for advice.  Then I would wait until they were finished to share my experience.  I would begin sentences with 'I' and I would avoid the words 'you should,' and 'you must.'

For more dynamics on dealing with family on a visit, see the Chapters, *Getting to Know the Internal Trickster* and *Bringing Your Household on Board*.

# PART III

## HOW DO I MAKE MY PROGRAM STICK?

# Chapter 12
## FALLING OFF THE WAGON

The trick to staying on the *SUGARS AND FLOURS* plan is to weave knowledge, support, and spirituality together to make a nest of protection for yourself. There are many features that distinguish the *SUGARS and FLOURS* plan from others. One of the main points is that we feel worse when we fall off than when we stick with it. This is not enough, however, to keep us on it. Support and spirituality play decisive roles. Part III discusses how to stay with this plan. It will show how our dark voices may want us to be sick and fat. It will show how to counter the dark voices by filling our lives with voices of compassion and love so that we don't have to suffer ever again from reactive foods.

At some point, almost everyone who gives up reactive foods tries to eat them again. They are usually surprised when they do. It is very hard to believe that we react so sharply to foods which we used to eat routinely. Scientists do not understand why our bodies reject allergic foods so violently once they are cleaned out of our systems. The literature reports reactions which range from projectile vomiting to severe hallucinations and delusions to aggressive behavior. This can happen with very small amounts. So, If you hear your internal voice say, "Oh, it's not enough to hurt me," or "Just this once won't make any difference," please think through your schedule and decide if you have a few days to work through a possible reaction. The first two stories happened to me, the rest I heard first-hand:

"Within 20 minutes of eating the chocolate peanut butter cup, my sinuses were swollen and painful."

"After I *thought* I had no reaction to a bite of bread made from lentil flour, I began to think that I could get away with other things as well. I thought I could get away with eating fast food hash browns even though I know full well that they have dextrose in them. I paid with a two-day headache."

"I decided to try a plate of pasta and two small glasses of red wine after giving up reactive foods for two weeks. I felt like I had a bad flu for next two days."

"The bread was so gorgeous that I ate about five pieces. I felt so lethargic and depressed I couldn't get out of bed the next day."

"When I accidentally ate a hamburger with bread crumbs, I felt woozy like I was drunk."

"I gave up sugar, flour, and wheat for Lent, then ate candy on Easter. The next day, I was completely without confidence. My self esteem was so low, I couldn't continue with the project that I was responsible for."

"After eating a lot of cheese in a few days, I was going to a breakfast meeting. As I pulled up to the building, I almost turned around because I had the thought that they didn't really want me there. Luckily, I recognized it as a food reaction and went in anyway to have a great time."

"When I have eaten sugar, I really feel it in my joints. I can hardly walk."

"I decided to finish up the wheat flakes for breakfast. I got a headache so bad that I had to come home from work. I did it again two days later. I guess I had to prove it to myself."

"After two days of falling off the plan, my little daughter was acting so badly that I could hardly stand to be around her."

"I didn't think that the vodka had any effect on me. But twenty-four hours later I had an out-of-control cookie binge. I'd had no cravings for cookies for the prior seven weeks of being clean. Now I know that when I started to withdraw from the last of the vodka, my internal addict tried to keep me from getting clean again. My support group met the next night. They explained what happened and still loved and accepted me. Thank God. But I couldn't stop the binging. It's now six months and thirty pounds later. I am clean and very grateful. I sure wish I hadn't tried that vodka."

"I just decided that I could eat pastries. I went into the bakery and ate two turn-overs. I woke up again after a three-year binge.

"I felt that surge of anger well up in me and I knew that I couldn't eat carob again."

"I have a great job, friends, and family, but when I eat sugars and flours, I am suicidal.

"I have learned that if I eat something reactive during the day, I will be unable to sleep during the night. It's just not worth it."

**If you fall off the wagon, get to the phone or to a support meeting, and tell someone as soon as you can.** This will take the shame out of the incident and vastly improve your chances of successfully climbing back on board. For the first seven weeks of trying the plan, I confessed something to my support group every week. I kept trying to kid myself that I didn't have reactions to first frozen yogurt, then wine. By talking about the lapses and the reactions, I gradually accepted my condition. The loving acceptance and patience that I found in my group gave me a bright alternative to the darkness of reactive foods and I too, decided that the reactive foods just weren't worth it.

# Chapter 13
## MARGINAL FOODS
## -OR-
## PLAYING NEAR THE EDGE OF THE CLIFF

Marginal foods are those which trigger negative results in some people, but not in others. **You run the risk of feeling like you can go off your plan if you eat a lot of foods from the marginal list. Some of the more senior, wiser members of my support group call these "gateway" foods. It means that they are the gateway to falling off the plan altogether. Tread carefully.**

**I would suggest *not* using these foods for the first three months of replacing reactive foods.** After the first three months, try a small amount and see if you have a reaction to it. Some reactions will be obvious such as sneezing or hunger pangs. Others might be more subtle such as irritability or obsessing, or even a binge twenty-four hours later. For example, if you decide to have potato chips one Friday afternoon and the next day you are thinking about potato, DO NOT risk having them again. If you drink a can of diet cola and rage at another driver four hours later, do not drink caffeine again.

This page gives each of us the choices which will define our individual plan. No one else can tell you whether these substances are OK for you. For example, I was able to give up popcorn the moment that I found out that I have an allergy to corn. But a friend of mine absolutely cannot buy the first kernel at the movies. It would be only a matter of days before she would be going to the theater, on the pretext to see the movie, but actually to get the popcorn.

Remember to think of these substances as cumulative. If you eat an item from the high fat list, then be extra careful not to eat from the high sugars list. Be especially attentive to this list during holidays. The messages of, "Oh this much can't hurt me," and "Well, there's not sugar, flour, or wheat in this!" play constantly during the holidays and they will play loudly when your internal addict sees these foods. The power of these foods to pull people off their food programs during holidays is so great that I wrote a special chapter on how to handle the holidays. If marginal foods are 'gateways' to falling off the wagon during normal times, they become positive 'trapdoors' during the holidays.

Also remember that these foods move us towards the threshold of illnesses. Since I cannot control the other elements that move me toward the threshold, I prefer to stay in the middle of the food plan and not stray toward the edge. For example, if I am eating high fat foods and neglecting vegetables, I make myself susceptible to infection. When I am at school, I am more likely to catch a student's bug. Or, when a stressful event occurs, like starting a new project, if I have been eating marginal foods, I am more like to succumb to anxiety instead of staying centered and grounded.

I will never forget standing in the back of my health food store with one of my wise teachers. We were looking at the list of ingredients for unsweetened carob chips. Between the two of us, neither of us could see any ingredient that was a sugar or flour. I was arguing that we ought to be able to eat them. Nonetheless, she was adamantly not interested. Finally in exasperation, she turned to me and asked, "Do you *need* to eat this?" Of course not. That question put everything into perspective with a bang.

## MARGINAL BECAUSE OF TRACES OF SUGAR

"All Fruit" fruit spreads (jams) contain concentrated fruit juice
Dark sodas such as diet caffeine-free Coke, root beer, diet caffeine-free Dr. Pepper contain caramel coloring and Aspartame.
Bouillon cubes contain caramel coloring.
Light flavored yogurt contains modified food starch, pectin, and Aspartame.
Non-fat and light sour cream contain modified food starch.
Bananas, grapes, cherries, and many berries contain high concentrations of natural sugar.
(In general, stick with fruits that contain the letter 'p'.)
Bacon and ham contain various sugars.

## MARGINAL BECAUSE REPEATED
## HAND TO MOUTH MOTION
## TRIGGERS THE URGE TO BINGE OR OVEREAT.

| | | |
|---|---|---|
| Popcorn | Rice cakes* | Cherries |
| Potato Chips | | Berries |
| | | Grapes |

*A rice cake runs the extra hazard of being a platform which invites marginal foods to be spread upon it. Butter, jams, cream cheese, and peanut butter may appear to be normal and acceptable on top of a rice cake. They are not!

## MARGINAL BECAUSE OF HIGH GLUCOSE CONTENT.

*Always* eat these foods with a protein. They make many people groggy, even with a protein.

| | | |
|---|---|---|
| Oat bran | Baked potatoes | White rice |
| Carrots | Microwaved | Instant rice |
| Parsnips | potatoes | Brown rice |
| Banana | Instant potatoes | Rice cakes |
| Apricot | French fries | |
| Papaya | Polenta | |
| Mango | Grits | |
| | Corn | |

## MARGINAL BECAUSE OF SIMILARITY TO WHEAT.

| | | | |
|---|---|---|---|
| Barley | Rye | Kamut | Spelt |

## MARGINAL BECAUSE OF HIGH FAT CONTENT.
## *WARNING*: USE OF THESE FOODS WILL BRING WEIGHT LOSS TO A SCREECHING HALT.

This is the one area where I staunchly support the measure rule. If your weight loss plan is going to run off the road, this is a likely place for it to happen. **The rule of thumb for using these foods is 1 tablespoon per day. But be sure to get that tablespoon of fat per day.** The speed of your weight loss depends to a surprising degree on not using these substances more than 1 tablespoon per day. However, if you use less, your skin and hair will dry out. When you reach your goal weight, add fat back gradually. See *Food Addiction: The Body Knows* by Kay Sheppard, pg 90 and 101 for more information.

Peanut butter*
Nuts**
Seeds (1/4c = 2T of fat)
Trail mix
Potato chips and shoe-
  strings
Unsweetened cocoa powder

Sour Cream
Cream
Whole milk
Cheese
Butter

Avocado
Boarshead beef frankfurters
Boarshead kielbasa
Unsweetened carob chips*
Cooking oil
Salad dressing

*These foods also make me irritable! **Nuts are highly problematic. They trigger people to do all kinds of things they later regret. Proceed with great caution.

## USING MARGINAL FOODS TO GAIN WEIGHT

High fat foods are excellent for slipping into the recipes of the person you would like to have gain weight. My daughters sometimes get pulled into the fashionable eating habits of their middle school which unfortunately means skipping lunch. So, when I am fixing dinner, I use these ingredients to make sure that they don't lose too much weight. However, if you want to gain weight using these substances, then be very careful that you still eat all 14 items on the daily list so that you don't displace balanced, complete nutrition with high fat foods.

# TOP TEN TROUBLESOME MARGINAL FOODS

People start down the road to relapse with these foods by saying to themselves, "But they're not sugar, flour, or wheat!" They inevitably regret the trouble that starts with these foods.

1. Popcorn

2. Nuts

3. Caffeine

4. Peanut butter

5. Rice cakes

6. Puffed cereal

7. Half and half creamer

8. Cheese

9. Dried fruit

10. Tropical fruit

*Notebook:*

## PERSONAL MARGINAL FOODS

Dear Reader,
    Use this page to keep track of your own personal marginal foods.

# Chapter 14
## BRINGING YOUR HOUSEHOLD ON BOARD

If you find yourself saying that you cannot do this food plan because your family would never stand for it, **have courage**. If you think it would be too complicated or too much work, **think simple**. If you don't want to monitor your family members, **don't worry!** If you bought this book to help yourself or only one of your children, this chapter will help you expand your horizon to seeing how you can help your whole family. It is virtually impossible that only one member of any family would benefit from removing refined carbohydrates from the diet.

> You will face the task of bringing your family on board with more energy, clarity of mind, and calm than you have right now.

The protesting and screaming will not last. Just like you, the other members of your household too will begin to see benefits within four days, including a reduction in irritability. Leave the house if you need to get away from your dependents. But whatever you do, don't leave them out of your food plan if you can possibly help it. Reread the chapter, *The Benefits of Replacing Reactive Foods* if you need motivation. Get yourself as clean as you can and then start to clean out your house. As much as adults need to eliminate reactive foods, kids' needs are even more profound. Let's listen to the experts:

"A child's brain has two to three times the energy needs of the adult. No wonder children flip out on an empty stomach."[66]

"In treating hyperactive kids nutritionally, I quickly found out that it was next to impossible to get them to change their diet without dealing with the diet of the entire family. Just try to get a child to be satisfied with a carrot (a CARROT? or an APPLE?) for dessert when the rest of the family is having cherry pie a la mode!"[67]

"Modern high-tech food additives have the same impact on children who experience learning and behavioral (hyperactivity) disorders and on adolescents who exhibit antisocial and later criminal behavior. I have seen how addiction to sugar has paved the way to violent behavior in adolescents and adults. These addicted children invariably begin to steal money from their parents, later from others in order to buy sweets. They may not be caught for a long time, for parents find it difficult to believe their children will do this. They may be caught only occasionally. If they are punished 10 percent of the time, this is a small price to pay for having gotten the desired sugar. Once the pattern has been established, it will continue into adolescence where the wants are different but the method of achieving them the same. Now they steal for drugs, for alcohol, for cigarettes until the criminal pattern of behavior is well established."[68]

"Because Jean's entire family decided to follow a four-day Practical Rotary Diet, her mother quickly pinpointed problem foods for each family member."[69]

On the topic of a junk-free diet for a hyperactive child, Dr. Smith feels that "The whole family has to change their way of eating. Many of the parents find they feel better on this diet as well."[70]

---

[66] Smith, Lendon H., M.D. *Feed Your Body Right.* 174.

[67] *Ibid.* 17

[68] Hoffer, Abram, M.D., *Hoffer Laws of Natural Nutrition.* 63.

[69] Rapp, Doris, M.S. *Is this Your Child?* 138.

[70] Null, Gary, Ph.D., *Nutrition and the Mind.* 225.

"I have seen the same realization in families where the mother and/or wife became my patient. I advised her to follow a good diet, usually eliminating sugar, junk foods and very often milk, plus any other food she might be allergic to, and outlined which vitamins to take. Very often, the husband, who was well, did not want to give up sweets and desserts, and my patient did not want to deprive him of these. After a few months my patient would often tell me the whole family had had the flu and she had remained well; in the past she would have developed the same infections that they had. Then, after many months of preparing two sets of meals, one for herself and one for the rest of the family, she would decide to place the whole family on her diet, primarily because she was now well. Then I would hear from her how her husband was more energetic, less irritable and more relaxed and the whole family was much healthier."[71]

The emotional impact that replacing reactive foods could have on household members is significant, both positive and negative. Try to have compassion for family members if they experience fear and uncertainty. Reassure them that they only do the program one day at a time. Discourage the despair that comes from thinking about not eating these substances for the rest of their lives. Avoid criticizing family members. Set boundaries on family member's behavior if they criticize you. And then, get out of their way.

## GENERAL HOUSEHOLD GUIDELINES

The concept is to focus on making the *home environment* safe and to studiously avoiding controlling others' behavior. My family relaxes at home knowing that all food in the house is safe and wholesome. Once I recognized the benefits of replacing reactive foods, I replaced them for my family too. However, I realized that if I forced my family or tried to control them or monitor them, they would resent it, rebel and possibly develop resentment toward the very foods that could support them. I needed to stay totally focused on my own responsibilities for the environment and avoid directing my household members as to how they should react.

I took as my guidelines the successful experience of Co-Dependents Anonymous (CoDA) and Al-Anon. CoDA helps people learn the elements of healthy relationships while Al-Anon is an organization that helps people who are in relationship with an alcoholic. Al-Anon encourages healthy behaviors such as detachment and trust: detachment from other's behaviors and trust that they will learn how to handle their addictions according to the will of their Higher Power. If you need help handling the transition to non-addictive, non-allergic foods for your household, find an Al-Anon or CoDA meeting. Soak up the hope, strength, and experience of these blessed fellowships.

If you are worn out or frustrated with your child's eating habits, hear these words of comfort from Al-Anon. I have substituted the words 'food-addict/allergic' for 'alcoholic':

"Detachment helps people to know a higher form of love than they may have known when they were preoccupied with the food-addict/allergic, always trying to second-guess the next move, the next disaster. Trying to keep the food-addict/allergic out of trouble, cheering him up, encouraging him to pull himself together - all these are loving things to do. But isn't a greater love required to help only when it is truly helpful and, finally, to allow the food-addict/allergic to know the consequences of his or her own behavior? Al-Anon thinks so. How is it possible to draw the line between the things to be done to make the situation better and the things that cannot be done? . . . Love turns to desperation when people are unable to recognize the point at which, in helping others, they have taken too much upon

---

[71] Hoffer, Abram, M.D. *Putting It all Together, The New Orthomolecular Medicine.* 164.

themselves. Al-Anon asks its members to stop obsessively devising new strategies for dealing with the food-addict/allergic. As this essential difference is defined, family members begin to feel more confident about themselves and, therefore, more patient with their loved one, more tolerant of them."[72]

"People who have lived for any length of time in a close relationship with a food-addict/allergic have found themselves engaged to some extent in trying to control outcomes, especially with regard to the food-addict's eating. It is a major adjustment to understand that one can only be responsible for one's own behavior and must therefore let go of a need to control the result - part of which involves another person's behavior."[73]

Perhaps the most powerful facet of dealing with another person's habits and addictions that Al-Anon teaches how to avoid **enabling and controlling.** For the food-addict/allergic, enabling means buying and preparing reactive foods for someone, or helping them to obtain reactive foods. It supports them in their poor habits or addiction. Enabling is not OK. On the other hand we do *not* want to slip into controlling. Controlling means constantly watching over your family members, questioning them about what they've eaten, making them account for their money, looking for evidence of illicit eating, insisting that they 'clean their plates', making them report their weight, criticizing, nagging, etc. This is destructive, controlling, co-dependent behavior. It will make you so crazy that you will want to numb out on reactive foods to make the pain stop. Don't do it.

I view my job as limited to shopping for and preparing clean food with help from my household members . . . and oh yes, to following the food plan myself. I take the responsibility very seriously. It is my top priority in life. The rest of my well-being and the well-being of my family start with our food. If our food is right, life is right. If our food is incomplete, or reactive, life's problems multiply like a fungal growth.

From the beginning, I have placed complete breakfasts, lunches, and dinners before family members. Often these meals were far from perfect. I only did my best. But, this practice made it easy for them to identify healthy foods. Today, they can visualize what well-balanced meals look like. The amount of snacking they do is their business. However, I have noticed that their tendency to forage for snacks diminishes greatly when I do a good job providing complete, *on-time* meals. This is especially true on week-ends and after school. On week-ends, if I have one large complete dish available to be eaten as needed, snacking is minimized. After school, I might need to bring the teatime meal in the car at pick-up time to ward off binging when the child reaches home. This is especially true if dinner is not ready at home.

In some regards, children are really no different than adults. They can develop binge urges if they experience incomplete nutrition or go too long between meals. I cannot control them. I absolutely do not want to control their eating habits. *However*, I can offer them the foods that they can use to stabilize themselves and thereby to control themselves. Although I am not responsible for how they eat, if I see them binging or eating too much marginal food, I do ask myself if there is anything I could have done differently in terms of executing my responsibilities to provide complete, timely food. Sometimes the food has been remiss. A meal has been too late, or incomplete. Sometimes the kids are eating extra because they have been under stress. In any event, I know what to do: stick strictly to my part of the deal, i.e. delivering four on-time meals per day and following the plan myself. End of story.

---

[72] Al-Anon. *Al-Anon Faces Alcoholism.* 25.

[73] *Ibid.* 32.

I absolutely do not try to control the quantity of food they eat, nor the timing. They can roam around the marginal foods list unless it gets out of hand. Even then I do not criticize what they are eating. I do not even comment on it or make suggestions. I just stop buying the marginal food that seems to have developed into a problem. I had to do this when we were eating too much fruit. I gradually reintroduced small amounts of fruit, while keeping up a steady flow of full vegetable servings in our meals. It worked. Fruit consumption is back to normal.

**Boundaries.** I am absolutely entitled to set boundaries with household members. If household members are pushing me too hard, I may ask them to stop. If I have the patience, I will listen to complaints and laments. If I have heard their comments before, but feel that it would be wise to hear them out, then I might tell them that I will listen without interruption for a specified period of time, like two minutes. I express empathy for their feelings. (What I usually hear is their unhealthy voice trying to regain control of their habits.) Then I leave the room. I absolutely do not have to listen if they are yelling, mocking, teasing, threatening, shaming, or being otherwise abusive.

In addition, I have set the following boundaries around what I am willing to do and tolerate to keep myself safe. My dependents all have their own money (baby-sitting, allowance, salary.) They all have access to the school cafeteria, a fast food restaurant, or a grocery store by foot.

---

**BOUNDARIES ON ENABLING AND CONTROLLING**

1. Family members can buy whatever they can afford whenever they want to go get it.
2. I will not take them to buy reactive foods and I will not pay for them.
3. They may not bring sugars, flours, or wheat into my house. My house is safe. I can eat anything in it and so can they.
4. They may not consume reactive foods in front of me out of consideration for not tempting me.

---

My sister made one pass through my cabinets about three weeks after I had given up reactive foods. We put products containing sugars, flours, or wheat in a storage closet and eventually gave them to a food drive. The kids knew where these products were in the storage closet. I knew that they were raiding this stash occasionally but I felt that perhaps it gave them some security to know that they were not cut off entirely. But after about six months, I went through the cabinets again very carefully, as well as the refrigerator. This time, I just threw the stuff away.

With the experience I have now, I would have done a thorough job of cleaning out the house and getting rid of all reactive foods right off the bat. The benefits of taking your household off of refined carbohydrates cold turkey as opposed to gradually are very important. I asked my own children about this and they said that cold turkey was the way to go for one very good reason: if you remove the substances gradually, the kids are upset because they're losing familiar foods. But, because they're still eating the substances, albeit at lower levels, they have not yet experienced the benefits. So gradually means the worst of both worlds: loss of familiar foods without the compensation of benefits. Gradually also means that the period of uncertainty about what foods will be left after the transition period is prolonged. I vote for cold turkey as much as you can manage. Remember that no one can do this program perfectly for themselves, much less for a household. Just do the best you can and discuss options with people who have been there.

If I pick children up from a party where I have seen them eating cake, I do not mention it. Whatever they do outside my presence is their business. Totally. (One exception, I do not let them eat sugars and flours before they get in the car for a long drive because I do not want to have to try to control their compulsive behavior when I cannot get away from them.)

Each member of my family has lost the weight that they desired. But the most important effect has been on the general atmosphere of the household. We have fewer crises, fewer upsets, fewer fights, and quarrels. We leave for trips calmly, without departure chaos. Homework gets done without tears and wails of frustration. This is a miracle.

It almost goes without saying that you cannot put a child on this program without going on it yourself.

> Modeling is one of only two activities that makes a profound, positive, and lasting impact on teaching healthy eating habits to anyone, but especially to a child. Experiencing consequences is the other.

## ADULT MEMBERS OF YOUR HOUSEHOLD

The adult members of your household are beyond your control. You cannot make decisions for them. However, as Al-Anon has demonstrated, YOU DO NOT HAVE TO BUY OR PREPARE SUGARS AND FLOURS FOR THEM. I often give my friends the following scenario: Suppose you and your partner were cocaine users and you decided to quit. Would you still buy the stuff for him/her? NO! Of course not! At least I *hope* not!

I know that I am lucky to have a supportive partner. If the adults in your household are not cooperating, then I would suggest that you make the four items in each meal for them and put the meal in front of them. If they insist on bread and desserts, ask them to buy these items for themselves. Your household members will eventually get cleaned out. They will eventually notice that refined products do not make them feel good. Gradually they will stop craving these products.

I have one friend whose husband suffers from terrible mood swings. One minute he's leaving her and the next he wants her around all the time. (I used to be this way with my husband.) She suffers and complains bitterly about his constant changes. But she still buys him sugars and flours. Why? Because she feels that she *has* to! Go figure.

I have another friend who knew that her husband would be very threatened by her end to sugars and flours. So she got herself clean while on a ten-day driving trip. She deliberately picked a time when they would not be making joint decisions about shopping and cooking. He ordered whatever he needed without compromising her program while she went through withdrawal. It worked. By the time she got home, she had completely lost all desire for reactive foods. This remained the case even though he kept reactive foods around the house. Over the following years, he gradually adopted a food program similar to hers.

I know of many households where wives keep their clean program while the husbands keep eating reactive foods and vice versa. They have managed to maintain this for years. Another friend maintains her own refrigerator. She sets her boundaries around that refrigerator just the way I set boundaries around my house. No one else in the household may put anything reactive in it. Every household works it out in its own way. But I beg you, please stop playing the role of supplier/enabler to your household.

129

My husband has set boundaries with me around the issue of alcohol. I tried to set boundaries with him and failed. I had to let go of my desire to keep alcohol out of my house. Yelling and shaming are not the answer. I have turned this problem over to God and because of my faith in divine power, I maintain my serenity in spite of having alcohol in my house.

I also have difficulty persuading him to stop bringing aspartame into the house. I asked him to read the material about the terrible brain diseases which have been linked to aspartame. He did and after that, he stopped buying aspartame for a long time. Then he started again. So, I ask him to keep it locked up. He solved the problem with a locked cash box that holds two sodas and stays in the refrigerator. Nonetheless, I still see a case of soda with aspartame show up in the house now and then. There is absolutely nothing more I can do about this. I take care of myself by remembering that the problem is in God's hands and out of my control. All I can do is model my own abstinence from aspartame.

## CHILDREN

For several months after replacing reactive foods at home, my daughters continued to buy sugars and flours at school. But the level of these substances in their bodies decreased. In other words, they started to complete withdrawal and get clean.

Then we went on a long family vacation. They didn't have the opportunity to eat anything reactive in front of me. At the end of the trip, they were really clean. When they returned to school and tried to eat refined carbohydrates again, their headaches, fatigue, depression, and runny noses returned. The difference was very clear to them.

> According to the USDA, only 1% of all American children eat enough fruit, grain, meat, dairy, and vegetables.

> My children's motivation to work their own food program comes from inside them, not from a nagging mother.

I have to bite my tongue to keep from lecturing them. When they were progressing through withdrawal, they came home sick with food hangovers from birthday parties where they ate sugars and flours. I had to let them experience the consequences of their decisions without interference. Today, I limit my role to education without retribution. Education might look like describing what I heard from someone else about a situation similar to theirs. I might wait a day or so after the kids have made themselves sick to share the story. When they are not feeling well, another technique is ask them if they have eaten anything out of the ordinary. If they know there is no punishment for whatever they've eaten, they are likely to be honest. The point is not to create an opportunity to lecture. The point is to reinforce the awareness that they themselves are developing about the relationship between food and well-being.

I deeply object to the idea of using food as a reward or withdrawal of food as a punishment. Food is nourishment. Food can also be celebratory such as at holidays and other special occasions. I would not offer food as a reward, because I would not want my children to think that the converse could happen, i.e. that withdrawal of food could be a punishment. Food should be extremely dependable. It should always be available in correct quantities. It should always be based on what the body needs, not what the kid has done. Good, regular food is the cornerstone of well-being. It should not appear or fail to appear based on any certain behavior. No sense of ambiguity should ever be connected with food. Food should be thoroughly enjoyed, but otherwise its emotional content should be minimized. Use money as a reward. Use praise. Use your smile. Use a hug. Don't use food.

In my children, their desire to avoid reactive foods developed from the inside out. This approach of providing good food, boundaries, and education worked insofar as they now recognize the benefits of replacing reactive foods and their food choices are astonishingly and consistently excellent.

A friend of mine took her two little daughters off sugars and flours. The four-year old in particular developed her own healthy voice that asks for fruit and turns down cake at parties. Remember that your children have unhealthy tricksters inside of them which are just as strong as yours. If you learn to recognize these voices, it will become easier to resist trying to satisfy them. Learn how to cope with the trickster in the chapter, *Getting to Know the Internal Trickster*.

> Even in a young child, the healthy voice emerges and takes control when the unhealthy voice is starved. You will find unexpected allies for your program in the "healthy voice" of your children.

Other care-givers are probably going to have a big problem believing that they should not feed your dependents pasta and pop. You can try telling them that your children are allergic to these substances. Give them the care-giver letter found in the appendix. You may be surprised at the extent to which your children can refuse reactive foods. If your children have a clear association between reactive foods and the ill effects they cause, your children are in a good position to say, "No, thank you!" when offered sugars and flours by a care-giver. You may want to reinforce this with role playing. If they come home sick, just ask them if they suspect any of the foods they might have eaten. See if they get the connection between the food and the reaction. Then let it go.

**Rejection by Peers** You may be worried that your kids will be teased or rejected by their peers because they will not be binging alongside friends anymore. All I can tell you about are my own experiences. Both of my teen-age kids have eliminated

> My kids are admired by their peers for their eating habits.

sugars and flours from their diet for two years. They eat other reactive foods moderately. They were both elected to the post of vice president of their respective classes this year. Last summer, they both received the citizenship award at camp which is given to only a few campers, and is voted on by both campers and counselors. At lunch, they must fend off other kids who would like to eat their lunch. They are admired for the way they eat. Several of their friends have tried the food plan and many have said they wished they could eat the way we do. Their parents are not in a position to help them, so they try the food plan and then fall off. It's sad, but at least they have the information and when the time comes, these kids will know how to eat.

**Eating Disorders.** My daughters especially have experienced the positive connection between eating a lot of food and maintaining a beautiful, slender figure. I pray that this keeps them from anorexia and bulimia which afflict 30% of teenage girls in this country. To experiment, they have both tried going without eating. (This is very chic at their school.) They can't do it. Their serotonin levels are normal, so their appetites are normal. Our house is filled with whole, clean food which coupled with their

> Never punish children for eating something. Never criticize them. Praise them for their good choices. Do not use food as a reward. In this way, avoid giving them an eating disorder in adulthood.

strong, healthy internal voices, takes the decision to miss meals right out of the realm of peer pressure. They can't help it. They eat well, in spite of national fads to the contrary.

**Adding items to the marginal list.** About ten months into the program, I started to focus on the mounting evidence against aspartame. When I suggested that I was going to eliminate aspartame from the household, the kids blew up. So, I asked them to listen to their bodies. I asked them to go without aspartame for four days, then, to drink a soda in isolation, i.e. without other drink or food. When they experienced the headache that resulted, they voluntarily gave it up. Because diet drinks are available at school, they still have them now and then. It grieves me to see this, but I have to trust that sooner or later, they will give it up because they themselves don't want the headaches any more.

The bottom line on adding items to the list of foods to be avoided is that it is traumatic. It is much better to get the list as complete as possible on the first go-around and avoid taking away new items.

## TRANSITION TECHNIQUES

**The "pick-one-from-each-column" sheets.** These are in the Chapter, *WHAT ELSE IS THERE TO EAT?*. I recommend using them for the purpose of including your household in the decision-making process around this food plan. I would suggest that you make one copy of these four pages for each person for whom you will be preparing food. Let them circle and cross off items to show their preferences. Try to honor these preferences as much as possible when you shop. Your dependents will feel that they have gained some control even while they have lost choices in other ways. Also, offer to take them to the store and buy them whatever they want from the lists. Even if they choose a few expensive items like raspberries and smoked salmon, spending the money to make them feel like there are immediate benefits to giving up reactive foods is worthwhile.

When I was taking my family off of reactive foods, I made one extra copy of the "pick-one-from-each-column" sheets for the door of the refrigerator so they would know what to eat if they so chose. I think it is extremely cool that now, for example, they know the difference between a protein and a vegetable. In restaurants, creative ordering to meet the requirements of the list of foods has become an amusing game for the family.

**Refrigerator Tubs.** When each child had picked items from the pick-one-from-each-column sheets, I put those items in a plastic tub in the refrigerator with their names on them. This was especially useful when we had to throw together lunches in a hurry. It helped answer the question of what to eat instead of sugars and flours. The tubs contained tomatoes, cucumbers, fruit, yogurt, carrots, etc. The fact that I kept the tubs filled with things that the kids like also reminded them that I cared about them deeply during the transitional process.

**Creative Projects.** You can do many fun things for young children. Let them decorate breakfast muffins with yogurt and bits of fruit. You can bake the muffin in a jelly roll pan, thin enough for children to cut with cookie cutters. (Shorten cooking time.) They can also do this with a flat, thin pan of polenta. Decorate with bits of vegetables. Kids can make "ice cream" by mixing frozen fruit with yogurt. Giving your children lots of attention during these projects will create good associations with the food.

**Learn by Doing.** Dr. Abram Hoffer gives an intriguing account of how one mother got her children to give up sweets. Dr. Hoffer had asked her two sons if they would follow the no sugar diet on weekdays if they could have all the junk they wanted on Saturday? They both agreed.

"In preparation for junk-food Saturday they had gone to a store. The boy who had been cooperative before was very upset because his brother was going to get all those sweets. His mother agreed he could also go onto the same program. But then the five other children in the family complained that they were being left out. Mother finally said the whole family could do so. The following Saturday one of the children became violently ill with nausea and vomiting after consuming sweets. Pretty soon every child in that family was sick with either headaches, nausea, or vomiting. After that the little boy who had been so determined he would never give up sweets told me, adamantly, that he would never ever eat sweets again."[74]

They key concept here is that the children learned to associate illness with reactive foods. Their bodies taught them. Their mother could have talked about it their whole lives. Until they could experience the illness themselves through the withdrawal and reintroduction technique, they could ignore the problem by disbelieving mom. By letting the kids have their process, mom avoided a potentially damaging power play. Provision of alternatives, permitting consequences, and modeling are truly the three keys to getting kids off sugars, flours, and other reactive foods.

## DAILY MECHANICS

Please don't think that you are going to make 14 items for each of your household members per day. The mechanics for a household are pretty much that same as for one person. We are still thinking about just three items per day. My family is conditioned to forage across kitchen counters and stovetop and through oven and refrigerator in search of the daily jackpot of great food. I make no effort to monitor servings. They make their own bedtime snacks.

> Once a day, think, 'Only three plus seasonings.'

Please find someone who wants to do this for their family too. Having a friend to talk over the day's successes eases the effort.

**Lunches.** School lunches are prepared during dinner clean-up. Leftovers from dinner are cut up into bite-sized pieces, tossed together, and put into plastic containers. My children pick up forks in their cafeteria. They do not like to take left-over fish. So, on the nights when we have had fish, or for some reason there are not enough leftovers, they might take 2 hard boiled eggs, unsweetened sliced deli meat, a stockpiled grilled chicken breast, a chop or meat patty, canned beans, chicken or tuna, cut-up vegetables, etc.

Some children may object to having to eat their lunch with a fork. I have to admit, eating a lunch that looks like salad might not appeal to a child who is trying to project a macho image. If this is the case, do not cut up their food. Put the items in plastic bags. The kids can eat with their fingers. I think this helps them blend into the crowd that is eating sandwiches with fingers.

**Parties.** Initially food for parties was a challenge to develop. In the beginning of our program, I relented on foods for parties. I permitted commercial ice cream, tortillas, and chips and dips in particular. I noticed that as we started into the second year of our food program, this was less of an issue. My children ask for particular dishes to be prepared for their parties, usually a Mexican buffet. I go out of my way to see that they get what they want. My own kids have no problem telling me on no uncertain terms which of our foods will appeal to their friends and which to skip.

I never need worry that visiting children might start into withdrawal from refined carbohydrates while at our house, because they bring their own stashes with them. One child even called her father to bring her fast food for lunch while spending the day at our house. And yes, the father did bring it over! Children nonetheless like to come to our house. Thanks to our food program, and other healing efforts, our household is safe, warm and attractive to our children's friends. Children who need to escape their own troubled households come to us.

I also spend extra money to send glorious food with my children to school parties. Strawberries are popular. Chicken drum sticks or grilled chicken breasts are also good to take to school parties. Raw vegetables and dip work. When candy is being exchanged, my kids might

---

74  Hoffer, Abram, M.D., *Hoffer's Laws of Natural Nutrition.* 26.

take flowers instead to give to their friends. The children come home content in having had their own special treat. They take a piece of breakfast muffin with them to birthday parties so they can eat with the other guests. On Halloween, we give out fortunes, coins, or small plastic toys.

**Sports Tournaments**. To maintain balance, alertness, and energy during athletic events, I would suggest making "half meals" of finger foods in plastic bags for your kids. In a sandwich-sized plastic bag, place a half serving of protein, one serving of vegetables, and a half serving of carbohydrate. The kids can dig these out of the cooler without having to find several different bags to get full nutrition. The food program will make a huge difference in their performance. Thick sticks of chicken breast, turkey breast, steak, carrots, celery, cucumber, boiled red potatoes, and polenta slices are good sports day finger foods. Their nourishment is steady, but they are never bogged down by a heavy meal. Nor are their brain chemicals and blood sugar levels whipsawed by the sudden intake of sugars such as are provided by "sports drinks". Increasing protein a little toward the end of the day will keep their mental capabilities sharp.

On sports days, do not supply your athlete with caffeine as this will mess up their coordination. (The exception would be the athlete who is already addicted to caffeine. Help them through withdrawal during the off-season.) A really alert coach will notice what the players are eating and avoid playing a child who is on a sugar high.

Sports diet is the subject of an informational brochure written for fellow team parents that I have included at the end of this chapter.

As I look back on my experience with my family, I think that I have given them a tremendous gift by implementing the food plan for my whole household. My children are strong enough to be different from other kids, but they are admired by their peers for their discipline and their healthy appearance. My kids are very thoughtful about what they put into their bodies. Of course, family members are healthier and their personalities are more pleasant. They like me better and I like them better, too. It's definitely worth the temporary upheaval.

# TOP TEN IMPROVEMENTS IN FAMILY DYNAMICS

1. We laugh more. We have more fun. We yell and quarrel less.

2. We are emotionally available to give positive support in completing projects and achieving goals. We are a mini-mutual support system.

3. We give more praise. We have more patience. We accept each other unconditionally more often. We criticize and nag less.

4. Discipline flows from logical consequences, not impulsive anger.

5. We are sick less often. We miss less school and work. We spend less time taking kids to doctors.

6. We resolve conflicts in an orderly fashion with mutual respect.

7. Adults have the self-discipline to set good examples for the children.

8. We experience reduced chaos and stress.

9. Our communications are clear. We delineate appropriate, effective, and clear boundaries. We identify and enunciate our feelings. We are free to express our love.

10. Family members are better able to execute responsibilities. We are less apt to shame and blame one another for mistakes. We are able to admit mistakes and apologize.

1. Get through your own withdrawal. Get through the first few weeks of the plan. Serve your family the same dishes that you are making for yourself. MODEL, MODEL, MODEL. Do not ask your kids to do something you are not doing.

2. Call your child's health care professional and tell the office that you are starting your child on a program that may rapidly alter their need for medicines.

3. Reread the chapter *Bringing the Household on Board.* Explain to your family what reactive foods are. Go over the rules for what you will and will not do about providing reactive foods. Explain the benefits that the plan will bring to the child. Explain that the child makes his or her own choices outside the home. Explain what reactions the child might experience when he or she chooses to eat a reactive food.

4. Share the Pick-One-From-Each-Column sheet with your children. Help them cross off items they do not like and highlight items that they especially do like.

5. Take them to the store and let them pick out items from the lists.

6. Buy them each their own special plastic tub to fill with the foods that they picked out.

7. Send the letter at the end of this chapter to your children's care givers, including teacher. You may want to consider the letter to fellow parents as well.

8. Keep a journal on your child's food consumption and reactions (both physical and behavioral). This is for the purpose of detecting food allergies and not to punish the child for eating reactive foods.

9. Praise your child for any benefits you might notice. This would include new behaviors or the absence of old behaviors as well as weight loss, clear skin, clear noses, etc. (Do not use that I-told-you-so tone of voice.)

10. Find a health care professional who can diagnose and neutralize any food or environmental allergies your child might have.

# TOP TEN 'DON'TS' FOR HANDLING FAMILY MEMBERS

1. Don't criticize.

2. Don't buy reactive foods for family members, or help them buy reactive foods.

3. Don't monitor, control, dictate, or nag.

4. Don't negotiate or compromise on buying reactive foods.

5. Don't use food as a reward.

6. Don't pry.

7. Don't search your child's room, book bag, purse, etc.

8. Don't force your child to eat something.

9. Don't let your child eat reactive foods in front of you.

10. Don't punish a child for eating a reactive food.

*Notebook:*

## WHAT BENEFITS DO YOU WANT FOR YOUR HOUSEHOLD?

Dear Reader,

Circle the problems that your household is experiencing. Visualize the benefits of reducing these problems.

| | | | | |
|---|---|---|---|---|
| Weight gain or loss | Despair | Allergies | Attention deficit | High |
| Cravings | Shame | Headaches | Hyperactivity | cholesterol |
| Hunger pangs | Anger | Sinus pain | Compulsive behavior | Numbness |
| Anxiety | Mood | Coughing | Obsessing | Fatigue |
| Depression | swings | Congestion | High blood pressure | Mental |
| Confusion | Humiliation | Asthma | Low self-confidence | fogginess |
| Fear | Critical | Infection | Pre-menstrual | Type B diabetes |
| Restlessness | nature | Swelling | syndrome | Anorexia |
| | Tension | | | Bulimia |
| | Irritability | | | Acne |

*Notebook:*

## HOW WILL YOU HANDLE YOUR HOUSEHOLD?

Dear Reader,

Take a quiet moment and think about what you're going to say to your household, what boundaries you will need to set, and how you will help household members adjust.

# SPORTS: EATING TO WIN

Last year, our team accidentally got signed up for a tournament beyond our capabilities. On the first afternoon of play, as the fourth seed team, we were beat soundly by the second seed and then by the third seed. During the break, the kids sat down and ate their fill of baked chicken, tuna salad, and raw vegetable salads. After the break, we returned to the court and *beat the first seed team decisively*. Why? Our opponents' blood sugar was low, their brains and muscles were starved, and they therefore made lots of mistakes. On the other hand, our team had all the steady, long-lasting fuel we needed. We were alert and our reflexes were sharp. The right food at the right time was *the* deciding factor.

After all the time and energy spent getting our children to the arena of competition, we can make a huge positive impact on success by providing the right food at the right time. This letter is about how you as a parent can feed your athlete to win. Rule number one: your child is most likely to do whatever *you* do. So, here are a few whys and wherefores about the questions:

# SIX BASIC RULES OF WINNING NUTRITION

> What do I want for my athlete?
> What do I want to avoid?
> How do I make it happen?
> What habits should *I* model?

- I want a steady supply of blood sugar in my athlete's bloodstream supplying fuel to brain and muscle to keep her alert and energetic. I want her adrenalin available for competition.
I don't want peaks and crashes in glucose levels leaving her mentally foggy, irritable, or tired. I don't want her adrenalin sidetracked into stabilizing blood sugar levels. So,
*We avoid sweetened products and refined flour products. We minimize fruit. <u>We eat at least every four to five hours.</u> Drinks are limited to water.*

- I want my athlete's muscles and organs to get a good supply of oxygen.
I don't want her bloodstream filled with fats. So,
*We eat low fat foods. We especially avoid hydrogenated fats.*

- I want my athlete's digestive system to release a steady stream of nutrients.
I don't want food stalled in her stomach. So,
*We eat the fiber found in whole foods. We avoid processed and refined foods.*

- I want my athlete's immune system to be available to repair the stresses of practice and play and to keep her healthy and available for practice and play.
I don't want the immune system to be preoccupied with disposing of chemicals from foods, or be deprived of rebuilding materials. So,
*We avoid processed foods that contain preservatives and additives. We prefer organic when possible. We eat plenty of protein.*

- I want my athlete's nervous system to be alert and available.
I don't want the nervous system to be frazzled and destabilized by stimulants. So,
*We do not use caffeinated drinks. I help her through withdrawal if she is already using caffeine. Bottled water is our first choice.*

- I want my athlete to have adequate electrolytes, minerals and vitamins.
I want to avoid attitude and energy problems caused by deficiencies. So,
*We follow our health professional's advice about electrolyte replacement, and mineral and vitamin supplements. We do not use high-sugar sports drinks for electrolyte replacement if necessary.*

# THE GOOD, THE BAD, AND THE UGLY FOODS

---

**FOODS TO ENCOURAGE**

Bell pepper strips, broccoli florets, cauliflower florets, celery sticks, cucumber spears, steamed green beans, lettuce rolls, spinach rolls, (a lettuce or spinach leaf wrapped around a meat strip or another vegetable), mushroom caps, steamed snow peas, zucchini spears, cherry tomatoes, baby carrots, apricots, raspberries, beef, pork, lamb, chicken, plain yogurt, and eggs. Cans of tuna, salmon or chicken. Beans with rice. Potatoes, sweet potatoes, rice. Dips of unsweetened mayonnaise and Paul Newman's Own Vinaigrette (regular only). Unflavored milk and water for drinks. Muffins made from oat bran, eggs, dried milk, fresh fruit, spices and baking powder.

---

**FOODS TO USE RARELY**

Nuts, cheese, popcorn, potato chips, taro chips, unsweetened juice, unsweetened peanut butter, fruit, and dried fruit.

---

**FOODS TO AVOID ALTOGETHER**

Cookies, crackers, cake, candy, ice cream, sweetened yogurts, breakfast cereal, donuts, bread, pretzels, pizza, corn chips, sodas, sports drinks, sweetened juice drinks, canned fruit, and tropical fresh fruit.

---

In restaurants, we focus on plain grilled or baked *proteins*, (beef, pork, chicken, fish, eggs, diary) that have been prepared without breading. We include raw *vegetables* like salads and coleslaw. We also eat steamed or grilled vegetables. Our *starches* are whole (baked potato, mashed potato, corn, peas, rice, sweet potato, beans, squash) and without sauces. We avoid foods that have been deep fried or covered in sauce. We chose not to eat sugary desserts. Fresh fruit is our only choice for dessert.

For breakfast, we always eat a *protein* such as eggs, steak, dairy (milk or yogurt) or soy milk. Ham is second choice since it is cured with sugar and preservatives. We have a *whole starch* such as oatmeal, cream of brown rice, grits, or potatoes. We eat one piece of *fruit* with breakfast. We chose not to eat sugary breakfast foods such as donuts or pastries, or foods that contain refined flours such as breads.

## SUMMARY

Breakfast: Protein, whole starch, fruit
Lunch: Protein, vegetables, whole starch
Dinner: Protein, vegetables, whole starch, fruit optional
Snacks: Protein, vegetables

# NUTRITION AT AWAY GAMES:

**Breakfast**: If bringing breakfast from home, pack small cartons of milk, instant oatmeal or grits, hard-boiled eggs, and fruit. Make instant oatmeal or grits with hot tap water, or bring a hand held heater coil to make boiling water. Scrambled eggs can be made with this coil. Another breakfast protein could be rice and beans, or sliced unprocessed deli meat. Pack all in a cooler and replace ice regularly.

If the hotel is too expensive for breakfast, find a cafe or diner. Order carry-out when you wake-up and pick it up on the way to warm-up. You will probably still need to provide your own fruit. Three scrambled eggs and grits, or two scrambled eggs with milk and oatmeal are two very cheap, readily available cafe breakfasts.

As a last resort, persuade a fast food restaurant to make you three scrambled eggs. The order-taker may not know that the restaurant can do this, but the manager probably will. All of the rest of the breakfast foods at a fast food restaurant are so saturated with fat and sugar that you will probably want to skip them.

Pleeeeease do not skip breakfast. Your team needs your child to be nourished and ready for the first game of the day. If she refuses to eat, get the breakfast, take it to the sports arena, let her decide when she wants it. See if she notices that she's making more mistakes before than after eating.

**Snacks** Whether your athlete eats breakfast at 6:30 before a morning tournament, or lunch at 12:00 before an afternoon tournament, she will be out of fuel four to five hours after the last meal. For a morning tournament this will be around 10:30-11:30. In the afternoon, it will be 4:00-5:00. Waiting until after the tournament is finished to eat means that from these times until the end of the last match, your child will be playing with low blood sugar. A snack of protein and vegetables will give her an astonishing advantage over players who have not eaten or who are trying to jack up their glucose levels with candy or soda.

One way to handle the snack is for a few parents to make a run to the nearest grocery and provide snacks for the whole team.

- Look for herbed turkey and chicken in the deli section. Ask for baked chicken to be cut up into eighths. Avoid high-fat cheese.
- The produce section often has containers of vegetables already cut up. If not, then find the bags of baby carrots and the cartons of cherry tomatoes. (The tomatoes will need to be washed, but the carrots are ready to eat.) Avoid the fruit.
- The salad bar may yield tuna, chicken, bean, corn, brown rice, or vegetable salad. Avoid pasta.
- Don't forget a bottle of salad dressing for vegetable dip.
- Buy small paper plates if needed. Pick up forks and napkins on the way out.

Back at the sports arena, just spread a blanket on the floor, put out the packages of food, and let the kids gather around. Parents get the leftovers!

Here are a few don'ts: Don't ever *make* your child eat anything. If she wants an avoids food, briefly try to dissuade her, but in any case don't help her get it by fetching it or paying for it. If she gets it with her own money, be quiet and let her experience the consequences of her choice on her own. Don't make food the object of a power struggle. Be proud of your child and praise him or her *a lot*.

144

# LETTER TO CARE-GIVERS

Dear Teachers and Care-Givers,

I am writing to inform you about a condition which my child has. It is called carbohydrate sensitivity. When he/she eats refined carbohydrates, i.e., sweeteners and flours, he/she experiences elevated insulin levels. Even small amounts can trigger this response; "just a little" *can* hurt. On days when the class is eating refined carbohydrates, I will be sending snacks with him/her. The foods he/she can have versus those he/she should avoid are shown below.

You may be interested to know that carbohydrate sensitivity is believed by some experts to affect as many as a quarter of all American children. Symptoms are numerous including weight gain, uncontrolled eating, extremes in energy levels (vacillating between hyperactive and sluggish), lack of motivation, mood changes, confusion, lack of coordination, perspiration without reason, irritability, crying, insecurity, clinging, distancing, becoming isolated, lack of ability to focus or concentrate, sitting and staring (or falling asleep) headaches, feeling faint, shakiness, craving for sugars and flours. Frequent infections, nasal congestion and asthma are also associated with carbohydrate sensitivity.

Please let me know if you would like more information on this subject. And thank you very much for helping me with my child.

Sincerely,

_____

Phone number:

| SNACK FOODS TO ENCOURAGE | SNACK FOODS TO AVOID |
|---|---|
| Bell pepper strips, broccoli florets, cauliflower florets, celery sticks, cucumber spears, steamed green beans, lettuce rolls, spinach rolls, (a lettuce or spinach leaf wrapped around a meat strip or another vegetable), mushroom caps, steamed snow peas, zucchini spears, apricots, raspberries, strips of beef, pork, lamb, chicken, plain yogurt, and hard boiled eggs. Dips of unsweetened mayonnaise and Paul Newman's Own Vinaigrette (regular only). Unflavored milk and water for drinks. Muffins made from oat bran, eggs, dried milk, fresh fruit, spices and baking powder. | Cookies, crackers, cake, candy, ice cream, sweetened yogurts, breakfast cereal, donuts, bread, pretzels, pizza, corn chips, sodas, most juice drinks, canned fruit and tropical fresh fruit. <br><br> **SNACK FOODS TO USE INFREQUENTLY** <br> Nuts, cheese, popcorn, potato chips, unsweetened juice, unsweetened peanut butter, and dried fruit. |

# LETTER TO SCHOOL PARENTS

Dear Fellow School Parents:

I am writing to you about carbohydrate sensitivity in children. I am sharing this information with you in hopes that we might reduce the amount of refined carbohydrates in the snacks we send with our children to school.

You may be interested to know that carbohydrate sensitivity is believed by some experts to affect as many as a quarter of all American children. Symptoms are numerous including weight gain, uncontrolled eating, extremes in energy levels (vacillating between hyperactive and sluggish), lack of motivation, mood changes, confusion, lack of coordination, perspiration without reason, irritability, crying, insecurity, clinging, distancing, becoming isolated, lack of ability to focus or concentrate, sitting and staring (or falling asleep) headaches, feeling faint, shakiness, and craving for sugars and flours. Frequent infections, nasal congestion, asthma and skin rash are also associated with refined carbohydrate usage, especially sugar.

The best way to minimize the effects of carbohydrate sensitivity is to avoid refined carbohydrates. This may sound difficult, but it is really as easy as choosing among the lists shown below.

If you would like more information on carbohydrate sensitivity, please call me.

Sincerely,

_____

Phone number:

| SNACK FOODS TO ENCOURAGE | SNACK FOODS TO AVOID |
|---|---|
| Bell pepper strips, broccoli florets, cauliflower florets, celery sticks, cucumber spears, steamed green beans, lettuce rolls, spinach rolls, (a lettuce or spinach leaf wrapped around a meat strip or another vegetable), mushroom caps, steamed snow peas, zucchini spears, apricots, raspberries, strips of beef, pork, lamb, chicken, plain yogurt, and hard boiled eggs. Dips of unsweetened mayonnaise and Paul Newman's Own Vinaigrette (regular only). Unflavored milk and water for drinks. Muffins made from oat bran, eggs, dried milk, fresh fruit, spices and baking powder. | Cookies, crackers, cake, candy, ice cream, sweetened yogurts, breakfast cereal, donuts, bread, pretzels, pizza, corn chips, sodas, most juice drinks, canned fruit and tropical fresh fruit.<br><br><br>SNACK FOODS TO USE INFREQUENTLY<br>Nuts, cheese, popcorn, potato chips, unsweetened juice, unsweetened peanut butter, and dried fruit. |

146

# Chapter 15
## THE INTERNAL TRICKSTER

So, what good is it to know that reactive foods destroy our head, heart, body, and soul? What good is it to know how to buy, prepare, and store glorious whole foods? What good indeed if the voice of our internal trickster retains the power to blow up the whole effort?

A saying comes to mind, "Keep your friends close. Keep your enemies closer." We learn how to keep a very close eye on our internal trickster. A VERY close eye.

> Our internal trickster is the culmination of all the negative things that have been said to us, or done to us, or just happened to happen to us. When the trickster speaks, it sounds like reality but it's really just brain chemicals and conditioning.

What does a trickster sound like? Lynne, in the chapter, *Stories of Personal Triumph*, describes her ordeal with refined carbohydrates as like having a trickster inside of her. It controlled her thoughts, emotions, and behavior. However, even after the refined carbohydrates were out of her system, the voice of the trickster continued to try to trick her into returning to her old habits where it had supreme control.

By starving the trickster and feeding our internal healthy voice, we keep the trickster from controlling us. The trickster can derive a surprising amount of strength from a trace amount of refined carbohydrates. It is very clever. It can make the most outrageously awful ideas seem normal, acceptable, and even desirable. It takes an alert, well-fed healthy voice to countermand the crafty trickster. Outflanking the trickster usually requires the healthy voice of a friend, possibly a group. For myself, I take what my trickster suggests to the elders in my support group and check it out before I act. I have been so grateful for their experiences with the cunningness of their own tricksters. They can detect the voice of my trickster from a much greater distance than I can.

Although the trickster is the persona who seems to control my internal addict, other people with susceptibility to carbohydrates struggle with other personae or archetypes. You may feel like you are controlled by a kidnapper. Or that you have accepted a large amount of exhilarating money from a lender who gradually exacts crushing, compounding interest. Your control figure may be more like a lover or a romantic outlaw or rebel. In the latter stages of the addiction, you may feel the vibrations of a madwoman or bear the pain of a critical judge. All addicts know the presence of the killer who daily shapes the world of the addict.[75]

If you are having trouble imagining what your trickster might look like, start writing down your dreams. Pay particular attention to figures that make you uneasy. Develop these figures by describing their characteristics and motivations. Transform these characters into personae that will help you by rewriting their personalities with positive traits.

This chapter describes a few of the operating archetypes of the person who is enslaved to carbohydrates or any other substance. There are other archetypes that run more deeply and broadly through us whether or not we are struggling with carbohydrates. When children are oppressed by their parents, they develop syndromes of ravaged personalities which express themselves as eating disorders. In this regard, I will talk about the work of Marian Woodman in

---

[75] Leonard, Linda Schierse. *Witness to the Fire*. (Boston: Shambhala, 1989).

the chapter *Related Conditions.* For the moment, I would like to introduce you to my personal addiction operator.

## MY TRICKSTER AS WARRIOR

I have approached my life as a battle. It is not surprising that I write about my trickster as a warrior. My trickster comes in many forms and has the ability to transform itself if one form doesn't work. Warrior tricksters can be like battering rams, hoping for immediate short term goals. They can be long-term strategists, patient, and wearing. They can be political underminers, spreading dissension among friends who otherwise seem to support us. Like a submarine, they can strike silently, without warning. They have an impressive ability to exploit any weakness by whispering rationalizations in our ears until the most destructive suggestions seem reasonable. Then, they can disappear and come back as false comforter and lover.

**The Trickster as Battering Ram.** This voice is perhaps the easiest to pick up on, but it pounds on us with incredible force. It likes to tell us:

> You're not really sensitive to reactive foods.
> You don't really need this program.
> You're not like the other people in this meeting.
> You can handle a piece of cheesecake.

It's not necessarily easy to fend off this voice because each of us would like to believe it. But it is easily recognized. When we hear this voice, we laugh, thank it for sharing, and call a friend to report on its latest brazen attack.

**The Trickster as Long-Term Strategist.** This form of the trickster is very patient. It is content to make little holes in the bulwarks while no one is looking and then watch the whole structure cave in. It knows that there is more than one method for getting its way. It particularly likes to work on self-esteem. It steals strength from other crazy-making quarters like job, relationships, and family members. It is even encouraged by factors which affect our physical strength over time like pollution and pollen. It attacks our sense of well-being until it can transform itself into a SWAT team and push our food program over the edge. It lets panic seep into the void that good food should fill. It says:

> I don't have to eat everything.
> I don't have time to eat.
> If I'm not hungry, I can skip a meal.
> This is too much food, I can't eat it all.
> If I don't eat everything, I'll lose weight faster.
> Now that I've lost my weight, I don't need to go to meetings any more.
> I ate this yesterday and it didn't seem to affect me. So I'll have some more today.

Along with the rationalizer, the long-term trickster is delighted when we think the thought, "There's not enough sugar in this to hurt me."

The best defense against the long-term strategist is to work a spiritual program in all areas of our lives. Avoid people who make us feel bad. Create peaceful surroundings in our workplace and home. Make time to have fun. Get lots of rest. Meditate. Exercise. Take vitamin and mineral supplements where necessary.

We make our food plan a reflection of life and vice versa so that they flow together. When relationship problems threaten our sense of well-being, we can attend support meetings such as Co-Dependents Anonymous, Sex and Love Addicts Anonymous, Co-Sex Addicts Anonymous or Al-anon, and open Alcoholics Anonymous. With the example of caring for our food before us consistently through the day, we carry this practice of self-care into all areas of our lives.

**The Trickster as Underminer.** This trickster works on our self-confidence. It likes to prey on isolated victims of reactive food. It aligns with friends and family members who are uncomfortable with change and would like to discredit the food program. (I wonder if these 'friends' are uncomfortable because they know they need the food program and are afraid that they can't do it.)

My Underminer likes to work on me at social events, during family disputes, and on holidays. It perked up once when a friend told me that I was imagining the benefits of the food plan. It tries to make me feel like a deviant from the society; as if there's something wrong with me because I don't eat like other people. It would like me to feel awkward. It would like me to forget the benefits of the plan in my rush to be accepted by my peers. It says:

Well, if my hostess prepared this, I really ought to eat it.

My dad will make fun of me if I don't eat like him.

My mom will be mad if I don't eat what she made.

If my friends can eat this, I really can too.

Since everyone else is eating one vegetable, I can skip the second vegetable too. Nobody else weighs and measures so I don't have to either.

I don't have time for a meeting today.

This program doesn't work for me anyway.

P.S. The friend who told me that I was imaging the benefits did eventually get on the food plan. She lost so much fear and anger (and 20 pounds) that she was able to save her marriage. Take that, you trickster!

The best defense against the Underminer is a good offense. For example, when I am going to a social event, I put myself in the role of a teacher. It is somewhat inevitable that the subject of my food plan will come up since people will see that I eat differently from most. Once I have explained what the plan is about, people either ignore it, or they become very curious. They begin to watch closely and question me about what I eat and what I avoid. In this role, I lose the desire to eat something reactive lest I give a potential newcomer the wrong impression. I surround myself with new recruits in this fashion and my trickster must retreat. I give my healthy voice so much air time that my trickster cannot get a word in edgewise.

One new friend told me recently that she listened to me because I was confident and slender. I do look different from most people. They notice the nice qualities I have and want them for themselves. I couldn't let them down by setting a poor example.

The Underminer also works through children. We hear its plaintive voice rising up from our beloved little sons and daughters in the form of wails of despair over food treats lost. Over time, the voice wears us down. We question whether we are being cruel to our children, whether we are depriving them of symbols of their acceptance by their peers. In this situation, all I have to do is remember what it was like before the plan. I remember the agony of hearing my children cough and wheeze and feeling helpless to do anything about it. I relive the waits in the doctor's office for antibiotics too soon after the last round. I remember the nights of yelling over homework left undone. I recall the bewilderment and helplessness I felt about not being able to help them address their weight problem. I especially remember the family quarreling. I regain my resolve to do my part.

If this is a problem in your household, review the list of benefits that you made in the chapter, *Bringing Your Household on Board*. Keep it in a prominent place where you can find it easily when you feel like you are losing your mind over your children's pestering. Reread it. Then with a knowing smile, silently thank the children's tricksters for visiting and go start the next fabulous meal.

**The Trickster as Submarine Attack Master.** This trickster is silent but deadly. It doesn't have a voice. Its tactic is the sneak attack. We don't hear it until the ship is sinking. The only thing to do when we are victims of the submarine attack is limp into port and call our support group for repairs.

When I had a close encounter with this trickster, it was like an out-of-body experience. I literally watched myself pick up a peanut butter cup and eat it without the act entering my consciousness. It was the day *after* Valentine's Day when I had been on the program about six weeks. I had gotten through the Day itself just fine. I had made beautiful food and had enjoyed it. I just wasn't looking.

The submarine trickster waits for a real crisis. It likes a loss situation like a death, end of a relationship, surgery, family fight, job loss, financial problem, accident, illness, even unexpected travel.

It's very hard to defend against the submarine trickster. At a moment of crisis, it is important to put our support teams on full alert. We call food plan friends and talk about the crisis until we feel our feet under us again. We ask them to walk us through our food, meal by meal until *they* feel that we have our senses back.

A time of crisis is absolutely *the* worst time to fall off the wagon. It is a time when we need every benefit that eating cleanly gives us; our mental clarity, our clean access to emotions, our steady energy, and our spiritual connections. We need to process emotions as they come up by crying and screaming in a safe place if needed. We seek consolation, prayer, and counseling. We keep expressing the emotions as they come up. We don't make one crisis into two by falling off the wagon during a tough time.

**The Trickster as Rationalizer.** I enjoy this trickster the most perhaps because I appreciate its keen intellect. It makes up wonderful reasons for eating reactive foods. And it supports other tricksters in their strategies. I think of it as the brains behind the maneuvers. However, its sayings are so ludicrous it's almost funny:

Since it's in a restaurant, it's probably OK.

I'm eating this at a party so it doesn't count.

Well, it's frozen so it probably won't hurt.

It's mixed in with other things so I probably won't notice.

Now that I'm at a normal weight, I can eat these things.

Well, it's corn flour, not wheat so it's probably not as bad.

It doesn't have any sugar, flour or wheat in it, so I can have as much as I want.

I was raging because of what my boss said, not because I ate the sugar.

Since I was drinking the soda, it must have been what I needed that day.

The rationalizer achieves its supreme triumph when it can get you to say, "I got on this program once. I can do it again. It doesn't matter if I fall off." It makes us forget that getting back on the second time is much more difficult than the first, the third time even worse and so on. It would like us to forget that carbohydrate sensitivity can be fatal.

As you think about what your trickster says to you, try to organize the messages into a persona. See how many of the persona mentioned in the beginning of this chapter are operating on you. Here is one more.

# THE TRICKSTER AS FRIEND AND LOVER

This is how my friend's trickster talks to her:

## SUGAR, FLOUR, AND WHEAT, I THEE WED

So you've been abstinent and living a sane life.
This will happen when you take that first bite:
I will seduce you and make you my slave.
I'll climb in your head, you'll start to feel crazed.
You'll start seeking me out and sneaking around.
Soon, I'll be your lover, your friend.
Once I've gotten into your veins,
The insatiable craving will drive you insane.
You, one day, will realize the monster you've grown,
Then solemnly promise to leave me alone.
If you think you have that mystical knack,
Just try to get me off of your back.
You'll go through withdrawal and feel really bad.
Unless you have support, I know you'll be back.
And when you return, as I have foretold,
You'll ultimately give me your body and soul.
You'll give up your morals, your conscience, your heart.
And then you'll be mine, 'till death do us part.

This may sound dramatic. However, to people who have been repeatedly unsuccessful in their struggles to stop using refined carbohydrates, the power of the addiction is enormous and frightening. Fortunately, there are many means to combat the trickster.

## GENERAL DEFENSIVE MANEUVERS

**Calling for Reinforcements.** All other attempts to control the trickster pale in comparison to getting reinforcements. Limitless reinforcements are just there for the asking. The consistent success of people who call on reinforcements almost makes me feel sorry for the trickster. These people ease through life while those who cannot call for reinforcements struggle with their tricksters almost constantly. We give ourselves a break and learn to call for reinforcements. Read the chapter on *SUPPORT* and get yourself some.

> Divine power, friends, support groups, therapy, writing, and reading are the heaviest, most unrelenting artillery we can throw at the trickster.

**Starving.** This may sound a little obvious, but our trickster weakens without reactive foods. As long as it is not fed even a trace of refined carbohydrates, it has a hard time getting up the strength to harass us effectively. However, a curious phenomenon happens for many people. The longer the trickster is starved, the greater the strength it derives from smaller amounts of reactive foods. One little taste of a sweet can bring the trickster roaring back on the scene and prowling around our consciousness for days. Don't ask me why. I just know that it's not worth taking that little bite, or ordering food without asking questions, or forgetting to read a label. Dealing with the consequences is a drag.

**Gathering Intelligence.** Learning everything we can about our trickster helps us anticipate its moves. We can fend off attacks by fortifying our forces at critical moments, or just by moving our troops to a safe haven instead of meeting on the battlefield. We avoid ambushes by skirting locales in the terrain where the trickster could spring a trap, or where the trickster would hold the higher ground.

Some people for example, cannot go back into the kitchen after dinner. If I'm hungry, I cannot go into the coffee shop where the cookies are right at the cashier's counter without feeling the presence of my trickster making me feel sorry for myself. On the other hand, I can go in the coffee shop just fine with my supportive husband after the movies and not even see the sweet baked goods. When I am hungry, angry, lonely, tired, and stressed, I do not go into the coffee shop at all. I have analyzed my data to identify the trickster's behavior patterns. I exploit this information through offensive and defensive measures.

> Any military officer will tell you that intelligence on the enemy makes the difference between victory and defeat.

Until you are familiar with your tricksters, I would suggest writing down what the trickster does and says. Tell a friend. Reread this chapter. Listen to other people's stories about their tricksters' antics. Figure out what personality your trickster has, now and under different circumstances in your past. Think about times when you ate inappropriately. Who were you with? Where were you? What foods gave the trickster control? Look at the four days prior to a trickster's successful attempt to push you off the wagon. What time of day, month or year was it? Was a holiday involved? We have daily, monthly, and annual cycles that leave us more vulnerable at some times than others.

**Naming Your Trickster.** The naming of your trickster serves to bring its persona into focus, so that we can recognize when it is at work. It gives boundary to the voice, making it less amorphous and overwhelming. Naming also gives us a little distance from the trickster. Most importantly, it enables us to converse with this persona. We thereby get a degree of power over it. We can learn more about its tactics, its way of thinking. We can come to appreciate its power if we can congratulate it for its victories, concede defeat to it when it has tricked us into losing ground. We can also diminish its power if we can joke with it, make it cartoonish, even pretend to be on its side when evaluating a particularly clever attempt to pull us off balance.

We choose a name that gives honor to its strength, patience, and intelligence, a name which reminds us instantly of what a formidable foe our trickster is. We may even want to include a royal title in its name. My own trickster is named Attila the Honey. I chose the name because Attila was relentless and usually successful. I added the Honey to bring humor to the name. (Humor is one of the best offenses against the trickster.) Attila is my constant companion. My trickster will be with me for the rest of my life.

**Do Not Kill Your Trickster.** One thing we must not do is try to kill our trickster. It is part of us. As such, it must be honored as part of the guiding force that brought us to this point of divine grace. Trying to cast it off sends the message that we are not OK. While committing to change, we also commit to accepting ourselves as we are today. The degree of self-condemnation that killing the trickster requires is too great to allow us to sustain our sense of self worth and self dignity. Plus, it's really not possible to kill the trickster. If I permit the delusion that I have done so, then I let my guard down and give it the advantage.

**Do Not Negotiate.** Giving in to our trickster does not have any place in our strategy. The trickster does not take prisoners with the intention of eventually letting them go home. The trickster takes prisoners only for life-long torture. There is never a long-term gain to be had for a short-term compromise. The trickster views compromise as a sign of weakness and moves full force to exploit its advantage.

**Transforming Our Trickster.** Our trickster has characteristics which we can use by transforming them. It is interesting how little transformation is needed to turn the emotional forces of the trickster into a positive force for our food program. For example, a sense of deprivation becomes a sense of deserving great health. A sense of needing just one bite becomes a sense of needing ALL of our well-being, i.e., whole head, heart, soul, and body. A sense of loneliness in the midst of a society of poor eaters becomes a sense of connection to their pain, and compassion for them. Anger at our loss of access to reactive food becomes a passion for self-care. When we feel the presence of our trickster, we ask ourselves what we are feeling, then we turn the emotion into a positive affirmation for our food program.

## HEALING THE WOUNDS THAT CREATED THE TRICKSTER

The ultimate diminution of the trickster comes when we return to the various moments when its voice was instilled within us, i.e., times of trauma, either extreme or routine. These are moments that occurred in our childhood when we were helpless and vulnerable to the dysfunctional adults who were our care-givers. We were vulnerable to their need to abuse us verbally, emotionally, physically, sexually, and through neglect. However, when we return to childhood wounds with our own adult powers, we reclaim helpless moments with the adult capacities to defend ourselves, assert our needs, and set boundaries. We thereby regain our dignity, our sense of self-worth and our ability to trust other people.

We heal the pain caused by the traumas and eliminate reasons for using food to numb out. This is like cutting off the trickster's supply lines, or perhaps even deeper, like subverting its political support in its homeland. Your trickster will never be the same.

This is where a skilled, compassionate, confident, humble, respectful healer comes in. Whether he or she is a therapist, social worker, counselor, spiritual director, or sponsor, find a good one who is unafraid to accompany you on your journey to reclaim your core sense of well-being from your childhood. This healer should respect your timing and not push you to go back until you are ready. It works.

Don't expect your healer to understand about the effects of sugars and flours. This is new information and very few health professionals understand the scope of the problems these substances create.

For this work, I can also recommend the healing arts of two organizations: Woman Within for women and New Warriors for men. These two groups have perfected the art of retrieving lost parts of the heart and soul in a safe environment. Call around to the big cities in your region until you find a directory assistance listing for them.

I am glad you chose to read this section of the book. A clean food program, self knowledge, and support are everything you need to keep your trickster in check. Your chances of success rachet skyward every time you recognize the voice of the trickster and take appropriate action. Good luck. May *The Force* be with you.

# TOP TEN WAYS TO TAME YOUR TRICKSTER

1. Avoid fatigue.

2. Avoid isolating.

3. Share food decisions with a friend.

4. Learn the location of your trickster's hide-outs.  Avoid those places.

5. Figure out who your trickster's best friends are.  Avoid those people.

6. Learn to recognize your trickster's favorite phrases.

7. Name your trickster.

8. Refuse to negotiate or compromise with your trickster.

9. Develop sources of countervailing voices.

10. Intensify vigilance during holidays.

*Notebook:*

## WHAT DO YOU NEED TO KNOW ABOUT YOUR TRICKSTER?

Dear Reader,

Please use this page to start tracking the 'who, what, where, when, and how' of your trickster:

# Chapter 16
## SUPPORT

Suppose you were in the business of shipping freight. A customer asked you to ship a cargo that was so valuable that its loss would mean financial ruin for your business. Two cargo ships present themselves. The first has a poor record. It has just a few crew members, mostly inexperienced but full of heartfelt promises. The second ship has plenty of well- experienced, strong, motivated crew members. The financial cost of both ships is the same. But the well-staffed boat requires you to stay in touch with it for a few hours per week. The crew wants to hear what's going on in your life and tell you about what's happening in theirs. The second crew has safely carried many cargos to their destinations. This crew is ready to dedicate themselves to carrying yours.

Which ship do you choose? Well, of course you choose the second one. Who wouldn't? But plenty of people choose the first as they try to make the long voyage of a life-time change in their eating habits all by themselves! Their precious cargo is their own physical, emotional, mental, and spiritual well-being. The crew members on the first boat are their own individual thoughts, behaviors, time, energy, and creativity. The track record is their own life-time of poor eating choices.

The crew members on the second boat are members of support groups. The people who choose the second boat improve their chances of a safe voyage infinitely. Sometimes this requires walking through a fear of the unknown. There are support groups already out there and there are support groups waiting for you to create them. As a rule of thumb, try six meetings of a support group before you decide whether to continue.

> Choosing our internal resources over those of the support group creates the very problem that brought us to this book. Use of our own resources *must* have a terrible track record or we wouldn't need to change eating habits.

Some of the reasons to attend support meetings are to learn new techniques, to be in touch with the power of the program by witnessing healing, and to counterbalance unhealthy messages from our culture.

There are many possible adjustments to any food program that would make it run more smoothly and effectively. No one could possibly remember them all. Even though I am a passionate teacher in this field, I still need to be reminded of the guidelines and benefits of a well-run program. Also, not all of the techniques for managing a good program have yet surfaced. New ideas pop up all of the time. I'm still learning from my support system.

Another good reason to attend support groups is to have the opportunity to witness the miracles that occur constantly in food programs. We see people released from depression and low self-esteem. Before our very eyes, we watch a body turn from blimp to graceful willow. Witnessing a miracle makes it easy to happily rededicate our efforts to our food programs. We naturally avoid thinking in terms of deprivation. Instead, we carry images of bountiful healing. We stay in feelings of joyful fulfillment. These experiences are enormous gifts to be had from support groups.

Support also provides messages of reassurance that our food path is right for us. The media bombards us with advertisements for snacks that would harm us, for restaurants that would numb us, and for drinks that would devastate us. I know that these messages are toxic, but they are nonetheless relentless, exquisitely engineered to reach my subconscious through my best screening devices. In addition to the media, friends and family who might be threatened in some way by our food program might try to dissuade us from our path. My support group is an oasis of sanity in a world which has left its senses about food.

## SUPPORT MEETINGS

Before I attended my first support meeting, I didn't have a clue about what they were nor about why they were critical to making significant changes in my life. Support meetings have become vital to my well-being. Not only do I attend my food support group, but I also attend a group for relationships, one for healing childhood traumas, and one specifically for my marriage. I don't attend all of them regularly. In some weeks I need more help than in others depending on what stress I might be under.

The rules that should apply to any support meeting are: there is no cross talk, no advice, no interruptions, and no criticism of anything that anyone says. Confidentiality is everything to these meetings. Nothing about the people who attend or what they said is ever discussed outside of a meeting. Meetings are either open to the public, or restricted to invitation only. In the latter case, members commit to attend for a certain number of weeks (6 or 8) and prioritize attendance. Recommitment occurs at the end of the 6-8 weeks. Meetings begin and end on time.

These rules are essential for keeping meetings safe. Safety means people can speak without fear of being judged. Participants also know whatever they say or do will not be the subject of conversation outside of the meeting.

Routine attendance at support groups grows a profound respect and acceptance of humans and their pain. The healing that occurs when secrets come out of our internal shadows is miraculous. People who attend support groups live out their lives with a grace that eludes people who choose to struggle alone.

## 12 STEP GROUPS

This is the most powerful tool available for healing compulsive eating. The original 12- step group is, of course, Alcoholics Anonymous (AA). Founded in the 1930's, it is widely recognized as the only effective method for controlling alcoholism over the long term. I believe that 12-step groups for controlling ingestion of refined carbohydrates and wheat will also be recognized some day as the only effective method for keeping compulsive eating in remission.

There are several such groups in the United States, Food Addicts in Recovery (FAIR) and Food Addicts Anonymous (FAA). Overeaters Anonymous (OA) is also a 12-step group, but it does not define the complete range of substances to be avoided. Since it condones the use of some sweeteners and flours, in my opinion, it is doomed to failure. I have listened to men and women eliminate sugars and flours after having been in OA for years. Their stories are the same. They lose weight initially, then it starts to come back. They are told to pray harder, work the 12 steps more diligently. Still the weight comes back as their serotonin levels peak and plummet.

Because participants are unable to control their hunger and cravings, they begin to think that not only are they physical and emotional failures, but also must now define themselves as spiritual failures as well. Within days of eliminating refined carbohydrates from their diets, they triumph in the struggle with cravings. The spiritual discipline they acquired in OA begins to serve them well in their drive to stay away from refined carbohydrates.

In a city that does not have an FAA or FAIR meeting, an "open" AA meeting would provide excellent support for a person who is trying to avoid refined carbohydrates. ("Open" just means that non-alcoholics are welcome to attend.) Substitute the words 'food, bite, and eating' for 'alcohol, sip, and drinking'. If you can't bear the thought of being seen at an AA meeting, then go to the OA meeting, but be prepared to screen out any mention of substances. OA permits members to define their abstinence in any way they want. Yours will be defined as abstinence from sugar, flour, and other binge foods.

**The Format.** Twelve-step meetings start with a welcome and a reading. The reading is the same every week. The leader, who rotates, asks for newcomers to identify themselves by their first name only. A collection basket is passed into which people put whatever amount they want. Monies go for rent and literature. "Positive pitches" might be requested: attendees describe whatever benefits come to mind, from weight normalization to mental and emotional serenity. The 'leader' tells his or her own story of recovery from refined carbohydrates. Then the leader reads from the AA big book, or from *Food Addiction: The Body Knows* by Kay Sheppard, LMHC, CEDS. One of the twelve steps is read once per month. The leader describes what the meaning of the reading, then opens the meeting to general discussion. (Note: the leader is a volunteer position which rotates after every meeting.)

One particularly joyful element in a 12-step meeting is the celebration of anniversaries. These are the number of hours, days, weeks, months or years that have elapsed since we knowingly took the last bite or sip of sugar, flour, or wheat. Breaking abstinence, losing an anniversary, and having to start counting over is a powerful deterrent to temptation.

Any person with a desire to avoid sugars, flours, and wheat is welcome to a FAIR or FAA meeting. The rules described above for safe meetings apply to 12-step meetings absolutely. If you happen to attend a meeting where back-talk is permitted, leave.

## OTHER METHODS OF SUPPORT

Talk to a non-judgmental, empathetic friend who will LISTEN WITHOUT GIVING ADVICE

Reread the reasons for replacing reactive foods that you wrote in Part I of this book.

Keep a journal of your experience.

Call a FAIR or FAA member.

Listen to a Kay Sheppard tape.

Read the AA Big Book (substitute the words 'food, bite, and eating' for the words 'alcohol, sip, and drinking').

Get a FAIR or FAA sponsor.

Call in your food plan daily to a sponsor or friend.

Work the 12-steps with a sponsor.

*Notebook*:

## HOW WILL YOU DEVELOP SUPPORT?

Dear Reader,

Please reflect for a moment on whom you will call to start your support network:

Many books have been written about the twelve steps. The Twelve Steps as originally written by Alcoholics Anonymous are as follows: Step One *"We admitted we were powerless over alcohol-that our lives had become unmanageable."* Step Two *"Come to believe that a Power greater than ourselves could restore us to sanity."* Step Three *"Made a decision to turn our will and our lives over to the care of God <u>as we understood Him.</u>"* Step Four *"Made a searching and fearless moral inventory of ourselves."* Step Five *"Admitted to God, to ourselves, and to another human being the exact nature of our wrongs."* Step Six *"Were entirely ready to have God remove all these defects of character."* Step Seven *"Humbly asked Him to remove our shortcomings."* Step Eight *"Made a list of all persons we had harmed, and became willing to make amends to them all."* Step Nine *"Made direct amends to such people wherever possible, except when to do so would injure them or others."* Step Ten *"Continued to take personal inventory and when we were wrong promptly admitted it."* Step Eleven *"Sought through prayer and meditation to improve our conscious contact with God <u>as we understood Him,</u> praying only for knowledge of His will for us and the power to carry that out."* Step Twelve *"Having had a spiritual awakening as the result of these steps, we tried to carry this message to alcoholics, and to practice these principles in all our affairs."*

They apply to any situation where people suffer from their behavior, want to change the behavior, but cannot. Alcoholics Anonymous was the first Twelve Step program. Adaptations are now available to work on relationship obsession (Al-Anon, Adult Children of Alcoholics, and Co-Dependents Anonymous), overeating, sex addiction (Sex and Love Addicts Anonymous, and Sex Addicts Anonymous), gambling and nicotine addiction. The organizations that work the Kay Sheppard food plan are Food Addicts in Recovery (FAIR) and Food Addicts Anonymous (FAA). The chapter that follows uses the FAIR and FAA definition of abstaining, i.e. sugar, flour, and wheat.

Working the steps is different for each person and can also be different under different circumstances. Although the Twelve Steps call on spiritual power, they are not tied to any religion. People might labor over a particular step for months, or at some other time, do the whole 12 steps while stopped for a red light. Sometimes people jot down thoughts and prayers in a journal. Often they talk over their progress with a friend who has also been working the steps. People share their experience with how the steps have transformed their lives in meetings with others who are trying to make similar changes in their lives.

While I was writing much of this material, the streets around my house were being rebuilt. Bright blue pipes lay on the side of the road waiting to be put into the ground. These pipes will not stay clear forever. They will develop cracks and leaks and eventually the dark, oozing mud that passes for soil in the southwest will seep in and clog the pipe. The maintenance department will send scouring equipment through the pipe and it will be free-flowing again.

Our relationship with the divine universe that created us is like the pipe insofar as it is meant to carry material freely, but becomes clogged with negative thoughts and emotions. The factors that clog our conduit with God are mind-altering substances and foods, memories and experiential conditioning that create fear, anger, shame (guilt) and sadness. The Twelve Steps

---

[76] Adapted from *Twelve Steps and Twelve Traditions*. Alcoholics Anonymous World Services, Inc.

are the scouring equipment that removes the dark, oozing mass of obstruction from our conduit to God. As such, the Steps are the foundation for a spiritual life.

**STEP ONE**

Admitted that I was powerless over sugar, flour, and wheat and that my life had become unmanageable.

This is a lengthy way of saying, "I asked for help." I knew that I was coming to this step when I set goals for myself and then somehow those goals just weren't realized. I was *in* this step when I said "I am not making it by myself."

I have done this step many times. Anytime I catch myself eating too much of a marginal food, I do Step One. To start this step, I make a list of the actions I am taking that are harmful to me. When I first started doing this step, before I committed to eliminating sugar, flour, and wheat from my food, I put very fundamental foods on the list of substances that I was eating without wanting to. I also wrote down the consequences of using these foods. My first list looked like this:

| ACTIONS | CONSEQUENCES |
| --- | --- |
| Went into a fast food restaurant on Friday afternoon and ate an ice cream cone. | Felt off-balance all week-end. Felt jumpy. Felt ashamed that I could not control myself. Felt afraid when I told my support group about it. |
| Drank half a bottle of wine with dinner Saturday night. | Denied myself the opportunity to accept my condition as a food addict. Set myself up for future problems. Felt numb. |
| Drank a glass of wine without eating. | Fell into a deep pit of despair. Experienced a frightening sense of absolute hopelessness. Would have blamed my husband had I not realized that I was having a food reaction. |
| Ate a peanut butter cup | Had swollen painful sinuses for two days. |
| Ate just one piece of bread in a restaurant | Got a headache and cravings. |

Another time that I needed to do a First Step was after a struggle with high fat foods. Although my abstinence from refined carbohydrates was not at stake, I still needed to stop eating in a manner which was out of control. High fat foods are a gateway to relapse. I started noting how and when I was eating too much fat. I looked at salad dressing, mayonnaise, cheese, butter, cream cheese, oil for frying, high-fat cuts of beef, nuts, seeds, and butters made from them, etc. I thought about the time of day that I seemed to be unable to resist. I thought about what I had eaten or skipped in the hours and days leading up to the mistake. I thought about what foods I was eating *with* the offending food. My list looked like this:

| ACTIONS | CONSEQUENCES |
| --- | --- |
| Ate two rice cakes with cream cheese. | Gained weight. Began to think I could eat other high-fat foods. |
| Ate cereal with cream, without measuring the cream. (I am allergic to milk, but not to | Gained weight. Began to think that I could get away without measuring cream. |

| | |
|---|---|
| cream because cream is all fat and no liquid.) | |
| Ate a rice cake with tahini butter. | Gained weight. Began to think that I could eat other nut/seed butters without consequence. |
| Ate salad dressing without measuring. | Gained weight. Began to believe that I was different from other people who work this program. |
| Made ice cream with heavy cream "for my children," but ate it with them. | Gained weight. Failed to address a painful emotional condition because I stuffed it with food. Modeled for my children the destructive pattern of private bingeing. Used them as binge buddies. |
| Ate a rice cake with egg salad made with mayonnaise. This item was not on my food plan for the day. | Gained weight. Began to think I really didn't need to follow a food plan. |
| Used Half and Half in my coffee. | Gained weight. Believed that I could get away with Half and Half because I was close to my ideal weight. |
| Ate high-fat hamburger patties at a fast food restaurant. | Gained weight. Neglected to make a complete meal with nourishing vegetables. Lost touch with the fact that I deserve better and that I should give myself enough time to eat. |
| Used lots of oil in a stir fry. | Gained weight. Felt out of control. |
| Made mashed potatoes with cream and butter. | Gained weight. Fed my trickster who would like to believe that if I can't see it, it won't hurt me. |

When I looked at this list with horror, my first instinct was to thank God for the concept of admitting powerlessness. Once I realized the full extent of how far I had slid, I could put a halt to the problem by admitting that I am truly powerless over fat. I didn't have to regain the entire 30 pounds before I became willing to do something. Through the grace of God, I knew what to do. I knew to write down what I was doing with absolute honesty and to write down the consequence of doing it. And then I knew that I needed to share the list with a safe person or group.

By writing down what I had eaten, I also realized how deeply I had gotten into marginal foods other than high-fat foods. Rice cakes, puffed cereal, coffee, and mashed potatoes are not foods that I can eat without running the risk of being triggered into feelings of being out of control.

Once having spoken about what I had done, I was reassured that I do not need to be perfect. My friends accepted my report with understanding that recovery from food abuse is about progress, not perfection. I released guilt and shame. The speaking of mistakes is essential for letting go of them. It opens the door to regaining a sane, serene life.

I went on with this step by looking back over my emotional state when I had begun to overeat fat. I thought about whether I had been taking care of underlying emotions, particularly pain, shame or anger, that I might have been be trying to stuff with foods. I looked at what I was worried about and admitted that I had no control over most of it. So I did a deeper first step by listing the emotions behind the overeating.

| FEELING | CONSEQUENCE |
|---|---|
| Fear over financial matters. | Loss of trust in divine power |
| Annoyance with children. | Loss of compassion |
| Feelings of being overwhelmed. | Confusion, loss of spiritual connection |
| Fear of not being good enough. | Loss of connection with the preciousness of my soul |
| Fear that I won't be accepted. | Mistrust of my higher power's good intentions for me |
| Loneliness, isolation | Further encouragement of bad feelings due to not talking about them |

Left to my own devices, I could have sunk into a depressing spiral. But with the strength of nourishing food and of stable brain chemistry, I could make the choice to talk about these feelings with a friend. I was reminded that I do have the power of choice over how I feel, as long as I am not under the influence of a food substance which can alter thought patterns. I was reminded that by talking over feelings, I do not have to eat over them. I let them go through the process of acceptance. This is like cleaning a wound and exposing it to air to let it heal, rather than covering it without cleaning where it festers and becomes infected.

I took Step One to a deeper level by looking at some painful childhood traumas that I also had no control over. I looked at some controlling behavior that I was engaged in to no avail. I made a list of all these things and wrote down the consequences of my behavior in each case. Over-eating fat was the consequence of many of them. I need divine help with all of them.

| CHILDHOOD EXPERIENCE | CONSEQUENCE |
|---|---|
| Critical parents | Feelings of inadequacy, low self-esteem, not good enough, shame, need to overachieve, not loveable. |
| No one to listen to my feelings | Feelings of being unworthy and wrong. Learned to stuff feelings. |
| No spiritual guidance | Feeling of being lost. |
| Beatings | Feeling that pain is normal, an expression of attention. |
| Absence of displays of physical affection | Physical numbness, disconnected from my body. |
| Angry parents and siblings | Fear, drive to fix situations |

These very deep experiences and emotions can be released in a very safe, understanding, compassionate support meeting. By telling about the childhood experience and then receiving empathy and acceptance from the group, the pain is healed and no longer needs the medicating, numbing effects of refined carbohydrates. A therapist, social worker, counselor, spiritual director, or professional healing organization can also provide the special environment that we need to heal childhood wounds.

One of the wonders of the twelve step program is that it provides an alternative to destructive childhood feelings. Because of its emphasis on spiritual power, letting go of old feelings and behaviors does not leave a painful void. The space where old negative feelings were lodged is filled with feelings of divine love, hope, understanding, and compassion from new friends in the program.

It is very important to understand that Step One is worked over and over again. It doesn't have to be done in detail in order to go on to Step Two. It is normal for Step Two through

Twelve to provide the strength and courage to go more deeply into Step One. However, just saying, "I don't like the way I'm eating and I don't seem to be able to change it by myself," is a huge First Step.

By working Step One, I have a clear idea of what I need to work on and I am ready for Step Two.

## STEP TWO

Came to believe that a Power greater than ourselves could restore us to sanity.

For me, there were three avenues into Step Two. My belief came from listening to people's stories, from identifying my own barriers to belief, and from the mechanical practice of looking for divine power.

**Listening to Stories.** Over and over again, I have watched people sit with radiance in their faces telling about how horrible their lives were then and how happy they are now without sugar, flour, and wheat. After listening to so many and hearing again and again that it was divine power which caused the transformation, the point began to sink in. By the process of osmosis, I too began to believe that I have a Higher Power that could help me solve my problems. If you are not in a position to hear stories, then read the *STORIES OF PERSONAL TRIUMPH* in the back of this book. Every time I read that chapter, I cannot help but tear up joyfully as I once again witness suffering turning to grace through acceptance of divine wisdom.

Also, if you don't have a support group yet, get going. Make sure your meeting agenda provides for "positive pitches", so people have a chance to speak and hear about the benefits of the food plan. They will get a sense for the tremendous good of the program. Any sense of deprivation will be more than overcome by the clear images of the benefits being gained

Almost everyone I know who has successfully worked this food plan believes that divine intervention brought them into the program and faith in divine power keeps them from straying. The hymn "Amazing Grace" comes to mind when I think of this step: "I once was lost, but now am found." For many people, the experience of eliminating refined carbohydrates is very much a transformation of body, head, heart, and soul. When I hear their stories, I know from deep within my soul, that God was present on the journey.

**Identifying my own Barriers to Belief.** This step was also essential to ferreting out the negative images of divine power that had been imbedded in me during childhood. The 12 steps have engendered a trust in the divine universe which has never failed me. But my childhood religious training had taught me to be ashamed of myself before God.

My parents' demands of me were overwhelming and beyond my abilities. My mother and father were never satisfied. I could not please them. I transferred these feeling into my religious instruction. When my Sunday School teacher told me to be like Jesus, I really thought that I was supposed to wear brown robes and preach to my friends on the playground. As you might imagine, this did not make me turn to Jesus for comfort. I assumed that I had let him down just as I seemed to consistently disappoint my parents. I had to recognize this misunderstanding and let it go before I could trust God as a source of sanity and not a source of more insanity, i.e. feelings of inadequacy.

More commonly, children are taught to fear God, or to view God as a punishing figure. I hope that if you were brought up this way, you will find the willingness to at least try to view God as pure compassion, infinitely forgiving, and accepting. This view of God will open the door to recovery from all kinds of food reactions. The ability to trust God completely is a great gift of recovery.

**The Mechanical Practice of Looking for Divine Power.** This is just the practice of seeing God at work in all good things. Whether or not we believe that God is behind all good things, we can still practice, like a rehearsal, seeing Divine Intent behind the events of the day. For example, whenever there is a coincidence that eases my day, I thank God. When I witness a healing, I see God at work. When I walk my dogs, I admire God's work in the trees and sky. In the beginning, I didn't actually believe in Divine Intention to this extent, but at time went by, I found that I liked viewing life this way. I liked feeling in my heart that God was doing good deeds all around me all the time.

This part of Step Two really requires release from negative impressions of God's intent. I believe that there are negative forces in this world. I don't believe that God has the power to intervene in matters where Divine Will is not being sought. I do *not* see God at work when bad things happen. Suspending disbelief and looking for the good in all that happens helped me come to believe that God's power could perform one of the most difficult tasks imaginable, i.e. restoring me to sanity.

Coming into the belief that divine power could restore me to a normal life, led to the more difficult leap required for Step Three.

## STEP THREE

Made a decision to turn our will and our lives over to the care of God *as we understood God.*

Why wouldn't I? My own puny will and 'wisdom', learned through a dysfunctional family system, has brought me plenty of misery. Who else (including me) could possibly do a better job of directing my behavior? There is no more reliable, wise and loving entity in the universe than divine forces. So why wouldn't I put them in charge?

This is more easily said than done. I would like to think that I turn over my own thinking to Divine Wisdom. However, I am so deeply in the habit of viewing myself as intelligent, logical, and correct, that here again, I must adopt a mechanical device to help me get started on the road to God's wisdom, not mine.

In the case of Step Three, my mechanical device is a prayer from the Alcoholic's Anonymous Big Book which goes like this:

"God, I offer myself to Thee-

To build with me and to do with me as you will.

Relieve me of the bondage of self, that I may better do Thy will.

Take away my difficulties,

That victory over them may bear witness to those I would help, of your power, your love, and your way of life.

May I do your will always!"[77]

This prayer restores me to sanity quickly. The sensation that I experience when I give up my worrying is one of being surrounded and permeated with protection and care. If this doesn't happen, i.e., I am too determined to hold onto my misery, then I go to a more detailed rendition of the Third Step prayer. I take the specific problem and render it to God. This process goes something like this:

God, I offer this problem to you.

To build with and to do with as you will.

Relieve me of the bondage of thinking I can handle it without you.

Take away this difficulty,

---

[77] Op cit. Alcoholics Anonymous, 63.

166

That victory over it may bear witness to those I would help (including myself), of your power, your love, and your way of life.

May I do your will in this matter.

I may have to do the prayer a number of times before I can let go of a particular problem. I may have to offer up my thoughts in general, specific thoughts, my brain, my head, my history, my heart, particular emotions, sometimes even other people. But because of the miracle of the Second Step and the miracle of this Third Step prayer, eventually I return to serenity. I let go and let God.

The first three steps are worked over and over again by anyone who is trying to change their behavior. No matter how long a person has been a follower of the Twelve Steps, the first three are a part of daily life. Steps Four and Five, on the other hand are usually of a deeper, more reflective nature. I do believe that before Four and Five can be done effectively, some kind of trust in God is needed. Without a fairly firm conviction that God's compassion is available to me without reservation for any deed that I have committed, I think it would be hard to do a really honest and complete Fourth Step.

## STEP FOUR

Made a searching and fearless moral inventory of ourselves.

This is really just to know what behavior I am dealing with. What did I eat? Why did I eat it? What did it do to me, a precious divine creation? How did the consequences of eating the food affect my relationships with people and my relationship with myself? As I answer these questions, starting from childhood, I get a very clear picture of what went wrong. And I have a concrete sense of what I will gain from working the 12-steps, i.e. letting go of these behaviors and replacing them with divinely guided actions.

So what kind of behavior are we talking about? The most sweeping way to define the behaviors that fall under Step Four are those which harmed us in some way, either directly by damaging our body's organs, or indirectly by warping our relationships with people and the Divine.

**WHO?** This is a painful question to look at, but essential for recovery from any inappropriate use of substances (refined carbohydrates, drugs, alcohol) or activities (work sex, relationships). Who were our companions when we ate? We chose friends based on whether they liked to eat. We avoided people who were thin because we felt they judged us. We accepted food as gifts to please other people. We ate ethnic foods which are dangerous to us because we were with people of a particular ethnic background and we did not want to offend them. We chose particular restaurants because we liked the waiters. We bought bakery goods at the shop with the jolly clerk behind the counter. We ate because someone hurt us with pointed comments. We ate because our teacher or our boss criticized us. We ate to be unattractive and stave off unwanted attention from sexual predators. We ate because Mom said we had to before we could have dessert. We ate because our friend convinced us that we did not need this food plan. We ate because someone said, "Oh come on! One bite can't hurt. Over and over again, we ate to please other people, not because we needed to nourish ourselves. We think of bingeing buddies, people who give us food, people who make us feel guilty if we decline to eat or drink with them, family members, bosses, colleagues, co-workers, friends, clients, waiters, hostesses, vendors, teachers, coaches, doctors, our partners' families, co-workers, bosses, clients, etc.

Whenever we ate with the idea that it would please someone else, or make us more acceptable, or to give the impression of sophistication or worldliness, we harmed ourselves.

We need to make a list of all these people.  We need to ask ourselves if we resent them for their part in our eating of foods which we now know were harmful to us.  We need to take responsibility for our own behavior and not blame our eating on others.

**WHAT?**  This part is about identifying our problem foods.  At first, it will be easy to identify breads, breakfast cereals, candy, pastries, etc.  They are obviously full of sugar, flour, and wheat.  Down the road in this food program, the binge foods may creep up silently and overtake us before we know it.  These foods will come from the lists in the chapter, *Marginal Foods*.  We may have to work a Fourth Step if we discover that we are eating fruit in the middle of the afternoon, or eating rice cakes as the starch in our breakfast, lunch, and dinner.  Keeping a food log will help produce a Fourth Step inventory of foods eaten.  Taking with a friend will also surface any Fourth Step patterns that need adjusting.

**WHERE?**  Where did we get and eat the food?  We look at our behavior patterns in the car, in restaurants, in the grocery store, at other people's homes, at places of entertainment, and as we entertained others.

**Home.**  Where are the triggers to eating at home?  Obviously the kitchen is one.  We kept our binge foods there.  We prepared them in the kitchen.  We ate standing over the sink.  Do we need to give up spending time in the kitchen other than the bare minimum necessary to prepare our beautiful meals?  Do we need to make sure our kitchen has no binge foods in it, even if it means that other members of our household will be eating these foods only outside the house?

What about our reaction to sitting in front of the TV watching commercials for snack foods?  This is a common binge spot for many people.  Will we need to move to another room and read instead of watching TV.  Has the bedroom provided a cave for secret consumption of sugar, flour, and wheat?  Will we need to say a special prayer for divine assistance with resistance before we get into bed?

**The Car.**  Our society today is full of opportunities to abuse ourselves with food while in our cars.  Cars are relatively safe places to consume illicit foods because no one can see us.  We have stretches of time when we are alone.  Also, because we are going from one place to another, we can justify numbing out because of the pain of a situation just left, or the pain of a situation we are headed for.  Eating in the car is also seductive because we are actually doing something else (driving), so we're not so apt to notice what we're eating.  However, driving can also be boring so we can justify eating as a form of entertainment for the drive. Eating in the car is made easy because of drive-thru restaurants and convenience stores at gas stations.  It's no coincidence that 'convenience' stores are loaded with refined carbohydrates.  Have you seen the gas station billboard that features an over-weight man at the wheel of a convertible?  The caption is, "I brake for Twinkies." (Oh pleeeease help that guy!)  Drive time is prime food-abuse time.

**Restaurants.**  The first question here is how we choose restaurants.  The food addict thinks first of the bread, chips, and desserts.  Restaurants are attractive to a healthy person because they serve well-balanced meals.  The addict chooses the restaurant that serves a pile of corn chips or a loaf of hot bread, one for each person.  It's unusual these days to be seated in a restaurant without being given a refined carbohydrate right off the bat, even before ordering, or to get bread or crackers as soon as the waiter knows what's been ordered.  To inventory our restaurant behavior, we have only to think over the restaurants we frequented and the foods that we ate there.

Then, we ate or tasted companion's food because they insisted we try "a bite".  We listened to 'just one bite' can't hurt you!  We ordered dishes because our friends insisted we *had* to try them.  We ate a harmful dish using the excuse that it was a specialty of the house.

**Grocery Stores.**  How did we prepare to go to the store?  We went without planning.  We did not have a list of the foods which would have adequately nourished us for the week.  We picked foods that looked good on the shelf and these were inevitability foods that called to us because they would feed the vicious cycles of refined carbohydrate addiction. We went when we were hungry. We went with the coupons from the Sunday supplement that would support our carbohydrate habit. We justified buying products because they were on sale or because it was a really valuable coupon. We went when we were in a hurry and would not have time to read the labels.

Where did we spend our time in the grocery store? Did the bakery counter snare us before we could even get to the produce section? Did we go to the store that had the bakery in the front and did we buy cookies to eat while we shopped? Did we justify a treat because the bakery section smelled so good? When we chose 'healthy' products, did we conveniently skip reading the back of the label to find how much sugar these products carried because the front of the label used words like 'healthy', 'good for you', 'reduced fat', or 'well'? Did we focus on processed foods with the excuse that we didn't have time to cook? Which aisles did we spend the most time in? We look at how we lingered over the cookies, candy, and crackers.

We bought food ostensibly for others, without admitting that we ourselves were the most likely consumers. We failed to set boundaries on what we would be willing to purchase and lug home.

**Others' Homes.** This is about what we did when we visited in other people's homes. The big question here is, did we sacrifice our well-being because we thought we could make some one else feel better about themselves, or about *us*. Did we eat our cousin's pie because we thought she would enjoy seeing us eat it? Did we eat homemade cake at the boss' house because we were afraid we would not get a promotion? Did we eat Mom's cooking to avoid causing a scene? Anytime we gave away our power over what we put in our system, we need to look for the reasons if we are to break the pattern. A good question to ask ourselves is, 'What's the pay-off?'

**Places of Entertainment.** This is about going to the movies to get the chocolate covered mints, popcorn, and sweet soda. Or, going to the ball game to get the hotdogs, caramel popcorn, peanuts, and beer. I was two years into this food program before I realized why I was no longer interested in baseball. I thought it was the player's strike that had turned me off to the game, but now I know it was because I was no longer interested in stadium food. Movies and popcorn are particularly seductive because we sit in the dark where no one can see what we're consuming.

**WHEN?   Entertaining, gifts, celebrations, and holidays.** Inviting friends over was an excuse to make extravagant desserts. We chose friends based on whether they would enjoy eating sugar, flour, and wheat with us. Morning coffee breaks were a cover for consuming sweet cakes and Danish. Office birthday parties were the opening for a mid-afternoon mini-binge on heavily frosted cake. Halloween was the reason to have extra candy in the house. Christmas meant cookies first of all. We made desserts and breads with the expectation that they would make someone like us more. We labored over sweet rolls for teachers and cookies for school children because we thought it would bring us some connection to these people. Were we hiding behind offerings of traditional food because we thought it would express love that we could not otherwise convey? Did food take the place of words of affection and respect?

Did we consume extra quantities of carbohydrates and high fat foods during the holidays to cover fear of family reunions? We numbed out on food rather than face the pain of healing holiday traumas in support groups and therapy.

**HOW?** We use many behaviors to secure, consume, and justify our supply of refined carbohydrates. As habitual users, we hoard, hide, steal, manipulate, binge, eat fast, drive with one finger, stuff, graze, cook in secret, obsess, deceive, deny, cry, blame, beat up on ourselves, despair, isolate, cheat, numb out, pass out, suffer through hangovers, fail to set boundaries on saboteurs, justify, rationalize, criticize, over-order, and over-purchase at the grocery store.

**THE CONSEQUENCES.** It is essential that next to each action, you put down some idea of what your part in the transaction was. To just say that I ate the food my mother gave me, is not complete. I also need to look at the fact that I was a helpless little girl. This admission is the stepping stone to letting go of the feeling of being a victim of someone else. Without this admission, I might accept harmful food from a neighbor because she made the dish just for me. I might accept the food for the sake of pleasing someone else, without recognizing the action as "little girl" behavior. With the insight that the Fourth Step work provides, I can say to the neighbor that I am highly allergic to the food she made, but I am grateful for her effort. I choose to act from the position of an adult with adult powers, not the helpless little girl.

Here are some of the typical actions that I wrote on my Fourth Step inventory:

| ACTIONS | WHOM DO I RESENT? | MY PART |
|---|---|---|
| As a child, ate white bread squished into little balls between meals. Binged on white bread with sugar and butter. Binged on bowls of sweet cereal. Walked miles to buy chocolates. Ate white bread and a dessert with every lunch and dinner. Binged on freshly-baked cookies, grapes, and watermelon. Ate pastries after church on an empty stomach. Lied about milk money in order to buy ice cream. Stole pennies to buy ice cream from the truck. | I resent my mother for feeding me this way and food manufacturers for putting so much refined carbohydrates in processed food. | I was uninformed and overpowered. I was a little girl who was helpless and dependent. |
| As a young adult, abused myself by eating inappropriately. Bagel or pastry for breakfast, (pancakes on weekends), French fries and bread for lunch, Lorna Doone cookies for snacks, alcohol in the evenings. Heavy candy bars during pregnancy. Annoyed, depressed, unlovable, critical. Avoided life by eating and escaping to golf course. | I resent the medical community for not telling me about research that could have helped me. I resent my husband for traveling too much and making me feel abandoned. | I welcomed being pregnant as an excuse to overeat. I entertained as an excuse to eat desserts. I dieted while nursing to lose weight. |
| Middle-aged adult, abused self with food. More candy (M&M's), breakfast was sweet rolls, cereal, or huge muffins. Entertained as an excuse to have alcohol and desserts around. Baguettes at every meal. Heavily breaded fried chicken, pizza, white rice, tuna melts on greasy bread with French fries. Always had cake and cookies in the house. Sneaked chocolate peanut butter cups. Gained thirty pounds. Vacationed in France as an excuse to eat and drink. Drank consistently in the evening. Raged at children and husband. Cried uncontrollably. | I resent the media for promoting overuse of refined carbohydrates. I resent the FDA for approving refined carbohydrates without ever having tested them. | I didn't know how to handle the stress of raising children by myself. I had no concept of self-care. I indulged in workaholism. I did not have a spiritual life. |

170

| Attracted to dysfunctional, conflicted, high stress volunteer situations. Emotionally unavailable to children. | | |
|---|---|---|

Get going on your own story. You may want to reread the Stories of Personal Triumph in the back of this book for inspiration. Be as honest and thorough as you can, but be prepared to return to your story again and again as you gain more insight into the nature of carbohydrate sensitivity.

## STEP FIVE

Admitted to God, to ourselves, and to another human being the exact nature of our wrongs.

This step is about relief and a big foray into grace. When I told a safe person (someone who listened with unconditional acceptance and compassion) about my transgressions, I saw that she was not shocked. I was surprised. I had always assumed that when people found out about what I was really doing with my food, they would reject me. I thought they would be repulsed. In fact, not only did my friend not reject me, but she seemed to like me better at the end of my inventory than at the beginning. Guilt and fear flew away from my heart, leaving great spaces for divine light to fill.

The key word in this process is shame. Shame binds us to our addiction. Shame keeps us from speaking out. Shame feeds our internal trickster. Sources of shame are the bars on the prison windows around our soul. Shame is a dark, pervasive, corrosive enemy whose Achilles' heel is safe speaking.

When listening to people tell me something shameful, I help them release their shame through a statement of acceptance. When Jane Doe told me about her food and her children, I asked her permission to hold her hands, then I looked into her left eye (the window to the soul) and I said slowly, three times,

"Jane Doe, I heard you say that you ate a pint of ice cream every day and that you hit your children, and I accept you and love you exactly as you are."

Why does this usually generate tears of relief? I think it is because it is truly God speaking through me. I believe profoundly that this is what God says to me every time I speak about something that I am ashamed of.

When I have a big piece of shameful behavior to release, I might ask my most trusted friends to form a circle around me. I ask for their support as I release my shame. I tell them about what I need to release and then each of them, in turn, takes my hands and repeats the acceptance statement given above. As the acceptance statements move around the circle, I hear the words repeated, I gaze into loving eyes and I feel the layers of dark, heavy shrouds being removed from my soul. The infinite divine compassion available to each of us comes through the eyes and words of my friends and I am healed.

This release from shame removes one of the sources of pain that I used to try to numb with food. With the release, I am another step closer to the daily grace I need to keep my food where it will nourish and heal me, rather than constantly throw me off balance. The release from shame that we experience in Step Five gives us the courage to face the broader defects of character found in Step Six.

# STEP SIX

Were entirely ready to have God move all these defects of characters.

The key word in this step is willingness. I pray for willingness to do whatever I need to do next. When I first started giving up various foods, I worked this step frequently. I still have to work it, particularly whenever I have gotten into marginal foods beyond their ability to nourish me. I work Step Six when I am stuck eating foods that create allergic reactions and I can't see my way clear to giving them up.

Step Six can be done through meditation. When I do Step Six, I sit and pull up an image of the food that I am trying to let go of. I imagine my divine image taking the food from me and extending a beam of white light to the spot in my body that has been damaged by the food. The light comes to my head when I have sinus pain, headaches or swirling, obsessive thoughts. It goes to my voice box, when I have been holding back on speaking a Fifth Step out of shame. It goes to my heart when I have been raging at a family member because I relapsed on caffeine. It goes to my soul when I have been neglecting prayer and meditation.

I worked Step Six over and over when I discovered that I had food allergies beyond sugars, flours, and wheat. I had a hard time accepting this fact of my life. I felt that I had already given up so much. I kept eating allergic foods that I knew would make me miserable. I had to pray hard for the willingness to give up the character defect of self-abuse through eating allergenic foods. For an overeater, some foods may trigger bingeing even though they are not sugar, flour, or wheat. These can also be addressed through Sixth Step work.

Step Six was also useful when I needed to apologize to someone for bad behavior caused by not taking care of myself. Resentment often stands in the way of apologies. Working Step Six and praying for the resentment to be removed, are the answers. I must pray for the willingness to give up any emotion which stands in the way of my recovery. Pride, guilt, self-pity, greed, etc. all fall into this category.

What is meant by a defect of character in this step? The defects have terrible names which we, as good citizens, probably have never assigned to ourselves. Words like gluttonous and dishonest are not qualities we necessarily want to claim. Until we face them, however, we cannot hope to permanently escape our disease of refined sugar and flour addiction. These character defects are barriers to our recovery.

Steps Six and Seven are broken into two parts because they make up the long, complex task of crossing the bridge from old behavior to new. Giving up old behavior often means giving up ideals and self-deceptions. The task is made more difficult because the ideals and self-deceptions were probably given to us by people we dearly love, i.e. our family of origin. So, letting go of old behavior may feel like we're rejecting family members. These very members may have supported us in very fundamental ways (shelter, food, clothing, etc.) So rejection may bring up the fear of literally being put out into the cold. Step Six brings us the willingness to risk the rejection, even accept it with compassion, in favor of the healing that giving up reactive foods brings us.

This fear of reaction from family and friends to the adoption of new eating behavior must be faced squarely. The willingness to be different must be well developed to the point of being quite powerful. This willingness must be rooted in the trust generated by Steps Two and Three, the awareness gained in Steps One and Four, and the acceptance experienced in Step Five.

Where Steps One and Four focused on actions and behavior, Step Six is about qualities. When we're listening to people who have a lot of recovery, we notice certain qualities that we might like to have for ourselves. These people strive to be honest, willing to serve, humble, spiritual, inquisitive, open to change, self-examining, courageous, confident, strong, articulate, grounded, centered, wise, open to help, communicative, supportive, accepting, reflective, disciplined, aware, alert, grateful, generous, forgiving, energetic, engaged with life, trusting, joyful, respectful of self, respectful of others, and so on.

Dear Gentle Reader, Step Six is where the tire meets the road. This is where we focus on the qualities that we need in order to make ourselves whole again. We pray for negative qualities to be removed. We need to accept that we might actually have some these qualities.

We look to ourselves and recovery friends for information about what these qualities might be. Since refined carbohydrate sensitivity is not a well-known condition, it can be hard to find out from society how far gone we are. Most of our friends will not recognize the signs of carbohydrate sensitivity. We might not have the recognizable deteriorated reputation that an alcoholic might have. Most of our misdeeds have probably taken place privately. We don't hit "skid row" or lay in the gutter as alcoholics are traditionally portrayed. (This is not to say that carbohydrate addicted people do not suffer the condemnation of society. Being fat is one of the most judged conditions in the country by far. It is to say that the general public does not understand that being fat for about 80% of the overweight population is an allergic reaction to carbohydrates.)

Our disease is more devastating and consuming than alcoholism. Steps One and Four have made apparent how deeply it invaded our lives; How many of our activities and thoughts revolved around food. Fortunately, our determination to best this scourge grows in proportion to our awareness of how devastating its effects have been.

So, let's take a deep breath and look at our defects of character. We have been dishonest, selfish, arrogant, egotistical, self-righteous, closed-minded, needy, scattered, fearful, narrow-minded, prejudiced, resentful, manipulative, judgmental, critical, controlling, gluttonous, distrustful, untrustworthy, rejecting, vengeful, gossipy, sarcastic, neglectful of selves, faithless, lazy, isolating, numbed, confused, lost, jealous, perfectionist, inadequate, not good enough, emotionally unavailable, withdrawn, and so on. Whew! Of course we were not all of these things all of the time, but we need to ask ourselves to be ready to have God remove all of these defects of character.

Why did we not give up these defects long ago? Well, two reasons come to mind: 1) they enabled us to feel like we were surviving and 2) they were enjoyable. On the first point, we thought the pain of overeating was less than the pain of withdrawal and abstinence. So our poor chemical-soaked brains chose to eat and suffer. On the second point, we enjoyed the eating, let's admit it! We also sometimes enjoyed the socializing that went along with it. I have memories of sitting over ice cream or pastries with friends while we gossiped and chatted. The feeling of being bloated and stuffed are distinctly associated with memories of holidays and parties.

For some period of time, before the disease overcame us, refined carbohydrates were a playful, joyful companion. So we must recognize the shift from friend to foe as we do Step Six. Step Six asks us to give up the destructive elements of activity like gossip and self-abuse through refined carbohydrates, but keep the good elements like the company of blessed friends eating genuinely beautiful food.

Step Six may also involve some grieving. As we look at the behaviors were are letting go of, we may experience a grave sense of loss. How could we not? We will lose parts of our character, some of our relationships, familiar illnesses, a few of our haunts, and many pounds of body fat. I even doubt that I could have gone on to Step Seven had I not taken the time to shed cleansing tears over the loss of old ways. New friends in support circles comforted me as I moved through this phase. Grief *does* pass through the expression of tears, so with mounting excitement, we move to Step Seven.

Humbly asked God to remove our short-comings.

It's fairly obvious that all steps have led up to this one. From here on out, we are just mopping up and installing routines on the foundation built from Steps One through Six. Step Seven is when we finally give up our old ways and let divine light shine into the dark places where our old patterns thrived.

Step Seven is where we really have to look at whether we can continue to visit with our former binge buddies. Whether we can cook with Mom at the holidays. Whether we can go to the movies without eating a meal first. Whether we can see the people we used to eat with and go to the places where we used to get our binge foods. We find the courage to ask God to remove the urges to get close to our old habits and to actually change our behavior. We get a clear picture of the role of our new friends in support groups as providing new social activities in addition to support.

I work steps One, Six, and Seven in combination over and over. Before I sleep at night, I think of any food that I have eaten or behavior that I have engaged in that I should not have. I work a First Step - admit that I am powerless over that food or behavior, then a Sixth Step where I pray for the willingness to give it up, and then the Seventh Step to get the security of knowing that I am without the desire for that food or behavior. If I don't feel the release and relief that I associate with the Seventh Step, then I start over with One, add Two and Three, then try Six and Seven again. If I fail again, then I know I need to review the resistance with a friend, or talk about it in my support group meeting.

Most often, we can take old defects of character and turn them into positive characteristics just by slightly changing their focus. We can build new behaviors by seeing what was good in the old behaviors, and where we were giving in to the cunning, seductive part of the addiction. Some of the ways to do this follow:

| THE OLD BEHAVIOR | THE QUALITY WE WANT TO RETAIN | THE NEW BEHAVIOR |
|---|---|---|
| I obsessed over what I would eat and when. | Planning | I sit down weekly to make a shopping list. I review what I'm planning to eat daily with a friend. |
| I visited bakeries, bagel shops, convenience stores, to find refined carbohydrates. | Devotion to shopping | I select stores with great produce, meat, poultry, fish, grain, and diary departments. |
| I stashed candy and cookies where no one could find them. | Care about storing food | I store fresh foods carefully, properly refrigerated or frozen. Grains go in air-tight jars. |
| I baked and consumed goodies secretly. | Devotion to cooking | I cook a good variety of tasty, clean foods. |
| I entertained as an excuse to make high-carbohydrate food. | Socializing | I make clean food which beautifully nourishes my friends. |
| I used traditional dishes on | Devotion to observing the | I carefully prepare special |

174

| holidays to overeat. I numbed my spirit. | holidays. | foods which nourish and celebrate my spirit. |
|---|---|---|
| I gave into the cravings and demands of my minor dependents for excessive refined carbohydrates. | Careful attention to desires of dependents | I pay attention to the true nutritional needs of my dependents. |
| I chose friends who would binge with me. | Careful selection of companions | I spend time with people who support my recovery. |
| I isolated in order to eat. | Comfort with solitude | I find time to meditate and pray alone with my soul. |

In the first column, we see negative qualities that we decided in jettison in Step Six. In Step Seven, we make the decision to move on to the last column. We pray daily for the courage to leave old behaviors behind. And, because our soul has been liberated from its bonds of shame and fear, it is available to us to make life in the last column comfortable and natural. We constantly seek visions for the new behavior we want to adopt. Where we used to seek these visions from our ego, we now find them emanating from our soul. We find that Step Seven gently builds barriers to returning to our old ways. We find that we gradually build the desire to live in the last column where we find grace and serenity. Step Eight will also do this for us, in yet another way.

## STEP EIGHT

Made a list of all persons we had harmed, and became willing to make amends to them all.

This step is about making sure that we don't carry forward the destructive forces of guilt and resentment. Sure, we did what we did. We isolated, made ourselves sick, emotionally unavailable, etc. But with the help of these steps, those days are rapidly coming to an end. It's time to repair relationships that were strained as a result of our eating patterns. It's time to further clear our conduit to God by removing the sticky substances of guilt and resentment. By looking at the damage we have caused, we not only clear it from our souls, but we also build barriers against engaging in destructive behaviors again.

Intention is not the issue here. No one wakes up in the morning intending to eat foods that will make them crazy, sick, and fat. So the question is simply, "What did we do and did it harm anyone?

Working this step is, to some extent, made easier by two factors: One is that for most of my life, I did not know that sugar, flour, and wheat had so many devastating consequences. So, as I made my list for this step, I could do so without self recrimination because I simply didn't know. I still have to answer to the questions raised by my resistance once I did know. Why did I have to go on testing substances once I was told that they were harmful? I don't know the answer to this question, but I do know that the more I work Step Eight, the less likely I am to use myself as a human guinea pig.

The second and perhaps more important factor is the expectation of forgiveness that I have begun to take for granted because I have been working the Twelve Steps. I had a loving experience when I went through the painful process of reporting a relapse into high-fat foods in Step One. I received acceptance and empathy from my friends and support group as I took Step Five. I felt release from a divine source when I took Steps Six and Seven. I have surrounded myself with safe people who do not expect me to be perfect by any means. I have received the grace to look at myself through forgiving eyes. I receive knowledge of God's infinite compassion through regular prayer. With these experiences as fortification, I am ready to work Step Eight.

**MYSELF.** First, what did I do to myself? I think about all of the benefits that I have received from this program and remember their opposites. I accept responsibility for having caused myself harm. For me, the most important consequences that I must take responsibility for, are the myriad of negative emotions I lived with. Reactive foods made me angry, diminished my sense of worth, depressed me, made me fearful and caused me shame - the whole gamut of negative emotions. Physical self-abuse is the next category I must look at. The substances made me fat and puffy, caused terrific sinus pain and allergies, and exhausted me. The diminishment of my intellectual capability was another high price of eating reactive foods. Intellectually, the substances caused my brain to feel groggy. I was also often confused. And perhaps saddest of all, my food cut me off from my divine contact. Spiritually, sugar, flour, and wheat clogged the conduit between me and my Higher Power, my source of all divine bliss. So, the things I did to harm myself are extensive.

**MY HUSBAND.** My husband and I had just celebrated our seventeenth wedding anniversary when I started eliminating reactive foods. Our marriage had been punctuated by anguish caused by his frequent absences, but now I realize that the craziness caused in my mind by sugar, flour, and wheat was a much greater factor. Since these substances had my brain in a constant ebb and flow of chemical neurotransmitters, I was subject to mood swings. My husband might hear that I was very much in love with him one night, and the next day, I would scream that he was the worst husband possible. I was in constant fear that his career was faltering and I did not hesitate to communicate these fears to him with much blaming and shaming. I cried because I felt that he ignored our daughters. I had tantrums if he was late for appointments. I berated him for his lack of social graces. I rarely complimented him. I thought he was a burden when he asked me to do anything for him. I resented him.

About three weeks after eliminating sugar, flour, and wheat from my diet, I found myself thinking that my husband had gone quite a while without screwing something up. I can remember exactly where I was standing when I realized that, indeed, it was not he who had changed, it was I. I was so shocked and ashamed that I held onto this information for several days before I could move to Step Nine.

**MY CHILDREN.** This may be the most painful paragraph in this book for me to write. I have to face the fact that I neglected my children because I was too tired to be with them, or I was sick with sinus headaches. I neglected them emotionally because I was angry or depressed. They could not get much nurturing from me while I was in this state. My state of anxiety drove me to work monumental projects outside the house, which took me away from them even more. The raging is perhaps the most painful to write about. Yelling at them to clean up their messes is my most vivid memory. Little beautiful girls who should have been cherished were being squashed by my tantrums. Their self esteem was damaged by my constant criticism. My impatience with them made them feel inadequate. I heard the echo of my own mother's relentless, destructive controlling behavior and I was helpless to stop it.

**FRIENDS AND CO-WORKERS.** I kept my temper under control with co-workers and friends bowing to the pressure to be professional and to have social graces. I think the greatest harm I did them was to be distant and judgmental. I felt so defective, I could not let them be near me. I was also afraid of them, so I kept my guard up. I could not be there for them emotionally because I did not know how and I was too miserable to share left over emotions anyway. I was also controlling and took too much on myself instead of sharing and delegating responsibilities. Many of my relationships could be described as co-dependent. I think of co-dependency as an outgrowth of carbohydrate overuse.

## STEP NINE

Made direct amends to such people whenever possible, except when to do so would injure them or others.

This step finishes the attack on the self-destructive emotion of guilt. It's a tough step, but essential for staying on track. We forgive ourselves first and in as much detail as possible. When I sensed how helpless I was and how ignorant about my behavior, I was able to forgive myself.

I also did not apologize to anyone for any behavior until I was as sure as possible that I was capable of stopping the behavior for which I was apologizing. I am not perfect about this, but I catch myself progressively earlier in the process of a misdeed.

Forgiving myself is an important prerequisite for letting go of expectations about how people might react to my making amends. Their ability to forgive or understand is a reflection of their emotional state and *not* a reflection of the appropriateness of my apology. In contrast to my loving husband's reaction, I once listened to a husband tell me the story of his wife's amends. He indignantly stated that her apology had been inadequate and that he had told her so. My own heart twinged at the thought of his wife getting up the courage to apologize only to receive this terrible response. I hope she held onto the benefit of the amends by remembering that her husband's dissatisfaction was his illness and that she did not have to dance with his illness by feeling inadequate.

I apologized to people that I had raged at. I apologized to my family for buying and preparing food that harmed them. I apologized also to them for being sick and unavailable to them so much of the time. I apologized to my children for eating reactive foods while I was pregnant and causing their food sensitivities and possibly weakened organs.

Making amends helps keep me on track because I never want to have to do it again. When I crave caffeine especially, I think of having to apologize to my kids for terrifying them. It stops me cold. Thank God.

In the case of the bolt of lightening I experienced in Step Eight about my husband, making amends seemed very scary. Fortunately, we were very blessed at that time to be members of a circle of couples dedicated to helping one another with the problems that arise in the normal course of relationships. These were safe non-judgmental, accepting people. My husband and I sat in the middle of this circle with two particularly safe friends on either side, one of which my husband had chosen and the other of my choice. With this buffer of safety all around me, I told him that I thought that my criticisms of him were the result of eating refined carbohydrates. It only took a few minutes, but it was one of the most difficult tasks I have ever undertaken. His reaction was one of gratitude. At the next meeting of this circle, he took time to honor me for my courage and my dedication to my family.

The case of my two children who were then aged 11 and 12 was different. I was afraid that a big apology would overwhelm them. I thought carefully about the fact that as children, their ability to gain perspective on a situation was limited. They only had a child's ability to understand what had happened to them. I didn't want them to have to cope with all of the ramifications of having had an inadequate mother all at once. I have had the sacred duty of witnessing women who open up memories of how abusive a parent had really been. The process can be quite devastating, requiring another long process of healing and forgiving. I did not want my children to become aware all at once of how bad my emotional unavailability and raging had been.

So, I began apologizing for specific behaviors as they came up. If I praised them, I also apologized for criticizing them. If I let them do something new without supervision, I also apologized for having been controlling. If I admired their new figures, I also apologized for having fed them poorly when they trusted me to do better. If we do something in the afternoon, I apologize for having been too tired or sick to do anything in other years. Did apologizing help? Oh God, yes. They are very grateful for my efforts to improve myself. They notice in many ways and they do thank me. (Do not be confused, dear reader. They are angry about the fact that they adhere to a food plan that is different from their friends, but they *do* like the results.) The mending has been gradual.

If you are in the position of making a very large amends, don't hesitate to call in friends to support both you and the person you're making the amends to. Reactive foods create the sensation of shame, they tend to make us accustomed to doing things alone, in isolation from other people. We don't have to be ashamed anymore, so we can ask for help.

It is important for me to remember that the layering of experiences that my children received at the hand of my carbo-soaked person, does not go away just because I apologized to them for so many misdeeds. I must let go of the guilt so I can stay in my adult with them. I must not continue to serve penance for my misdeeds after a clean apology. I must not give into demands for treats to 'compensate' them. However, if they bring up memories of things I did to them, I must apologize again. I always say how sorry I am when they remember me yelling, making sarcastic remarks, trying to control their homework, or expressing despair over why they couldn't make a mark of 100% instead of 95%.

## STEP TEN

Continued to take personal inventory, and when we were wrong, promptly admitted it.

I feel sorry for people who never identify a reason to go into recovery. They miss out on the opportunity to fully surround themselves with love and protection. Steps Ten and Eleven are two parts of a daily routine that cleanses our souls of the daily accumulation of emotional gunk. They are a gift to those in recovery that provides maintenance of the conduit to our divine power. Step Ten surfaces items that we need to pray and meditate about in Step Eleven.

This society hardly has a clue about carbohydrate sensitivity. There are tremendous pressures from all around us to relapse. The media pressure us to buy foods and medicines which contain refined carbohydrates. Dramas portray attractive characters inhaling refined carbohydrates with impunity. Food manufacturers and restaurants are constantly pushing reactive products at us. Our co-workers place the stuff in front of us, our friends try to give it to us and tease us when we refuse. Classmates make fun of our food, or fail to include us in activities that evolve around candy. These pressures, combined with the deceptive invasion of sweeteners and thickeners into our food supply can wear down our vigilance and cause drifting and mistakes.

The daily inventory called for in Step Ten is just the constant checking and correcting that takes place on any long journey. A sailor constantly reads navigational instruments to pinpoint current location against the destination. Even on an auto trip, the driver reads the frequent road signs to reconfirm that the trip is proceeding on the right track.

For the recovering carbohydrate addict, there are two sets of inventories which need to be reviewed daily to ascertain that we're on the right path. The first is the mechanics of our food. The second set is our ancillary behavior. If we made a list of our planned food in the morning, then it's easy to compare our actual consumption with what we had planned. Deviations are carefully thought over, we forgive ourselves and let it go. Periodically, we also look at daily food lists to see if we have enough variety in our food, especially diary. Are we rotating among cow, goat, soy, oat, quinoa, salmon, etc? Another area is breakfast. Are we stuck on just one breakfast, like the breakfast muffin or grits and eggs? Are there other common foods that we are overeating? Are we eating eggs more often than once very four days?

Perhaps once every few weeks, we need to review the basic guidelines:

Are we eating on time?

Are we eating everything at one sitting?

Are we weighing and measuring?

Are we using fat in volumes appropriate to our weight?

We can also look at our written Steps One, Four, Six, and Eight and ask ourselves if we're drifting back into old behaviors. Are we reviving relationships with former binge buddies? Are we visiting old refined carbohydrate haunts? Are we planning events that include marginal foods on a "just-this-once" basis?

This is like a daily shower: Routine and cleansing. We make brief, to the point apologies so that we're not carrying guilt. We apologize to ourselves with comments such as, "I'm sorry I ate those almonds. I know they give me asthma," "I am sorry I ate the cheese that is making my stomach hurt," "I'm sorry I ate the peanut butter that is making me depressed," and " I'm sorry I had butter at all my meals today." To family members we might say "I'm sorry I yelled at you in the car." "I'm sorry I accused you of wishing me harm." "I apologize for calling you irresponsible." "I'm sorry I tried to tell you what to eat." We don't beat ourselves up. We move on.

Including the triumphs of the day is essential to recovery. In fact, I suggest doing the triumphs first, before inventorying the wrongs. Triumphs are going to look quite different for each recovery program. For the beginner, substituting oatmeal for a Danish might be a huge triumph. For a person who's been in recovery for years, admission that she needs to go back to weighing and measuring would be an enormous victory for her program. For the anorectic, eating four items in one day could be cause for establishing a national holiday.

One the second set of inventories, i.e., ancillary behaviors, we are looking at broader recovery issues, including our emotional states. All recovery programs, no matter what the substance or activity being healed, include the attempt to stay out of anger, guilt, and resentment. Love, compassion, and tolerance are the goals. So, our daily inventory includes a look at whether we've indulged in these emotional minefields.

Enjoy your Tenth Steps. Wallow in your triumphs. Reaffirm the presence of divine support in your progress. Ground yourself in the joy of recovery.

As I described in Step Seven, I take my personal inventory daily before going to bed. I find that taking this cleansing step makes my sleep easier. If I owe someone an amends as a result of taking this step, I rehearse what I'm going to say so that I am at least over the hurtle of forming the words. For my triumphs, I bring up gratitude as I prepare for Step Eleven. For wrongs, I prepare to ask for forgiveness from my divine universe.

We accept that we are not perfect. We express gratitude that we have a spiritual means for dealing with our imperfection. Holding on to an apology is like crippling ourselves. By making the amends, we release the guilt and our conduit to God is wide open for business as usual.

# STEP ELEVEN

Sought through prayer and meditation to improve our conscious contact with God as we understood God.

I sometimes think that every one of the Twelve Steps should end with, "and do Step Eleven". By the time I reached Step Eleven, I was already doing most of it without even realizing that frequent prayer and meditation had become a natural part of my life.

A prayer can be as short as one word, "Help!", or even two words, "Thy will!" These quick appeals are useful in emergencies when we otherwise might move into fear, shame or anger. For recovery from overuse of refined carbohydrates, these emergency prayers are most useful at moments of temptation. Since we know with clarity how harmful these substances are and how much our divine force wants us to be free from pain and illness, reconnecting with the divine at a moment of temptation can bring the negative consequences of relapse into sudden and sharp focus.

I work this step after One, Six, and Seven. I wait with clear mind and open heart. Upon entering divine space, I know what to do. The pure compassion and love that I experience in this space always direct me in the path of forgiveness, grace, compassion towards others and myself, trust in divine processes, quiet confidence, and love. These are such powerful forces that, even though I might not want to put aside pride and resentment, I must, because I prefer to live in divine light whenever I manage to open myself to its grace.

Take time to meditate. Designate a quiet spot to be your meditation space. Concentrate on each part of your body and listen to it. Think healing thoughts. Be confident of your body's tremendous healing powers. These powers surely have a Divine source. Call up these powers in your imagination. Give them form in your mind. Ask for their help in recovering from any ailment you might have. Ask your friends to pray for you.

Here is a meditation I say for myself, or any part of my body, or for a friend. I say this meditation for someone who has hurt me as a release from my own resentment and anger. The first stanza is a traditional Buddhist meditation. The second stanza came to me after a vision quest.

> May I be filled with loving kindness.
> May I be well.
> May I be peaceful and at ease.
> May I be happy.
>
> May I be open to nurturing.
> May I be accepted exactly as I am.
> May I have faith.
> May I be patient.

Please say this meditation for yourself first. Then repeat it for any entity you wish.

A healthy meditation practice will reflect well on your other planes of being: physical, emotional and mental. Feed your soul daily, just as you are learning to feed your body.

# STEP TWELVE

Having had a spiritual awakening, carried the word about reactive foods to others who still suffer.

This step rules my life joyfully. I have a visual treasure trove of people's faces as they tell me about regaining their serenity, their clarity of thought, their bodies, their personal relationships, their health, their sense of well-being, their happiness, even their right to a place on earth. Maybe I have replaced my addiction to food with an addiction to witnessing divine will at work!

What I must be very careful about is replacing an addiction to food with an addiction to getting into other people's business, i.e., co-dependency. Co-dependency comes from thinking that we know better than God what is good for someone else. We tend to think of the other people instead of turning our thoughts towards God's will for ourselves.

Do not get hooked into the *results* of carrying the word. We carry the information, but we're not responsible for anyone else's program. Taking care of myself is generally as much as I can manage. Planting the seed of knowledge and then sharing my experiences is all I can do for someone else and it is enough. People come back to me months after I have mentioned the program and tell me that they are ready to start. They also sometimes tell me that if I had pushed them initially, they never would have started at all.

When someone tells me they're not interested, I reaffirm my faith that God has them firmly in hand. My experience is that about one person in fifteen is ready to open him- or herself to the message about reactive food. A much smaller number will be ready to take action. I am in absolutely no position of judge whether the time is right or not for anyone else. With the passage of time and more experience with the Twelfth Step, I have come to appreciate what a complex decision asking for help is. People need space and time to consider how desperate they are and whether they have the resources to undertake a new journey. They will know what is right for them.

As always, keeping myself healthy and vigorous, (i.e., modeling the results of the program) is the most effective means of carrying the word. Family members, co-workers, and friends will approach you with questions when they see how good you look and sense how good you feel.

I do find myself being self-conscious when I eat around other people who are curious about my program. I reassure myself that my path is right for me. I am reaffirmed in this when I see how beautiful my food is. The colors on my plate sing nature's praises while other plates are pasty and pale by comparison. Sooner or later, someone will notice that, not only do *I* look better than most people, but my food looks better too. They think about the connection and sooner or later it begins to sink in.

A few rules of the road: I never talk about people's food while they are eating it. If they ask me why I don't eat something they're hauling into their mouths at the speed of light, I give a very brief answer and catch them after the meal. I give them reassurance that I am not the food police. I am not monitoring their intake. Low key is the *modus operandi* which will get the best results.

If someone does want to start the plan, I give them a very enthusiastic start, but I also try to stay one step behind the beginner. What this means is that I support what they are doing, not what I think they should be doing. I never ask them how their food is going until they have brought it up. When I help them, I start my suggestions with the word "I". (This is a short-hand way of saying I share my strength, hope, and experience, without giving advice.) I would never suggest that they try something if I had not tried it myself. No matter what they are telling me, I do not criticize them. To the contrary, no matter what they're going through, I find some aspect of their story to praise. I like to term any progress "a triumph." I remind them constantly that progress, not perfection is the objective of recovering from refined carbohydrate use.

Even if my friends say only that they are thinking about starting the program, I stop what I am doing, look them in the eye and say something like, "I am really exciting that you are considering this program. It has been a source of great joy to me." I try to be a good listener by mirroring back their thoughts to them, rather than injecting a lot of my own ideas. Even if I judge that they are in denial about being able to still use some substance, I just rephrase their statement as an answer rather than correct them. Later in the conversation, I might share a not-so-great experience I might have had when I experimented with whatever substance they want to keep using. Sometimes, they just have not been aware that the substance and effect could be related.

People are enormously sensitive and wounded about their eating habits, so a gentle, caring, celebratory approach will promote the healing process whereas a frontal attack may bring on embarrassment, shame, and avoidance of the program. If confrontation is inevitable, lead into it with love. The rewards of patience are great. I have often had people tell me how grateful they are that I didn't expect them to adhere to some rigid schedule as they undertook their initial attempt to eliminate and replace reactive foods.

I end every conversation with a detailed review of their progress and triumphs. I always tell them I am proud of them. At these moments, I have the distinct impression that God has been close by.

People who practice the Twelve Steps try to limit their teaching to sharing their own experience, strength, and hope. Here are some of mine:

# HOPE, STRENGTH, AND EXPERIENCE

Hope is walking into the first support meeting.
> Strength is making meetings routinely.
>> Experience is knowing when you need to make every meeting in the week.

Hope is putting together the first abstinent meal.
> Strength is getting to the other side of withdrawal.
>> Experience is forgetting that there's any other way to do it.

(False) hope is thinking, 'Maybe I can still eat _____.'
> Strength is feeling 'My body will tell me what I can eat.'
>> Experience is accepting 'God will tell me what I can eat.'

(False) hope is thinking, 'I am different. I can eat more things.'
> Strength is knowing 'I don't need to be different.'
>> Experience is, 'I accept myself and everyone where they are without needing to be the same or different.

Hope is buying the first book on food addiction.
> Strength is rereading it for the third time.
>> Experience is living the book.

Hope is eliminating sugars, flours, and wheat.
> Strength is eliminating marginal foods.
>> Experience is eating only foods that honestly work.

(False) hope is thinking, 'Oh, it's probably alright.'
> Strength is saying, 'Waiter this is not what I ordered!'
>> Experience is planning, 'I'll call the chef before I go.'

(False) hope is thinking 'I just need to loose a few pounds.'
> Strength is admitting, 'Oh maybe I should work on a few relationship issues along the way.'
>> Experience is praying 'Thank God for every aspect of 12-step recovery.'

Hope is focusing on, 'I can't wait to get this weight off!'
> Strength is moving to, 'I will work the program and forget about my weight.'

Experience is admitting 'I use weight gain or loss as an aid to being honest about my program.'

Hope is dreaming, 'I'm sure Aunt Tilly will have something I can eat'
> Strength is calling Aunt Tilly before hand and asking, 'What's for dinner?'.
>> Experience is taking your own food to Aunt Tilly's house because she doesn't have a clue.

(False) hope is that one bite won't hurt.
> Strength is accepting that what others say is not true.
>> Experience is the days of craving that come after one bite.

Hope is realizing, 'All I have to do is ask God to get this weight off me.'
> Strength is knowing, 'All I have to do is ask for knowledge of God's will for me.'
>> Experience is accepting 'I must work a full program of recovery in order for God to work fully in my life.'

Your spiritual life can be enhanced by replacing reactive foods. Each meal becomes an act of honoring the body and the Spirit within. Because the food is so glorious it reminds us of how important we are in God's eyes. We are reminded of our connection to Divine power each time we eat a meal made up of whole foods.

Because most processed foods have sugars or flours in them, we use mostly whole foods. This brings us closer to nature because these foods come more directly to the consumer from the earth than do processed foods. The foods we eat look the way they did when God created them, instead of the way a food manufacturing account executive might have conceived them. The foods actually look like a gift of God. It is much easier to remember that Nature created this food to nourish me because I am precious. It is much easier to believe that Divine Spirit loves me when I see the effort that nature exerts in order to feed me.

> No one, not the wealthiest nor the most powerful, can eat any food more glorious and healthy than the food described in this book. This is what the Divine wants for each of us, all of the time.

Because the foods I eat leave me feeling calm and centered, meditation and prayer become much easier. When I listen for Divine guidance, I will hear clearly because I no longer experience the chaos of body rhythms which are out of balance.

A subtle way in which replacing reactive foods works is that people become less fearful and distrustful. There is support for this in the medical literature and I hear it frequently in the support group. Therefore, it is easier for me to see the goodness in other people. I am more in touch with how God works through other people to my benefit.

There are many prayers and meditations which we can use to call on spiritual power. An example would be this prayer for help at the moment of being tempted to eat a reactive food:

Dear Divine Power,
Please bring me into the light of Your love and compassion, so that I hear Your voice clearly. Please remind me at this moment of how important my soul and body are in Your eyes. Please remind me that I am a part of Your precious universe. Please bring me to that place in my soul where I know with calm clarity that this body which shelters holy spirit is entitled to food which will gloriously nourish it. Thank You for Your guidance.
A prayer that could be said at each meal might be:

Dear Divine Power,
Thank You for reminding me, by the presence of this glorious food, that I am a precious child of the Universe. Thank You for showing me that my body, as well as my mind and soul, can be nourished by You any time I am open to receiving Your gifts. Thank You.

When someone tries to persuade you that you do not need to avoid reactive foods, or that you are imagining the benefits:

Dear Divine Power:
Please remind me that You have Your own plan for this person. Bring me to the conscious awareness that You bring light to people in different ways. Please give me the

trust I need to know that You will care for this person according to the way that he or she can best understand. Thank You.

When a waiter is impatient, or fails to tell you that there is flour or sugar in your food:

Dear Divine Power:

Please give me the strength to stay serene. Please let the goodness of Your light shine through me so that this person can see the glory of Your ways. Please let me maintain my purpose, which is not to please this person, but rather to care for myself in a way which glorifies the miracle of Your creation, my body. Please remind me that I did not cause this person to be impatient. Give me something humorous to say, or at least the ability to smile. Thank You.

When a child eats something reactive and comes home sick.

Dear Divine Power:

Please ease the pain of this child. Please remind me that I do not need to chastise this child about what he/she has done. The miracle of the body which You have given this child will convey the message about toxic foods far better than my willful ego can. Please keep me in compassion and out of anger. Please take from me the tendency to heap on recriminations. Remind me that I am not the one who grants forgiveness. Give me the grace to assure the child that the pain will pass.

When a partner becomes demanding, uncooperative, or derisive. Or when the partner eats or drinks something which makes him/her critical, irritable, or unconscious.

Dear Divine Power:

Please remind me that my partner is not in my charge. Please let him/her see Your light as clearly as possible. Fill my thoughts with the power of Your love so that I may protect myself from the dark emotions that may from time to time control my partner.

Other times that you may want to ask for God's help: when you need to talk to someone and no one is available; when someone shows unwanted attention to your new, slim body, or when you inadvertently eat something reactive and you are sick or confused.

A prayer that I need daily is based on Kay Sheppard's most important guide lines for avoiding relapse:

**DEAR DIVINE POWER,**

**JUST FOR TODAY...**

PLEASE LET ME: Weigh and measure all food. Eat on time. Know what I am eating. Read the list of ingredients or question the preparer. Eat only what is on the plan. Eat a variety of foods. Eat everything that is on the list for that meal

PLEASE KEEP ME FROM: Eating something without knowing what quantity it is. Eating late so that my body is not nourished for a period of time. Eating something without knowing what is in it. Eating something that is not on the safe list. Eating the same foods every day. Skipping something from a meal so that my body is undernourished. Thank-you.

# Chapter 19
## HOLIDAYS

Our internal addictive voice will be especially plaintive over a holiday. It will say "Just this once won't matter. It's Christmas! (or New Year's, or Thanksgiving or Halloween or Valentine's Day or Easter or my birthday or whatever.) This voice is particularly accustomed to being numbed out during holidays and it will try very hard to bring you back to the days of yore.

Try to remember how chaotic your life was when you ate reactive foods: the weight gain, depression, headaches, clogged nose and throat, coughing, fatigue, self-criticism, anger, etc. When the addictive voice says, "I'm so deprived," answer it firmly and clearly. Tell it that having health, sanity, serenity, and slenderness is having great wealth. This is hardly the stuff of deprivation.

> It is highly ironic that, on the very days set aside to recognize the spiritual love, tenderness, and hope that flow through us, we would be most tempted to thwart divine intent for our well-being by eating substances that harm us. The spiritual message of the holiday is there to remind us of how precious we are and how much we deserve the very best food possible. We have only to open ourselves to that message to find the help we need to avoid reactive foods.

If you know that one bite of a reactive food could make you sick, or worse, set you up for many other bites, then call a friend or say a prayer before going to a party or sitting down for dinner. Know where your friend or a back-up will be. Best of all, go to the event with an abstinent friend for support.

Don't hesitate to TAKE YOUR OWN FOOD to holiday events! Consider taking traditional dishes that are likely to be offered with lots of reactive substances. Examples would be a cranberry dish, sweet potato casserole, pumpkin pie, buche de Noel cake, fruit pie, birthday cake, ice cream, etc. Clean recipes for all of these dishes follow. It may not be practical to take gravy, but remember that most cooks thicken it with flour. Ask the person who cooked your meal where the sugars and flours are. Be warm and grateful if they make something special for you.

> Given the high reactive content of celebration foods, it's not surprising that depression and family quarrels are common themes of the holidays.

If you are the hostess, be of good courage and assign safe recipes to guests who offer to bring something. You are perfectly within your rights to keep reactive foods out of your house. A great gift that you can give your guests is a fabulous meal clear of commonly reactive foods. Your gift to them is the vision that life without these foods is glorious. I cannot tell you how many times my dinner guests have exclaimed "I had no idea that the food in your program was this good! I could certainly eat this way!" My guests notice that my relationships with my husband and children are loving, calm, and respectful. They notice that we are all slender and healthy. They leave my house with hope for their own lives. What gooey, thick dish could possibly compete with all of that?

Here's a plug for children. Please don't think that you are being wonderful to make an exception for candy and cookies around the holidays. Remember that candy sets them up for fear, temper tantrums, headaches, stuffy noses, infections, colds, etc. It is not a gift to make a child miserable around the holidays. Your loving, calm model, unfettered by stress and irritability, is the greatest gift you can give your dependents and friends. The example of a holiday which emphasizes the spiritual meaning of the day, is an experience that will benefit your dependents for their whole lives.

The food allergists tell us not to eat any food more often than once every four days. This is especially applicable during the holidays when we are presented with foods that might be more rich or more reactive than normal. I am particularly thinking about nuts which we don't eat because of their fat content, but which tempt us during the holidays.

# Thanksgiving

*BREAKFAST*
Pumpkin Custard

—

*LUNCH*
Raw Vegetable Relish Tray

Roast Turkey

Corn Dressing (1/4 c serving)

<u>Traditional Medley</u>
(1/4 c serving of each)
Pineapple-Sweet Potato Casserole
Mashed Potatoes with Gravy
Baked Squash

Cranberry-Orange Mold*

—

*DINNER*
Repeat lunch without Cranberry Mold

—

*BEDTIME SNACK*
Baked Apples
Whipped Topping

*Omit cranberry mold if you are trying to lose weight.

This menu has variations on the traditional dishes that my family has made for my whole life. It surprises me how many are carbohydrates. Considering that turkey is a natural source of tryptophan, it's no wonder that passing out is the traditional response to this meal. The three items under "Traditional Medley", plus the corn dressing should be taken as one serving of starch. In other words, the four servings in total equal one cup.

## BREAKFAST PUMPKIN CUSTARD
(1 serving)
1 c plain fresh or canned pumpkin
2 eggs
1 c evaporated skim milk
½ c applesauce
1 T cinnamon
1/4 t cloves
1/4 t allspice
1 t vanilla flavoring (or ground vanilla bean)
liquid saccharin to taste
olive oil spray

Place all ingredients in food processor and blend well. Pour into large custard dish which has been sprayed with olive oil. Bake at 350' for 35 minutes until knife inserted into center comes out clean.

## TURKEY
Most frozen turkeys have been injected with sweetener. To avoid this, order your turkey fresh from your butcher. Since there are proteins (eggs) present in the rest of the Thanksgiving menu, you will want to take a 3 oz serving of turkey, rather than the normal 4 oz.

Prepare your turkey as you normally would, using the stuffing recipe offered below.

## CORN DRESSING
(4 servings)
1 c cubed grits cakes. See recipe below.
Spray olive oil
2 cloves garlic chopped
2 c chopped celery
2 c chopped onions
2 t poultry seasonings
Salt and pepper to taste
½ c turkey stock

Sauté vegetables and seasonings in olive oil. Toss with cubed corn cakes. Moisten with turkey stock. Pile loosely in turkey cavities. Put remainder in casserole dish and reheat for the last twenty minutes of turkey roasting time.

## CORN GRITS CAKES
(4 servings)
2 c grits or Polenta
1 c plain yogurt
4 t baking powder
1 t salt (optional)
4 eggs
Mix grits and yogurt and let sit for ½ hour. Mix in remaining ingredients. Spray skillet with olive oil. Heat skillet, drop mixture by 1/4 cupfuls. Cover skillet and fry for about 3 minutes on a side.

## PINEAPPLE-SWEET POTATO CASSEROLE
(4 servings)
2 large baked sweet potatoes (appx. 4 cups)
2 c fresh pineapple, or canned in juice and drained
1 t Maple flavoring (optional)
2 T butter (optional)

Cube sweet potatoes and pineapple and place both in food processor with (flavoring) and (butter). Blend until smooth. Garnish with bits of fresh pineapple and place under the broiler until brown. Given the amount of other starch dishes in this menu, the serving size for this dish is about 1/4 cup. If you don't want to serve four starches in one meal for fear of over-eating, serve this casserole at lunch, the mashed potatoes at dinner and skip the squash. "Tradition" should be thrown out the window in favor of controlled eating even at holidays.

## MASHED POTATOES AND GRAVY
(4 servings)
12 medium red potatoes, quartered
1/4 c hot skim milk
2 c turkey stock and pan drippings (skimmed of fat)
salt and pepper to taste
other herbs (oregano, sage, thyme, rosemary) if desired

Place potatoes in stock pot and cover with cold water. Place on high heat until water boils. Reduce heat until water simmers and cook for 25 minutes more. Drain. Place potatoes in a food processor, add hot milk, and blend until chunky. Serve immediately. For gravy, heat stock and drippings in sauce pan. Serve in gravy boat

## BAKED SQUASH
1 acorn squash per two people
Salt and pepper

Place whole squash in 350' oven for one hour. Remove, cut in half, scoop out seeds, season and serve.

## CRANBERRY-ORANGE MOLD
2 T water
1 envelope unflavored gelatin
½ c boiling water
5 oz fresh cranberries (appx 1 c)
1 whole orange including rind, cut into slices
liquid saccharin to taste
spray olive oil

Place 2 T water in food processor. Sprinkle gelatin on top and let sit a few minutes until gelatin has softened. Add ½ c boiling water and blend until frothy. Add berries and orange and process until coarsely ground. Add drops of liquid saccharin to taste. Turn mixture into a mold which has been sprayed with olive oil. Refrigerate until firm. When ready to serve, fill a large bowl with very hot water. Set the mold into the hot water up to the edge of the mold form. Hold until edge of gelatin mixture is loosened, lift out form, and cover it with a serving plate. Hold serving plate firmly against the top of the mold form and flip the mold over onto the serving plate. If necessary, shake the mold form until the gelatin mixture falls onto the plate. If the gelatin mixture does not fall, repeat the process.

## BAKED APPLE

(1 serving)

1 sliced baking apple, such as a Rome

1 T cinnamon

½ T allspice

1/4 t nutmeg or cloves

Olive oil spray

Toss all ingredients together and spoon into baking dish which has been sprayed with olive oil. Bake at 350' for 45 minutes.

## WHIPPED TOPPING

(1 serving)

1 c evaporated skim milk, thoroughly chilled or skim milk

1 T vanilla or ground vanilla bean

2 t cinnamon

Add cold milk and flavorings to food processor. Let run until milk thickens. Spoon over apple slices. This topping must be used immediately. Unlike high fat toppings, the skim milk does not have the stiff fat to keep air bubbles trapped. Thus this topping begins to fall as soon as it is made.

# Christmas Eve

*DINNER*
Roast Beef
Roast Onions
Corn Pudding
Horse radish
Spinach and Water Chestnut Salad
Walnut Oil and Balsamic Vinegar Dressing

—

*BEDTIME SNACK*
Eggnog Flan

# Christmas Day

*BREAKFAST*
Buche de Noel

—

*LUNCH*
Cucumbers Stuffed with Smoked Salmon

## ROAST BEEF AND ONIONS
1 roast beef, 2-3 oz per person (this is less than a normal protein serving because there are eggs and milk in the corn custard)
1 egg
1/4 c milk
1 large onion per person
3 T combination of dried rosemary, thyme and oregano, powdered garlic, salt and pepper
2 T oat bran

Avoid high fat beef.  Buy a bottom round or sirloin.  Ask your butcher to tie these cuts into a roast for you.  Dredge beef in a mixture of egg and milk then in a mixture of seasonings and bran.  Place on lightly greased roasting tray.  Surround the beef with peeled onions that have been cut with an X across the top. Brush the onions with olive oil.  Roast 10 minutes at 450', then reduce heat to 350' and finish roasting for a total of 12 minutes per pound of beef for rare.  Remove from oven and if necessary, replace onions until they have baked 1 hour.

## CORN PUDDING
(4 servings)
3 eggs, slightly beaten
1 c milk
salt and pepper to taste
4 c frozen corn, or 4 c cooked fresh corn cut from the cob (appx. 16 oz)
Spray olive oil

Combine all ingredients in the order shown. Pour into oiled 1 quart casserole dish. Bake 1 hour or until knife inserted into the center comes out clean.

## CHRISTMAS SALAD
(4 servings)
3 c fresh spinach
½ c canned whole water chestnuts
½ c coarsely chopped sweet red pepper
4 T walnut oil
4 T Balsamic vinegar

Wash spinach by immersing it in a sink of water, letting it stand for a few minutes and lifting it from the water. Drain water, rinse out sink, and repeat. Remove stems. Dry in a salad spinner. Drain water from canned whole water chestnuts. Slice thin. Toss with spinach and red peppers. Toss with walnut oil and Balsamic vinegar.

## EGGNOG FLAN
(4 servings)
2 c milk
2 eggs
4 pears, cored and sliced
1 t cinnamon
½ t nutmeg
Spray olive oil

Heat oven to 350'. Place all ingredients except oil in the food processor. Blend until smooth. Pour into four custard dishes which have been sprayed with olive oil. Place dishes in a pan of water, so that the water is about half-way up the side of the custard dish. Bake until set, appx. 30 minutes. The flans will be soft and a little runny because of the moisture in the fruit puree. But if you miss Eggnog, this dish will substitute nicely.

Note: This recipe takes advantage of the rule that a half serving of protein can substitute for a 'dairy'. The two cups of milk are two servings of dairy, while the two eggs are the other two for a total of four servings.

**BUCHE DE NOEL**
(2 servings)
This beautiful traditional French Christmas cake looks remarkably like a log when finished. It must have been inspired by the Yule Log. The name translates, 'Christmas Log'.
CAKE
8 eggs, separated
2 c applesauce
1 t baking powder
2 c oat bran
2/3 c dried milk
1 t vanilla
Preheat oven to 350'. Spray two jelly roll pans with olive oil, line with waxed paper, and spray heavily again. Beat egg yolks until light in color and foamy. Fold in applesauce. Mix baking power with oat bran and fold into yolks. Beat egg whites until soft peaks form and fold into yolks. Spread mixture in jelly roll pan and bake for 20 minutes. Immediately upon removing from oven invert cake onto a damp dishcloth. Carefully remove waxed paper. Some of the cake may come off with it. Gently roll cake with the dishcloth , so the dishcloth covers the outside when finished. Refrigerate until chilled, at least 1 hour. The cake may be made the day before.

FROSTING
1 c double strength coffee, or 3/4 c espresso coffee
1 ½ envelopes unflavored gelatin
2 c canned evaporated skimmed milk thoroughly chilled, or chilled skim milk
1 t maple flavoring (optional)
1 t vanilla flavoring (or ground vanilla bean )
Put 4 T water in food processor. Sprinkle gelatin over it and let stand for a few minutes until gelatin has softened. Add very hot coffee and process until gelatin has dissolved. Freeze or refrigerate until gelatin mounds slightly. Start processing gelatin mixture while slowly adding milk and flavorings. Process until stiff. If frosting is not stiff, return the mixture to the refrigerator for 15 minutes.

Promptly unroll cake and remove dish towel. Frost inside of cake. Roll and frost outside. Drag a meat fork through the frosting to simulate the bark on a tree. Garnish with holly leaves. Do *not* eat the holly leaves. Refrigerate until ready to serve. Because the frosting contains gelatin, which turns rubbery with age, the Buche frosting should be made no earlier than the day it will be eaten. A serving is one half of a cake.

**CUCUMBERS STUFFED WITH SMOKED SALMON**
(4 servings)
4 cucumbers
16 oz smoked salmon
4 T low fat yogurt

Slice cucumbers lengthwise and scrape out seeds. Blend salmon and yogurt. Spread salmon mixture into cucumbers. Slice on diagonal in 1" sections. Arrange on platter and serve. This elegant simple dish will be welcome in the calm following the frenzy of the holiday season.

# New Year's Eve

*DINNER*
Cornish Hens
Baked Wild Rice
Roasted Green Beans and Onions
Boston Lettuce
Watercress Dressing

—

*BEDTIME SNACK*
Cappuccino Mousse

# New Year's Morning

Oat Bran Pancakes
Pear Sauce
Light Sour Cream
Baked Apples
Unsweetened Chicken Sausage
Fried Potatoes

In this menu, you would eat only one half of a serving of pancakes. The other items on the menu, when eaten in half portions, will make up the balance of a complete breakfast.

## BAKED WILD RICE
(4 servings)
1 c wild rice
1 c brown rice
3 c chicken stock
1 t poultry seasoning
1 chopped clove of garlic
1 T olive oil or butter (optional)
Combine all ingredients, except brown rice in greased casserole dish. Cover tightly. Bake at 350' for 45 minutes. Add brown rice and bake 45 minutes more.

## ROASTED GREEN BEANS AND ONIONS
(4 servings)
1 large onion, sliced into rings (appx. 1 cup)
3 c fresh green beans
2 T olive oil
Salt and pepper to taste
Preheat oven to its highest temperature. Place all ingredients in a plastic bag. Toss well. Turn into a jelly roll pan. Bake until edges turn brown, 25-30 minutes.

196

## WATERCRESS DRESSING
(4 servings)
½ bunch watercress, cleaned
1/4 c olive oil
1/4 c vinegar
Salt and pepper to taste
Place all ingredients in food processor.  Blend slightly and serve.

## CAPPUCCINO MOUSSE
(4 servings)
4 T water
1 c espresso
1 ½ envelope gelatin
2 eggs, separated
2 t vanilla
2 c canned skim evaporated milk, thoroughly chilled, or skimmed milk
3 t cinnamon
4 oranges

Put 4 T of water into food processor.  Sprinkle gelatin on top and let stand for a few minutes until gelatin has softened.  Add very hot coffee and process until gelatin has dissolved.  While processing, add egg yolks.  Place food processor bowl in microwave for one minute on high. Remove, add flavorings and spices, and process again briefly.  Place coffee mixture, still in the food processor, in freezer until coffee mixture gels slightly.  When the coffee mixture has gelled slightly, return the bowl to the machine and begin processing while slowly adding milk. Continuing processing until mixture forms soft peaks.  Beat egg whites until soft peaks form. Fold egg whites into milk mixture.  Turn mixture into four large custard dishes.  Arrange orange sections around the edge of the plate and enjoy!

## OAT BRAN PANCAKES
(1 serving)
½ c oat bran
1/3 c dried milk
1 t baking powder
½ t salt (optional)
2 t vanilla (or ground vanilla bean)
½ c applesauce
2 eggs

Mix all ingredients except eggs.  Separate eggs.  Beat egg whites until soft peaks form.  Mix yolks into bran mixture.  Fold egg whites into bran mixture.  Heat frying pan until hot.  Spray with olive oil.  Drop spoonfuls of mixture into pan, reduce heat, and cover.  When tops are beginning to be solid, flip and brown.  This recipe serves one person for a complete breakfast. On a holiday occasion, I eat a half serving of this recipe and accompany it with toppings and side dishes to make a complete meal, i.e., half servings of diary (light sour cream), fruit (pureed pear), protein (sausage), and starch (sautéed potatoes).  When served with a half order of pancakes, this makes a luxurious breakfast that fits perfectly within the safe guidelines of the food plan.

**PEAR SAUCE**
   (1 serving)
   1 large ripe pear
   Core and slice pear.  Place in food processor and process until smooth.

# Valentine's Day

*DINNER*
Grilled Salmon
Polenta Hearts
Sliced Tomatoes
Sliced Cucumbers

—

*BEDTIME SNACK*
Raspberry Parfait

This pink and red meal will delight your eyes and bring pleasure to your peaceful, loving heart. The first year we had this meal, we exchanged outrageous boxer shorts. We laughed and rejoiced in the joy of celebrating the true loving message of Valentine's day.

## GRILLED SALMON
(4 servings)
1 ½ lb salmon filets, raw weight
juice of one lemon
1 t dried dill
salt and pepper to taste
spray olive oil
Heat grill. Prepare salmon by squeezing lemon juice over it. Sprinkle with dill, salt, and pepper and spray with olive oil. Place salmon in microwave until it is hot and edges have started to turn opaque. Grill salmon on a medium hot grill until it flakes.

## POLENTA
(6 servings)
5 c chicken stock
3 c grits or Polenta
Spray oil
Bring broth to a boil. Add Polenta slowly, stirring constantly. Lower heat. Stir Polenta until it is thick, scraping the bottom often. Spray oil into any kind of casserole dish or bread pan. Pack Polenta into the casserole dish, pressing down with spatula or cutting board. Note on chicken broth: Bouillon cubes generally contain caramel coloring, so choose canned chicken broth or make your own by boiling a chicken carcass.

## POLENTA HEARTS
1 recipe of Polenta
½ red pepper sliced very thin
Sprigs of dill
Instead of pressing Polenta into a loaf pan, press warm prepared Polenta into heart shaped cookie cutters. Remove cookie cutter and garnish the edges of the Polenta hearts with thin slices of sweet red pepper. Place small sprig of dill where the lobes of the heart come together at the top.

**CUCUMBER HEARTS**

  (4 servings)
  4 cucumbers (to make 4 cups)
  ½ c yogurt
  1 t dried dill

Cut a narrow, long triangle from the side of the cucumber, so that when sliced the cucumber slices will resemble hearts.  Arrange in a curve along the side of the dinner plates and drizzle with yogurt which has been mixed with the dill.

**RASPBERRY PARFAIT**

  (1 serving)
  2 T water
  1 envelope unflavored gelatin
  ½ c boiling water
  1 c frozen raspberries
  sweetener (liquid saccharin) to taste
  2 T cold water
  ½ envelope gelatin
  1 c skimmed evaporated milk, thoroughly chilled
  Sprigs of mint

Place 2 T water in food processor.  Sprinkle gelatin on top.  Let soften for a few minutes.  Add ½c boiling water and blend until frothy.  Add berries and  process until smooth.  Add drops of liquid saccharin to taste.  Turn raspberry mixture into a bowl and rinse out food processor.  Sprinkle gelatin over the water and let stand for about two minutes or until gelatin has softened.  Add ½ c boiling water.  Run the food processor while adding cold milk and let run until milk thickens.  Drop raspberries and whipped milk into a parfait glass in alternating layers.  Eat promptly.

# Easter

*BREAKFAST*
Bunny Cake

—

*LUNCH*
Marinated Butterflied Leg of Lamb
Grilled Eggplant
Stuffed Herbed Potatoes
Field Greens Salad with Feta Cheese Dressing

Hide hollow plastic eggs filled with small treasures such as coins, toiletries, miniature soaps, candles, and jewelry. Including scrolls of paper with prayers, poems, and loving messages also helps deliver the day's message of hope.

**BUNNY CAKE**
(4 servings)
2 c oat bran
2/3 c dried milk
3 t baking powder
1 t salt (optional)
4 t vanilla (or ground vanilla bean)
4 c applesauce
8 eggs
Mix all ingredients. Pour mixture into two 8" round cake pans. Bake at 350' for 25 minutes.

**FROSTING**
4 T water
1 envelopes unflavored gelatin
½ c boiling water
2 c canned evaporated skimmed milk, thoroughly chilled or skim milk
1 t maple flavoring (optional)
1 t vanilla flavoring (or ground vanilla bean )
Put 4 T water in a food processor. Sprinkle gelatin over it and let stand a few minutes until gelatin has softened. Add boiling water and process again until gelatin has dissolved. Process gelatin mixture while slowly adding milk and flavorings. Process until stiff. If mixture is not stiff, refrigerate fifteen minutes. Because the frosting contains gelatin, which turns rubbery with age, the frosting should be made no earlier than the day it will be eaten.

Slice one layer of the cake in half to make two semi-circles. Frost one half and place the other half on top. Stand these two layers on the narrow, straight edge to form the body of the rabbit. Cut the second layer as if you were cutting out a large triangle from inside the circular layer. Use two of the remaining crescent-shaped pieces for ears. Cut a small circle out of the triangular piece for the tail. Frost with remaining frosting. Use coffee beans for eyes and nose (but don't eat them). Be sure to eat the remaining scraps of cake so that no nutrition is missed.

201

## MARINATED BUTTERFLIED LEG OF LAMB

1 butterflied leg of lamb (1 ½ lb. raw weight for 4 servings)
½ c red wine vinegar
8 cloves garlic chopped or 1 T garlic powder
1/4 c fresh oregano
1/4 c olive oil
Salt and pepper to taste

Place all ingredients in a plastic bag. Toss well and refrigerate at least several hours. Toss periodically. When ready to grill, microwave until edges are opaque. Then run skewers through thin edges. Bunch these edges along the skewer so that they are as thick as the thickest parts of the meat. Grill over moderate heat about 15-20 minutes to a side.

## GRILLED EGGPLANT

(4 servings)
1 large eggplant, cubed to make 4 cups
1/4 c olive oil
1 chopped clove of garlic
Salt and pepper to taste

Toss all ingredients in a microwave-proof bowl. Microwave until eggplant is steaming. Place eggplant into wire grill basket and grill until slightly brown on each side. For a more festive presentation, substitute 1 c green peppers and 1 c onions cut into big chunks for 2 c of the eggplant.

## STUFFED HERBED POTATOES

4 small baking potatoes or 2 large, weighing a total of 2 lbs.
1/4 c hot milk
1 t each of rosemary, thyme, and oregano
Salt and pepper to taste

Bake potatoes one hour in a 400' oven. Slice potatoes in half lengthwise. Scrape potato from skin and blend in food processor with butter. Restuff potato skins and return to the broiler until brown. Note: Using a pastry bag with a large serrated tip will make restuffing the potatoes easy and festive.

# Fourth of July

*DINNER*
Grilled Scallops
Brown Rice with Dill
Grilled Vegetable Medley
Cucumber Slices with Yogurt and Dill

—

*BEDTIME SNACK*
Strawberries and Blueberries on
Frozen Vanilla Yogurt

## GRILLED SCALLOPS
(4 servings)
1 ½ lbs. scallops, raw weight
juice of 1 lime
salt to taste
½ c cilantro
Toss scallops with lime juice and salt. Refrigerate overnight. Microwave until just steaming. Turn into a grill basket and grill over medium heat until firm.

## GRILLED VEGETABLE MEDLEY
(4 servings)
4 c of any mixture of the following, cut into large chunks: green pepper, carrots (sliced, not chunks), onions, zucchini, yellow squash
4 T Balsamic vinegar
4 T best olive oil
½ t rosemary
½ t thyme
½ t oregano
salt and pepper to taste
Toss vegetables with vinegar, oil and seasonings. Refrigerate overnight. Microwave until steaming. Turn into a grill basket and grill over moderate heat until cooked through.

## FROZEN YOGURT
(4 servings)
4 c yogurt
4 t vanilla flavoring or ground vanilla bean
4 t cinnamon
Mix ingredients together and turn into an ice cream maker. Process until frozen.

The powerful impacts of foods on our bodies, on our mental and emotional states, and on our behavior is something which most people do not understand. If someone had simply listed what changes would occur in me once I took refined carbohydrates out of my diet, I would not have believed. The best way I know to communicate the significance of the changes is to recount real life stories.

The people on these pages have had a miraculous change in their lives because they eliminated sugars, flours, and other reactive foods from their diets. Men and women, aged 12 to 64, of European and African extraction, have solved weight problems that have plagued them for their whole lives. They have solved physical problems in areas ranging from respiratory membranes to joints to skin. Their moods have improved from depression, anxiety, and rage to daily serenity.

## JOAN

My own story begins at the end of 1995 when I was getting ready for Christmas vacation. I was overweight by 30 pounds. I was depressed, anxious, afraid or angry most of the time. Physically, I was at the end of a year in which my respiratory allergies had made me miserable. I had suffered four sinus infections and countless episodes of sinus attacks similar to migraines. I was tired in spite of getting all the sleep I needed. My asthma had improved as the result of intensive emotional recovery work, but I was discouraged about ever healing my lungs. For the two previous years, I had worked a number of personal growth programs simultaneously to heal the wounds of my childhood so that I could get my emotional and respiratory problems under control. I had experienced improvement, but I was far from satisfied with the results.

I read about an eating disorders program that I decided to try. This program eliminates sugars, flours, and wheat in order to control brain chemical reactions that stimulate appetite. I was extremely pleased to lose my hunger pangs along with two pounds per week on this program. But I was positively stunned to also lose my allergies, sinus pain, fatigue, mental fogginess, depression, and rage. I removed all the sugars, flours, and wheat from my house. My family lost weight and a wondrous calm descended over my household. The crying and fighting over homework quieted down. My husband became less irritable. We left for outings calmly, well-organized, and without chaos. The sound of morning coughing disappeared. The children's daily afternoon headaches eased off. It was a miracle. With stability established in my body rhythms, I eventually was able to discern that citric acid and tomato sauce were contributing to my asthma.

I began to spread the word about reactive foods. I developed summary sheets of what to eat instead of foods containing reactive substances. Eventually I started teaching a system of eating that eliminated sugars and flours and allowed identification of other commonly reactive foods. I developed a network of abstinent people to track their progress, to offer them support, and to get support.

Today, I feel like I have walked away from a train wreck. I am shaken by my narrow escape, but I am otherwise unscathed. I turn around to go back and help people who are still on that train. Every time I talk someone into giving up reactive foods, I feel like I have pulled them from that train wreck. Through the grace of God, they also can walk away.

# CANDICE

I am a 12-year-old girl. I stand 5'3" and weigh 104 pounds. Last January, nine months ago, my mom took sugars, flours, and wheat out of my family's diet. A lot has changed since then, things like, I lost weight, my headaches stopped, my nose is clear, I don't wheeze, and I'm not so sad. Also, my mom is nicer and she's around more.

I can't get all sugars and flours out of my diet. Like today, I ate cake at a birthday party. About 80% of the time, I eat the cake and pizza at parties so I won't go hungry. I'm getting better about having my mom get me something special that I can take with me to parties. If a friend's family is having something I can't eat, I eat the side dish. But this morning, I spent the night at a friend's house. All they had for breakfast was bagels. So I had one. Next time, I will bring oatmeal with me.

Now, my reaction to an allergic food usually starts the same day I eat it. A hammer starts pounding in my head and a faucet starts running out of my nose. Seven or eight hours later, it gets really bad. It takes several days after that for the effects to go away.

It would be impossible for me to eat this way if my family didn't. I couldn't watch my parents eat something different. Anyone who wants to stop eating reactive foods should get them out of the house. Parents would make a mistake by yelling or forcing their kids. They should just make sure that the stuff is not available. They shouldn't force their kids. This worked in my family and I think it's a good way to help kids. I'm glad we're off reactive foods. Although there are hassles, I like feeling and looking good.

# LINDA

I became aware that I had a weight problem at age 8. By age 13, I had taken my first diet pill. Over the next 35 years, that pill was followed by other drugs, diet candy, canned diet drinks, a liquid protein diet, an expensive avoidance clinic, starvation, overdosing coffee, and finally, Overeaters Anonymous (OA). I wish I had known that my weight problem was simply a reaction to sugars, flours, and wheat.

The refined carbohydrates caused swings in my brain chemistry which drove my appetite completely beyond human control. These substances caused horrifying changes in my moods and perceptions. I was miserable, isolated, angry, and disgusted with myself. No matter what I weighed, my self-esteem was gone.

When I first married, I made and ate one layer of cake every day. I remember with agony the intense feeling of isolation as I ate those cakes. I might as well have been shooting up drugs. I had a husband, a baby, a house, and two cars, but I was not happy. I was depressed and confused. I abused my child because her crying made me so irritable. I really didn't know what to do for myself, much less for her. My moods and foods were out of control.

This low self-esteem led me to other substance abuse. I used marijuana and alcohol to numb my feelings of despair. Over-the-counter decongestants made me float.

However, I had to "hit bottom" before I was willing to accept help. "Bottom" came one day when I was stuffing a bag of cookies into my mouth as fast as I could. I was conscious that I didn't want to be eating the cookies. I was painfully aware that some force, other than myself, had complete control over my actions. The terror and dark despair that I experienced led me to call a friend who had joined a recovery program that eliminated sugars, flours, and wheat. I was saved.

206

I gave up a heavy caffeine habit at the same time that I started avoiding reactive foods. Withdrawal from these substances took 14 days. I was extremely disoriented, insecure, fatigued, and confused for those 14 days. I never want to go through that again.

I would love to take up another addiction, but recovery is the only good substitute for addictions. I have spent my whole life asking myself, "Where am I going?" Today, I feel like I am here. Thank God.

## CLEMENT

I am a 13-year-old girl. I stand 5'7" and weigh 125 pounds, but 3 months ago, I weighed 145. Now that I'm not eating reactive foods, I have a lot more energy. I have fewer headaches. My asthma has improved a little bit.

When my family started this way of eating, a few things made me happy. We started eating red meat and eggs again. I realized that I could still eat potato chips. It was nice when my mom took me to the grocery with her and I could buy lox and raspberries.

My friends say they can't believe that I have so much self-control. It's not really that I have such great self-control, I just know that if I eat sugars, flours, or wheat, I will get sick. At school, when I eat little of something "illegal", I get a headache or hyperactive. I'm in a cloud. At camp last summer, I ate candy. I felt drowsy. I was much more moody. I got cranky. I gained weight, even though I was doing tons of activities.

After the first week, if I ate something reactive, I only got a little sick. But after a month, if I ate something, I got really sick. After about two or three weeks, eating reactive foods got much less tempting. But if my family were not eating this way, I wouldn't be able to either.

I thought it was cool that my mom didn't force me to stay off reactive foods for my birthday. If a friend asked me about eliminating reactive foods, I would tell her to throw away all the sugars, flours, and wheat in her house. I would tell her to learn to read labels. I would especially tell her not to give up on it in a week or two. It's worth it.

## LYNNE

I am 35 years old. I am the single mother of 3 boys and a full-time professor. I have anorexia. I have been fearful, depressed, co-dependent, and I have had a shopping addiction. I have contemplated suicide. Reactive foods played a role in my problems and their solution.

Nine months ago, I had a very traumatic break-up of a 3-year relationship. The break-up challenged every coping mechanism I had. Because I was so depressed about the loss, I started CoDependents Anonymous (CoDA), a 12-step program aimed at managing relationships. I was feeling good progress toward new behavior, but I also felt that there was a visceral, almost tangible barrier standing between me and the issues that I needed to deal with.

I had been in CoDA for probably four months when I heard that reactive foods might contribute to depression. I decided to try eliminating them. Looking back on it, the benefits really started within a few days, but I wasn't paying attention because I thought it would take a few weeks.

I was talking to a friend on the phone when it hit me like a ton of bricks. I was suddenly aware that for the last week, I had not fallen into the abyss of despair. Right before I eliminated reactive foods, I was suicidal. I was in the kitchen looking through the cabinets for enough pills to take to die. I took out a knife and I actually held it to the skin on my abdomen to see what it would feel like. There was no reason to go on living. I was filled with the most despairing, hopeless feeling. It was as complete a hopelessness as a human could experience. This despair disappeared when I eliminated sugars, flours, and wheat.

Today, it's hard to believe that it was all body chemistry. It felt like life. It can create a completely believable reality. The feeling is seductive, convincing. The terrible thing is that I am being taught to listen to my feelings. But now I know that it is very dangerous to listen to feelings that are induced by food. It is as if I had a translator inside of me that took life's events and translated them into despair. Without knowing it, I was allowing the food to mediate between my head and my heart. Now I know why I could think the thoughts that I learned in CoDA, but I couldn't feel them. The food acted like a saboteur between my head and my heart. It was sending out untruths.

I am trying to think of the right way that the refined carbohydrates and wheat acted. It is as if they had a persona of their own. Not exactly like a poltergeist, but like a prankster playing jokes with my perceptions. Like a magician who creates illusion. Today that prankster/magician is no longer in control.

I still have the same amount of sorrow over my ended relationship. I still think about the losses in my life. I hurt just as much. The difference is that it's my real life hurt that I'm feeling, not the despair brought on by the food. I have my feelings without the anxiety and despair. I have my sorrow, but it's not connected to an annihilated landscape. Three weeks ago, I felt so empty. I felt empty inside and out. There was absolutely nothing there. Desolation. Now, I exist and the world exists. When I feel the sorrow, it's in there, inside of me. But there are other things in there too.

I also feel more honest. I think I was feeling dishonest before because I was filled with shame and fear. I felt like there must be something I needed to cover up. Being free of the sugars, flours, and wheat made me more honest with myself. This is very important, because now I can be that way with other people since that is the feeling that I carry within myself.

I will give you a dramatic example of how my new honesty works. I teach an adult class in educational cultural diversity. I gave my class an assignment before I changed my diet. I told them to pick out a school, interview the staff, and make an assessment as to how well the school is handling their cultural diversity. I told the students to be very careful as to how much they told the staff about the real nature of the assignment. I was very afraid that if the staffs knew that we were evaluating them, they might be angry and refuse to cooperate, or even threaten my students.

After the diet change, I was listening to one of my students tell me about her interview with a school principal. My student said she had trouble questioning the principal and listening to the answers because she was so aware of what she was holding back. So I told her to be completely open, direct, and honest, but tactful. I advocated telling the staff ahead of time what we were doing and offer to share the results with them.

It didn't dawn on my for several days that the second round of instructions was directly opposed to the first round. I realized with a shock that during the first round of instructions, I was still under the influence of the sugars, flours, and wheat. They created fear in me. The second round was free of the food influence. I had my honesty and integrity to guide me. Thank God.

Another very wonderful and unexpected virtue of this change in diet is that I got a real appetite. I am a recovering anorectic. I can't remember the last time that I got hungry. I think that eliminating reactive foods has leveled out my serotonin because the other day, I was driving along and I had the thought that I was hungry. And I was! I hadn't eaten on time and I really needed to eat! I pulled into a grocery store and got a salad. It was awesome! I have my body back. I feel like I exist in my body.

The last story I have to tell you is about another problem that I am recovering from. I have a shopping addiction. I have it pretty seriously. Last Sunday, I left my sons in front of the television. I got in the car and drove down the highway to the department store for an afternoon of shopping. As I got near, I had the thought that I was driving into darkness. In one sense, I literally was. It was an absolutely beautiful fall afternoon and the store would be dark by comparison. But I was also driving into another kind of darkness, a kind of numbing. A place to go to obliterate problems. Problems that I now know were created and made unmanageable by chemical reactions to foods.

Well, I turned that car around. I went back home, picked up my sons and our dog, and went to the outdoor blessing of the animals at my church. I did something with my sons instead of going shopping.

I have a whole new definition of life. Life is not worrying. The life I used to have didn't feel like life. I did things like shopping to make myself feel as if I were experiencing life. The day that I took my kids and our dog to church, I got to be IN the day. I experienced life as life. Not as an addiction or as despair. I have gotten back my mind, heart, body, and soul. Thank God.

## DEBORAH

I would say that eliminating sugars, flours, and wheat has impacted my life most profoundly in the areas of weight loss, spirituality, and mental clarity.

I eliminated sugars, flours, and wheat from my diet eighteen months ago. For years before, I thought I ate to numb my feelings about having been sexually molested as a teen-ager by my uncle. Now I know differently. In middle age, I participated in an expensive hospital program needing to lose 100 pounds. I lost 95 and regained 60 within two years, in spite of joining Overeaters Anonymous (OA) in that time period. Now I know why these programs didn't work for me. Eighteen months ago, I learned that sugars, flours, and wheat might be causing my problem. I joined a 12-step group specifically aimed at staying abstinent from those substances. I have lost a total of 75 pounds since I stopped eating refined carbohydrates and wheat.

OA could never have stemmed the tide of my weight gain because it did not eliminate the substances which were driving my inappropriate appetite, cravings, and obsessing. But OA was wonderful for opening me up to the love of God. Through working the 12 steps, I came to believe that God's love was available to me. For my whole life, I thought that God didn't love me because He let my uncle molest me.

I made my connection to God clean and strong when I eliminated the reactive foods. I felt so much better about myself without the chemicals from the foods in my body and mind, that I was able to believe that God really loves me. I became confident enough to ask Him for the things I need. I gained the grace to forgive my uncle. I see that my life is full of God's good works.

The big surprise of eliminating sugars, flours, and wheat came in the area of mental clarity. I always thought I was dumb. I had a lot of problems in school. In multiple choice tests, I often thought there were two right answers. It was confusing and demoralizing. I now know that I suffered from confusion caused by fluctuating brain chemicals. I also suffered badly from test anxiety. Today, when I take a licensing exam, my internal voice tells me that I know the material and the questions are clear. I perform very well.

I am so grateful to know what was wrong with me and to have a 12-step group to help me recover from sugars, flours, and wheat. God has shown me His love by bringing me to this knowledge and this circle of support.

# NANCY

I am 47 years old and I'm not sure what I weigh because I want to emphasize that my weight loss in only one of many changes that eliminating sugars, flours, and other reactive foods has made in my life. The change in diet has been the cornerstone to an on-going revision of my life. Do you know that expression, "Put a spanner in the works"? It means if you want to disable a piece of machinery quickly and effectively, you throw a wrench into it at a vulnerable spot. The elimination of reactive foods is like the wrench and my life is like the machinery. The change in diet enabled me to stop doing lots of unsatisfactory stuff and start having life on my terms. This is particularly true of my body, relationships, and business.

I am so pleased with my body. I have lost a lot of weight. But my goal is not to be any particular weight, but rather to have well developed, readily available, physical powers. I want to feel strong and flexible. Eliminating refined carbohydrates and wheat is a way to become more aware of the body, more sensitive to it. What my body looks like is important, but looks are irrelevant compared to feeling. My whole life happens inside my body. Physical well being is the absolute root to everything else.

This concept shows up in my renewed attractiveness. A lot of middle-aged women feel invisible, but I feel conspicuous. It's a combination of blessing and curse. I'm a little uncomfortable as the center of attention, but I also sense the power that this gives me. I not only have the wisdom and experience which comes with middle age, but I also have the energy, suppleness, and freshness which are associated with youth. I have no trouble attracting partners. Health has been the prime criteria for selecting a mate from the beginning of evolution. The primal instinct is to find a mate who will perpetrate the gene pool. Guys have started to tell me all the time how pretty I am, but I think they are really attracted to my health.

My superb health showed up recently in my recovery from a broken ankle. It was a clean break that didn't have to be set. In six weeks it was completely grown over. I needed no physical therapy. I had resumed full normal activity within two weeks after removing the cast. The speed of the whole recovery was incredible.

I used to have red bumps below and outside of my left eye. My doctor said that the only cure was a massive, long-term course of antibiotics. Well, I didn't want to take that much antibiotics. And now, after a few months of abstinence, they're disappearing.

I have tons of work. My business is hot. This month I'm going to bill the equivalent of my best month ever out of the last nine years. I find that anytime I eat a reactive food, my ability to put out work diminishes. I got carried away at a party recently and had bread and wine. The consequence was that the next day, I couldn't do anything. I felt lethargic, sleepy and fatigued. I was still in bed at noon. Needless to say, I was worthless to my clients and generated no billable time that day.

I must also mention how much reduced my fear and anxiety are. I used to wake up at 3 o'clock in the morning, usually worrying about money. NO MORE! This change came really quickly, maybe on the fifth day after I starting avoiding reactive foods.

This simple way of eating would really appeal to a man. It only takes me twenty minutes to shop for the week. Preparing and eating a meal might take me thirty minutes. Eliminating sugars, flours, and wheat has got to be the easiest, cheapest approach to solving physical, mental, and emotional problems. Why wouldn't anyone try it?

# BARBARA

I stand 5'9" and I weigh 139 pounds. I definitely don't have a weight problem. I was moved to look at reactive foods because my 2-year-old daughter has big problems with sinus infections and asthma. The change in diet has helped her tremendously. However, I would keep my family off of these substances even if my daughter's asthma and infections had not improved, because the change in our behavior and emotions has been so dramatic. I now see how sugars, flours, and wheat were sabotaging our lives.

My two-year old daughter has responded to the elimination of these foods in several ways. Her infection is clearing up. She is actually relieved by the breathing treatments. Before the change in food, she had to have steroids in order for the treatments to be effective. However, more importantly, her behavior and that of my four-year-old have changed dramatically. My four-year-old is much happier. She has more energy. She's not mopey. Her head is not droopy. She has become more health conscious.

Perhaps I can best illustrate the meaning of the change by relating what happened when we ate some toaster waffles, half a piece of bread, and a few cookies yesterday. Those foods were enough to send me into raging. The kids were crying and having tantrums like they haven't had since we changed our food. It was beyond chaotic. It was nightmarish. Never again will I allow that to happen. So today, we're having a food hang-over. I am bitchy, and I have a headache.

I really love exercise, yoga, mediation, and teaching. They are the foundation of the well-being of my head, heart, body, and soul. The foods are like dark forces that would keep me from attaining my full potential in these areas. I look forward to running. But after ingesting a reactive food, I don't want to go. The sugars, flours, and wheat are absolutely toxic for getting into the proper meditative mood to do yoga. These foods numb the place where my spirit comes from. They absolutely crush my joy.

I have developed my meditation techniques to the point that I feel the oneness with the universe. But when I have had a particularly powerful meditation session, my internal critic comes on in my head and says, "Who are you to be wise and connected to the Divine?" That's when I am drawn to junk food. When I eat it, I feel crummy and that matches my inner critic that says I *should* feel crummy. It's consistent with my low self- esteem. It keeps me from being powerful.

These sugars, flours, and wheat also sabotage my family relationships. My life is absolutely perfect. I have a wonderful husband, a nice house and car, and two beautiful little girls. But when I ingest sugars, flours, and wheat, I have absolutely no patience for anyone. Two beers is enough to send me into raging and depression. I am not present after eating reactive foods. For example, I might be sitting here at the dining room table coloring pictures with my little girl. When I've been eating well, I can pay attention to her. But when I have ingested sugars, flours, and wheat, I am always worrying about something weird. I am here physically, but absent mentally and emotionally.

When I was in college, I had bulimia. I thought my feelings about food were the result of being emotionally messed up. Now I know that it's the other way around. I was messed up emotionally because of the foods I ate. In my junior year, I was in fabulous shape. I trained and trained for varsity volleyball, but my coach still rode me about my weight. I turned to bulimia for a solution. The first time I had a bulimia episode, I thought it was crazy. But I continued. I continued until I had beat the s--- out of myself. In the middle of my junior year, I quit the team and I quit school.

The underlying theme of this experience reflects society's expectation that we have to "do it all". I have so many regrets about my college years. I was really smart and I wanted to be a

211

doctor. But I got on a self-hatred cycle. I was so vulnerable to the society view that it was OK for me to dislike myself because I couldn't do and be everything that people wanted me to be. Now I think that this self-loathing was the result of abusing my body, not only with bulimia, but with sugars and flours too.

After college, I had a disease in which my thyroid was chronically inflamed and I had to have it removed. It's hard to regulate the amount of thyroid medicine that I need. I know that I must live within a narrow range of body chemistry reactions because my body is no longer capable of processing the swings. I am grateful to know that eliminating sugars, flours, and wheat helps keep my biochemical cycles within a comfortable range.

It's nice to know that our saboteur is just a few foods. It's nice to have a concept of what to do about my family's physical health and our moods. It's nice to know that I'm not crazy.

## JAY AND VERA

We're in our late 50's. We were both attracted to the idea of eliminating sugars, flours, and wheat as a way to lose weight. We also wanted to improve our general health and to create a healthy platform to stand on through the end of our lives. Vera in particular has been suffering from severe headaches which have kept her in bed for as long as four days.

We have been delighted with the loss of hunger, cravings, and obsessing as well as the weight and the headaches. We just don't think about snacking - even when we're watching TV, our former binge set-up. Neither of us have suggested jumping in the car to go get pizza or bar-b-que, another favorite binge activity. It is amazing to us that our desire for foods containing sugars, flours, and wheat should disappear so easily.

We've both experienced an increase in energy and a surprising willingness to exercise along with it. Vera's sinus problems have largely disappeared. This is after 40 years of being treated for non-stop sinus infections. Neither of us wake up with nose, throat, and lungs full of phlegm. We can eat dairy products which used to cause congestion. No one could have made us believe this would happen. We had to experience it for ourselves.

We are so grateful that we are eliminating these foods as a couple. For example, we're going on a cruise next month. We have already discussed which buffets we will avoid, which dining rooms we will use and what kind of foods we will eat at each meal. Unlike preparations for other cruises, we've made these plans calmly, without anxiety or fear. The support we give each other has reinforced the strength of our relationship.

Our sex life has always been good. With the weight loss and the general peace that the elimination of sugars, flours, and wheat has given us, our sex has gotten to be quite frisky. We admire the emerging physique in each other.

We see attitude changes in one another. Jay is much more confident. He has momentum and motivation which weren't there while he was eating refined carbohydrates and wheat. Vera has become less fearful, more forthright in her dealings with people. She used to be so afraid of hurting someone's feelings that it was hard for her to make herself understood.

We both went through adulthood with weight problems, sinus problems, and emotional discomfort. We tried every diet that came on the market for the last forty years. We have lost weight and then gained back every pound of it. Abstinence from refined carbohydrates and wheat is the only routine that has a built-in desire to stay with it. The side benefits in terms of relief from other physical problems and from depression and anger that derive from this abstinence are so extensive that we would eat this way even if we weren't losing weight. We will be on this plan happily for the rest of our lives.

# THEA

For me, sugars, flours, and wheat create the sensation of being empty inside. This has been true for me for my whole life. I have been trying to fill my empty hole for 45 years. I have tried to fill it with food, alcohol, drugs, nicotine, and relationships. Today, I know I would never have filled it. I know that the hole was a chemically induced by refined carbohydrates and wheat. It was an illusion. I could never have filled the hole anymore than someone could kill a ghost.

My struggle started with birth. I was born fat and fussy and then was fed a corn syrup formula. My mother was repulsed by my fat. She didn't cook, so we mostly ate *hors d'oeuvre*. I could handle a toothpick long before I learned to handle a fork and knife. I was doing the grocery shopping by age 7 and secretly buying candy bars. I picked them out with rising excitement, ate them alone, and basked in the peace that followed. I weighed 140 pounds by fourth grade. I hadn't any idea what a normal diet looked like.

School was a source of tremendous misery. I couldn't read and comprehend, much less retain. I became very fearful when I had to read something. I could read a paragraph 20 times without any idea of what it meant. Today, I know that the fear and confusion around reading was caused by the refined carbohydrates and wheat. The reaction of my brain chemicals to these substances drove both confusion and appetite. I understand now why the words "fat and dumb" appear together so often. Both conditions derive from maladaptive reactions to refined carbohydrates and wheat. It's a tragedy that no one knew then.

By age 13, I was trying to fill my internal emptiness with boys and alcohol as well as food. This set up a pattern that would endure through my early adulthood. Boarding school was time to go absolutely wild. I landed in the hospital twice with alcohol poisoning. Three schools expelled me. I never made it through college.

In school, I took diet pills and then ate to calm the jitters that the pills brought on. My weight was a constant struggle. I tried to control it with fasting and shots. As an adult, I drove one hour to get those shots, sometimes as often as once a day. I eventually got my husband to give them to me. I decided liposuction would take care of my weight problem. Fortunately, I saw a film about liposuction and was absolutely repulsed.

During my adult years, my weight swung between 145 and 185 pounds. It would cycle about every two years. I was completely obsessed with food - getting it, preparing it, eating it, and sleeping it off. I had no idea what was appropriate. I just ate until I passed out.

I stopped eating sugar a year before I learned about the flour and wheat. Sugar caused fatigue, so I thought, but eliminating only sugar didn't change much. The only benefit was that some bumps disappeared from my face. I ate much more bread when I stopped the sugar. I suspect that the increased flour from the bread canceled out any benefit from reducing sugar.

When I heard about abstaining from sugars, flours, and wheat, a clear voice in my head said, "This is it." Hearing the word "addict" also made an immediate impact on me. I stayed home for the first few days of withdrawal. I slept mostly. I wondered why I wasn't looking for food all the time as I had for every day of my life prior to these. The hole was gone. I sensed the presence of my stomach in its proper place. My body felt solid, instead of like an empty cavity.

The emotional benefits of eliminating these reactive foods center around being out of fear and into self-confidence. I no longer search for reasons why I feel so angry. I don't blame others for my bad feelings. I don't feel the drive to control others. I don't expect others to fix me. I have taken responsibility for my own behavior. I have the mental clarity to see that other people are not the source of fulfilling my needs. They do not hold me back, nor do they give me the power to move forward. These attributes come from within me. I have also lost my fear of reading. I can retain what I read.

I have done a substantial amount of personal growth work to heal the wounds from my past. In many of these sessions I have drawn pictures of myself, always as a big empty heart with a little head on top of it and little bird feet underneath. Then I drew a sign next to it which said, "Please fill". Now I know that the empty heart feeling was chemically induced by sugars, flours, and wheat. When I got rid of these substances, the empty feeling went away.

It's taken me a while to trust the daily serenity and this feeling of being solid. I have lost 33 pounds in 4 months. I am still in awe over how simple it was. I keep cookies in the house for my husband and I have no desire for them whatsoever. I have gotten off the food roller coaster and I am not tempted to get on it again. Thanks be to God.

## TED

I am 44 years old, 6'1" tall, 183 pounds, and generally healthy. I am co-owner of a firm in a high stress, financial service business. I live with my wife of 18 years and two teen-aged daughters. I have enjoyed good health all of my life, other than lots of cavities in my teeth, lower back pain, and persistent canker sores.

I exercise regularly, running 3 times per week and playing tennis once per week. I drink alcohol and coffee moderately. Since a short period when my cholesterol went over 200, I have been careful about what I eat, especially by reducing my intake of high fat foods. I abandoned virtually all consumption of eggs, rarely ate red meat, and chose non-fat frozen yogurt over ice cream. After receiving a cholesterol count of 240, I took niacin until the cholesterol reading came down to 209.

I have never had a serious weight problem. I did gain about 20 pounds since graduating from college at about 178 pounds. During the time that I was trying to reduce my cholesterol, I was also trying to lose weight. I lost about 10 pounds, but I later gained it back.

I eliminated sugars, flours, and wheat about 10 months ago. In the beginning, I tried it because my wife was doing it. Although it required some planning and accommodation, I was surprised at how manageable it was.

Within three months of going on it, my weight had dropped from 197 to 183, where it has stabilized for the last several months. I have not tried to limit the amount of food that I eat. In fact, the portions are larger than I'm used to.

Beside my weight loss, the other big changes I've noticed are an increase in my energy level and a decrease in my hunger. It's a great relief not to have the late morning and mid-afternoon slumps that used to be part of my daily life. I find that when I do get hungry, it's because it's time to eat: in other words, hunger pangs between meals are pretty much gone.

I have never had allergies or asthma, but I do notice that I don't get nasal congestion nearly as much now. When I do, it's usually just after ingesting a reactive food. I haven't had a cold in the ten months. I usually get them every 3-4 months, so normally I would have had 2 or 3 in this time period.

A minor but very annoying malady for me has been persistent canker sores in my mouth. I've had these constantly since I was a young child. In the last nine months, I have had only one small sore which cleared up in a matter of days, as opposed to a norm of several weeks.

Another curious development is that my gums no longer bleed. They used to bleed so badly that my hygienist had a note about it on my chart. On my last visit, she expressed surprise that they weren't bleeding even before I told her about my change in diet.

The longer I am abstinent, the more I notice the effects of food on my body. For example, whenever I have more than a few beers, I can feel the effects in my body the next day in the form of a hang-over or day-after impact. There's usually a tightness in my head and a gluggy feeling. I feel slow. Before my system cleared up, it took much more alcohol to produce the same effect.

I judge that I experience less anxiety, less tension at work. I am also less angry at home. It's very clear to me that the general atmosphere at home is much improved. Although my two daughters still have some fights, their conflicts seem less frequent and less intense. All four of us just seem happier and more at peace more of the time. Since both my wife and I eliminated sugars, flours, and wheat, we have had fewer radical mood swings and fewer times of despair.

Since all of my family eats the same diet, staying with it while at home is relatively easy. I need to be more careful about my choices at lunch during the week. There are several meals which I typically choose from, including red beans with rice and sausage and a salad; a potato with chili; or Japanese stir-fried dishes. For more up-scale dining, I just avoid breads and pastas. Most of the other foods seem OK. I am not strict about making sure that sauces are void of all sugars and flours. But for me, these seem to have little or no impact.

One change that I did not expect was in my cholesterol level. Since the food I eat now includes many more eggs, more meat, and a somewhat higher level of fats, I thought my cholesterol might rise substantially. But recently, I received a combined reading of 165 which is the lowest I have ever had and 44 points below my last test. I also had a very healthy level of the "good" cholesterol.

The bottom line is that I am healthier, I look better, and I feel better. As an added bonus, all of the same things are true for my wife and two daughters. I am extremely skeptical by nature. My advice to all of the other skeptics out there is simple: TRY IT!

## NORA

I think I've lost and gained about 1,000 pounds over my life time. My food reactions have kept me locked in a prison of shame and depression since I was a small child. I was 64 years old when God sent me the task of founding a support group aimed at helping people eliminate sugars, flours, and wheat from their diets. This mission has freed me from fat, shame, depression, and pain. Let me tell you about it.

I had a huge appetite from my earliest memory. I was fat and my mother was ashamed of me. I tried my first diet in high school. I starved myself and lost 40 pounds. However, in nursing school, I had a nervous breakdown and attempted suicide. I gained 55 pounds during recovery. I left school, moved across the country, married, divorced quickly, moved back to the east coast, gave birth to my first child, married again, bore five more children, moved to the southwest, and gained a net of 55 more pounds. I weighed 250 pounds. I watched what I ate and lost 100 pounds. It came back within a year. I lost 42 pounds on liquid protein and 67 pounds in Overeaters Anonymous and then gained it back. I started going to Co-Dependents Anonymous, thinking that if I could solve my relationship problems, my weight problem would go away. Of course it didn't. I weighed 296 pounds and became suicidal.

Today, I know the thoughts of suicide were partially because I looked so bad, but they were also because the sugars, flours, and wheat create a brain chemistry which depresses me. Shame, despair, depression, low self-esteem, and humiliation were my constant tormentors. I would have to shop on the largest rack in the store, the size XXX. I hid behind these racks so that no one would see me and know how fat I was. I imagined that they wouldn't notice how big I was unless they saw where I was shopping. During this time, my husband and I took a vacation together. Sitting at a restaurant table, I saw a truly obese woman enter. I said to my husband, "Have you ever seen anyone so fat?" He said, "Yes, you!" I utterly shut down. I was ashamed, humiliated.

I wanted to apply for a job at a department store, but I thought I was too fat. I was too afraid to apply. My self-esteem was so low in these years, that I thought I had no reason to take up space on the earth. I justified my existence by sewing my family's clothes. I thought that if I could do that, I was worthy to continue living.

I became suicidal again. Rather than commit suicide, I decided I was desperate enough to spend money. I entered a "protein-sparing" modified fast program at a local hospital. I lost 129 pounds in 7 months and gained it back within the year.

I tried therapy. I became desperate enough to go back to Overeaters Anonymous (OA). By the grace of God, two friends in OA had read *Food Addiction: The Body Knows* by Kay Sheppard. We decided to eliminate sugars, flours, and wheat and eat the large quantities of food that she advocates. It was a miracle. I have lost 104 pounds, but unlike any other experience, I have taken it off gradually over three years with no interim gains. Never in my life have I gone three years without gaining weight.

Two other benefits of eliminating sugar, flour, and wheat come to mind. I used to have constant headaches which are gone. I also had high cholesterol. The last time I had it checked before eliminating refined carbohydrates and wheat it was 253. Now it is 193.

I often say a prayer these days that goes like this, " God, help this child see how little I can get by with, instead of how much I can get away with." I am constantly amazed at how little I can get by with, without feeling hungry or deprived. In all of the abuse I have suffered in my life, from my alcoholic parents and my first husband, no one has ever abused me as much as I abused myself with food. From this experience, I will never let anyone abuse me again, including myself.

I now make wise decisions. I am not dragged down by cravings, or the constant focus on food, or the depression and shame, or the headaches. How could I ever have been joyous, happy, and free when I was eating sugars, flours, and wheat?

## ATTY

I am a miracle. Statistically I should not be slender and sober, but I have been for the last seven years. By the grace of God, I discovered that I am a food addict and my favorite binge food is alcohol.

For most of my adult life, I was a success professionally. I felt that my success made my obesity OK. I didn't have to be successful everywhere. But food addiction is a progressive disease, after a while, no amount of food or booze could numb the pain inside of me. Then, God sent me a baby boy to adopt and I knew that I had to stop bingeing on alcohol.

I was lucky to find a weight loss program run by recovering drug addicts. They knew how fierce addictions are and their techniques were effective for me. They eliminated all sugars so this is when I put down the booze. It was very hard. No one else in the program was withdrawing from alcohol so I had to go it alone. They had us write five new reasons every day that we would succeed in this program. Then we taped them and played them back all day. I am 5"1' tall. I weighed 250 pounds at the beginning of the program and 120 at the end. In the last session, the staff asked the group how many of us realized that we were food addicts. I was the only one who raised my hand and I am the only one who is still slender today.

For the next four and a half years, I attended Alcoholics Anonymous meetings. I ate vegetables and fruits for lunch and the same for dinner with 6 ounces of protein. I also lost a lot of my hair, I suppose due to insufficient protein. I lived those years in constant hunger, and terror that the weight would come back. I knew that if the weight came back, I would start drinking again. I knew that I couldn't drink and be around my young son.

God really helped me when He showed me the way to a 12-step program that treats sugars, flours, and wheat the same way that Alcoholics Anonymous treats alcohol. NOT ONE BITE! When I stopped eating flours and wheat, I immediately lost my constant hunger. And incredibly, I lost the terror that I had lived with for four and a half years. I knew that the weight would not come back. I had serenity for the first time in my life.

## OTHERS

Other friends have had remarkable experiences similar to those described above, with one or two differences. One friend has experienced lower blood pressure, while her husband, with the help of his doctor, has been able to reduce his diabetes medicine. Another friend reports that she no longer gets depressed and angry when she is premenstrual. And yet another no longer has excruciating spasms in her colon. Your experience will be as individualistic as your appearance and personality. Enjoy your adventure!

*Notebook:*

## WHAT IS YOUR STORY?

Dear Reader,
    Find the threads of your own food habits and consequences.

There are a number of reasons that you may be following the food plan without deriving the same benefits as the person next to you in a support meeting. It does not mean that the food plan is wrong for you, rather that refined carbohydrate sensitivity has left you with other problems. You may need to further restrict your food choices or you may have some other condition all together. When deciding on a plan of action to correct an illness, Dr. Abram Hoffer's advice is to fix food first by providing excellent nutrition and eliminating allergic foods. You may need to neutralize food allergies. In addition, a look at vitamin and mineral deficiencies may be necessary. Dr. Nancy Appleton adds skeletal alignment to this list.[78]

> It is unlikely that the carbohydrate sensitive individual has survived the condition without developing ancillary problems, especially allergies, and vitamin and mineral deficiencies.

Only after these treatments have been tried should the use of drugs be considered. Hoffer says surgery should be a last resort.[79] Most health professionals talk about improving lifestyles in terms of exercise and stress management. In addition, Dr. Doris Rapp mentions avoiding chemicals and pollution as well as making the home allergy-free and ecologically sound.[80] With so many areas to examine, where should you start if you are not deriving all of the benefits of replacing reactive foods?

Get a thorough checkup from a good diagnostician. You may have a condition unrelated to food. However, no matter what the diagnosis, remember that refined carbohydrates are a drag on your system and eliminating them will boost the resources available to your body to heal from any illness. And, before you go on to allergies and deficiencies, make sure you...

## TIGHTEN UP THE PLAN

Check to see if you have drifted from the plan as it is written (not as your internal addict might like to see you follow it!) If you are not losing cravings and weight, or you don't have a sense of well-being:

- Weigh and measure everything, especially proteins and starches and especially on weekends.
- Read EVERY LIST OF INGREDIENTS and put back on the grocery shelf anything that has even the slightest trace of sweetener or flour.
- Recheck with the chefs at your favorite restaurants to make sure that your food does not have any sugar, flour, or wheat.
- Eliminate any marginal foods, extra fruit, or artificial sweeteners.
- Eat on time.
- Write a weekly plan.
- Eat EVERYTHING on the plan to avoid binge setups caused by inadequate nutrition.
- Count fat carefully, including cream in coffee, especially on weekends.
- Tell a friend or sponsor what you're going to eat each day.

---

[78] Appleton, Nancy, Ph. D., *Lick the Sugar Habit*, 159.
[79] Hoffer, Abram, M.D., *Putting It All Together*, 164-165.
[80] Rapp, Doris, M.D., *Is This Your Child?*, 62.

- Rotate foods to see if cravings reappear on certain days, especially dairy days. You may be experiencing a hypoglycemic reaction to an unknown food allergy.

If your objective is to lose weight and all of the above do not help, consider replacing fruit servings with vegetables. See Dr. Appleton's food lists for help with eliminating fruits and dairy.[81] (But avoid the avocado, bacon, liver, or white rice from her lists as these are too high in fat to support weight loss, or in the case of white rice, too refined.) Under any circumstances, do not lose more than two pounds per week or you will set yourself up for a relapse.

If your problem is frequent relapses, then be sure to read *Food Addiction: The Body Knows* by Kay Sheppard, LMHC, CEDS.[82] This book contains brilliant work on the stages of relapse, particularly the subtle early signs of a relapse into addictive eating. Kay Sheppard's advice has kept me more than once from the sad suffering caused by relapse. Allergic reactions that take the form of hypoglycemic cycles can also contribute to relapse. The highly sensitive individual can be triggered even by handling sugars and flours.

If you are still experiencing physical, emotional, or mental problems and your health care provider is out of ideas, look for other reasons. For the recovering carbohydrate addict, food allergies and vitamin and mineral deficiencies are strong possibilities due to the particular way that refined carbohydrates attack the body. Skeletal misalignment and emotional traumas are also discussed in this chapter because they may be contributing to cravings and food allergies. They can prevent full realization of some of the benefits of eating well.

In my own case, I had lingering asthma and the occasional migraine that persisted no matter how perfectly I followed the food plan. After a few years on the food plan, my energy levels fell from the heights I had experienced at the beginning of eliminating reactive foods. I resumed my quest for optimal health in the obvious places for a recovering food addict i.e. other food allergies, vitamin and mineral supplements, skeletal misalignment, and emotional healing.

## ALLERGIES

As we saw in the chapter on Medical Theory, gastrointestinal walls become permeable or leaky for many reasons related to refined carbohydrate consumption. Food leaking through the wall is attacked by the immune system. This creates an allergic relationship between the food and the body. This is why, if you are recovering from refined carbohydrate usage, you are a good candidate for other food allergies.

If you are already keeping a food diary, look for patterns of feeling poorly, but don't forget that you will be more allergic on days when you're stressed from overwork, quarreling, or lack of sleep. You may be able to eat potatoes on Monday after a peaceful weekend, but not on Friday at dinner with your quarrelsome in-laws. Stress from losses can increase susceptibility to reactions. Loss of a job, a relationship, a home, or a pet may run down your immune system and set you up for an allergic reaction. Watch for reactions such as elevated heart rate, headache, runny nose, irritability, drowsiness, depression, skin rash, etc. Even a hypoglycemic response with accompanying cravings can be caused by a food allergy.[83]

Not all emotional illnesses are caused by food allergies, but a food allergy may cause *any* type of emotional symptom:

---

[81] Appleton, Nancy, Ph. D., *Lick the Sugar Habit,* 165-166.

[82] Sheppard, Kay, LMHC,CEDS. *Food Addiction: The Body Knows.* Health Communications. Deerfield Park, Florida. 1989.

[83] Hoffer, Abram, M.D., *Putting It All Together, The New Orthomolecular Nutrition,* 70.

"Any food allergy can reproduce almost every known psychiatric syndrome from infantile autism and schizophrenia to mood and behavioral disorders. I do not single milk out as the only villain in the reproduction of allergic reactions. Allergic reactions tend to develop against staple foods. Thus in wheat consuming countries, wheat allergy is much more common than it is in rice consuming countries where rice is a greater problem. In tea drinking countries, tea will more often cause allergic reactions than coffee, while the converse is true in coffee consuming countries. I have seldom seen allergic reactions to tea but coffee allergic reactions are more common in Canada. Milk is a major staple since almost everyone is introduced to it early, either directly or via their mothers who drink milk, and it is consumed for a long time. For this reason milk allergy is a major problem and amongst the allergic reactions it induces, the psychiatric ones are common. They include behavioral and learning disorders in children."[84]

The topic of food allergies is complex in several aspects. Theory as to origin and cure vary all over the lot. Techniques for diagnosing are still evolving and have been vehemently debated and defined sometimes narrow-mindedly to the detriment of the sufferer. Eastern and Western medical approaches still offer solutions that are a world apart.

So, how to approach the hunt for food allergies and treatments? This chapter covers the most practical and effective means. For a most exhaustive overview of approaches, see Ellen Cutler's *Winning the War Against Allergies and Asthma.*[85] One very striking feature of diagnostic techniques and treatments is that they vary widely in terms of time requirements, expense, and effectiveness. For persons with multiple allergies, these are very important factors. At one time, a blood test showed that I had 179 allergies to foods alone. If I had chosen a diagnostic technique that can only diagnose one substance per day, I would have spent nearly a year just establishing reactions levels. It was impractical.

> There are many approaches to allergies with a wide array of results.

The four diagnostic and treatment approaches I have tried are traditional skin scratch test and shots; allergy medication with no testing; rotation and elimination diet supported by a blood test, and muscle resistance testing followed by NEAT acupuncture (which will soon be explained.) Allergy medication does nothing to heal the underlying causes of the illness. I am not going to discuss skin scratch tests and shots because they did nothing for me, either in terms of revealing food allergies, or curing environmental allergies. Some traditional allergists have abandoned this approach altogether. A last approach which is discussed in the literature, but which was impractical for me is testing through injections beneath the skin and neutralization by highly diluted homeopathic drops.

The two approaches to investigating food allergies are presented in order of difficulty and expense. Rotating is presented first because anyone can start today with only the "Pick-One-From-Each Column" chart found in the chapter, *What Else Is There To Eat?*

---

[84] Hoffer, Abram, M.D., *Hoffer's Laws of Natural Nutrition*, 81-82.

[85] Cutler, Ellen. *Winning the War Against Immune Disorders & Allergies*. Delmar Publishers. Albany, NY. 1998.

# ROTATION, ELIMINATION, AND REINTRODUCTION

**Rotating foods.** Food rotation is the first line of investigation into food allergies. After the elimination of sugars, flours, and wheat, rotating food is the next most effective means for improving well-being through food. Rotating food simply means not eating food from any food family any more often than once every four days. Rotating foods discloses hidden food allergies. If a symptom occurs, write down the foods that were eaten in the prior 24 hours. Over time, patterns will appear and you can eliminate suspected allergic foods.

Rotating also prevents new allergies. This has not been scientifically proven, but has been observed by allergy experts. Most allergists suggest a four to five day rotation which means that any food family is eaten no more often than every four to five days. I think this is hard to keep track of, so I try to do a seven-day rotation, one food family per day in each category of protein, fruit, vegetables, and starch.

In this book, I offered a simple means for rotating in the chapter *What Else Is There to Eat?* As with eliminating refined carbohydrates, shopping is the key to rotating foods. If you buy foods from all the food groups on a weekly basis, you will naturally rotate foods as you work your way through the week. Finding variety in restaurants is more challenging. Just think through what you have found to eat in restaurants and rotate visits accordingly. Your favorite restaurant may be willing to keep special items for you. For breakfast, take to the chef boxes of cream of buckwheat, rolled quinoa, unsweetened oatmeal, and grits. If the chef is uncooperative, rolled quinoa and unsweetened instant oatmeal can be made in the bowl by adding hot water. Order an empty bowl and a cup of boiling water.

Seven starches to rotate include grains (grass), buckwheat, beans, white potatoes, sweet potatoes, squash, and tapioca. (Make tapioca pudding for breakfast from eggs, milk, applesauce and tapioca; and tapioca cooked in egg and milk for dinner dessert after an 'entree' of two vegetables.) There are easily seven families of protein. The most common

> Successful rotation is as easy as thoughtful grocery and restaurant selections.

animal proteins might be beef, pork, chicken, turkey, shellfish, freshwater fish, and saltwater fish. Vegetarians can rotate four proteins: eggs, beans with grain, quinoa, and buckwheat. If you buy seven different families of protein and starch, and you have used each for three meals in turn by the end of the week, you know that you have rotated without further thought. Suggestions for all seven proteins and seven starches for breakfast and dinner are found in the respective 'Top Ten Favorite' lists at the end of the chapter *Mechanics*. A similar approach works easily for fruit. Vegetables are more tricky because we eat four one-cup servings per day. On the other hand, vegetables, except for the nightshade group, seem to be implicated in food allergies less frequently than proteins, starches, and fruit.

For vegetarians, I think the probability of food allergies are especially high since there are fewer food families to choose from giving rise to the problem of frequently eaten foods. Wheat flour is a very frequently eaten food for vegetarians who rely on bread for protein. As noted, there are four vegetarian protein families to rotate: eggs, combined beans and grain, quinoa, and buckwheat. Quinoa and buckwheat are seeds. Quinoa is related to the lambs quarters (spinach) family and buckwheat is related to rhubarb. Nuts and other seeds would normally be sources of non-animal protein, but Kay Sheppard has eliminated them on the grounds of their high fat content.

As a vegetarian, if you find that you are allergic to eggs, make sure you rotate your grains and beans extensively with quinoa and buckwheat. Also, pick vegetables with high protein content such as artichokes, broccoli, brussel sprouts, mushrooms, mustard greens, okra, spinach, and some seaweed. Use sprouts as a vegetable on bean days. If you are vegetarian because you feel better without animal proteins, you might want to go back and retest the animal proteins. You may be allergic to a few but not all of them. If you are a vegetarian on moral grounds, stick to your guns and rotate to the best of your ability.

Experts wonder if rotating grains (all in the grass family) makes any difference. Would it make any difference if we ate oats on one day, corn the next, and rice the day after? Is this rotating, or is it eating the same family every day? Try this for yourself. I have different reactions to different grains. I have a violent emotional reaction to wheat. Rice makes me tired. Fresh corn makes me irritable. Barley and rye are so closely related to wheat that they give me cravings. Of course, if we rotate starch families over seven days, we don't really have to worry about whether we can eat grains for days on end because we are eating them less often than every four days.

Grains have bigger refinement issues than almost any other category of starch except white potatoes. Although oatmeal (rolled oats) makes me sleepy, I can eat whole oat groats without any adverse reaction. (I prepare oat groats like rice.) So how much processing a grain has undergone can determine whether or not you have a reaction to it.

Rotation may seem like it would give rise to the complaint of monotony along the lines of "If it's tuna, this must be Tuesday." Not so! There many foods within each family *and* there are many ways of preparing foods. Recipes for soups, stir fries, roasts, salads, grills, and toppings take ingredients from many different families. Go back to the chapter of *Favorite Recipes* for the inspiration to substitute with vigor!

> Rotating generates a list of suspected food allergies. Elimination and reintroduction confirm these suspicions.

**Elimination and reintroduction.** This technique calls for eliminating the suspected allergic food for at least four to five days, but no more than fourteen days, and then reintroducing it in isolation.[86] If it is indeed an allergic food, the reaction will be quite discernable. Over the four to five days, the antibody to the food will increase and the reaction could be quite dramatic. However, after fourteen days, the antibody may have disappeared as it was not needed and no reaction will occur. If you eliminate an allergic food long enough, two weeks to two months, you may be able to eat small quantities infrequently without consequence. If this works, then you can cautiously increase quantities and frequency.

Rotating works to show up reactions in general, while you might use elimination and reintroduction if you want to confirm an allergy to one specific food.

The foods that are most likely to be the allergic culprits are the ones that you and your family eat most often (and are therefore at least somewhat

> Your preferred foods are also likely to be the allergic ones.

addictive). If you are not ready for a full rotation diet, but want to begin looking for allergic foods, pick the two or five or ten foods that you use the most.[87] Eliminate them all any Monday through Friday, then reintroduce each one singly every four hours over the weekend. Please do not try eating fruit or starches in isolation as this may trigger a relapse into

---

86 Rapp, Doris, M.D., *Is This Your Child?*. 41.
87 Null, Gary, Ph. D., *Nutrition and the Mind*, 151.

carbohydrate addiction. When testing for reactions to fruits and starches, accompany them with a protein to which you are sure you are not allergic.

If you are testing a child, check pulse, breathing, writing, and drawing. A reaction could show up in any of these areas as well as a more commonly recognized symptom such as a skin rash, runny nose, or asthma.[88]

The greatest advantage to handling food allergies through elimination is that the technique is free and pretty effective.

There are a number of draw-backs. It is annoying to avoid a large number of foods. For multiple allergies, it is impractical. In some cases, the sufferer must even avoid touching the food. If the sufferer is also the food preparer for a household, this can limit the whole family's diet. There is also the problem of accidentally ingesting a hidden allergic food and becoming ill. If the substance is very common such as corn, and well hidden such as corn starch, or the person cannot easily ask for a list of ingredients as is the case with a child, then elimination may not work. Neutralization may be a better option. This may also be the case where the reaction is so severe as to be life-threatening.

Another disadvantage is that non-food allergies may confuse results. If you're allergic to cotton, and you happen to wear your favorite cotton shirt on Tuesday, you may come to believe that you are allergic to everything you routinely eat on Tuesdays because your eyes itch all day and you have cravings like crazy. Or, if you relapse in October every year, you may be triggered by pollen. Or, if you are allergic to leather and your favorite seafood restaurant has leather chairs, you may develop the idea that you're allergic to seafood because your skin breaks out after eating at that restaurant.

You can solve this problem by getting tested. Blood tests are available through physicians offices. This involves drawing a vial of blood which is sent to a lab to test for the presence of allergens. The advantage of this test is that it can test for 180 foods at the same time. The disadvantage is that if you have already been avoiding a certain food, it will not show up as allergic. Muscle resistance testing is also available from many nutritionists, chiropractors, and acupuncturists.

By avoiding the most allergic foods, and rotating the least allergic, I have improved my health. For those of us who suffer from multiple allergies, elimination and reintroduction are useful for developing lists of suspected foods to take to an allergist for neutralization.

## NEUTRALIZATION

Techniques for neutralizing allergies have existed for decades, but only recently have their effectiveness improved. Two evolving techniques are homeopathic and NAET. NAET stands for Nambudripad Allergy Elimination Technique. My talented and much appreciated general practitioner suggested I try it when I grew tired of eliminating so many foods as my main means of coping with food allergies. It not only helped with food allergies, but with other environmental allergies, emotional wounds, and wayward cravings too. It even cured my altitude sickness.

This method was developed specifically for allergies by a medical pioneer, Dr. Devi S. Nambudripad. Dr. Nambudripad had extensive allergies which had not responded to traditional treatments. Once during emergency acupuncture treatment for a severe reaction to carrots, she unintentionally laid down on top of the carrot. She fell asleep during the treatment and woke up feeling wonderful. She tested herself for a reaction to carrots and found that she had none.

---

[88] *Ibid*, 214.

On the basis of this serendipitous "accident," she developed a seemingly simple technique using muscle resistance testing and modified acupuncture.

**Applied kinesiology or muscle resistance.** This technique starts by a health care practitioner pressing down on the patient's extended arm to test for the strength in the muscle. When an allergic food is smelled or tasted by the patient, the muscle will weaken and the health care practitioner will be able to move the arm more easily. If you have never heard of this before, try it yourself. Stand up, extend your arm in front of you. Have your friend press down on your arm while you resist the pressure as much as you are able. Then, put a suspected allergen in your other hand. See if you are able to resist the pressure to the same degree. You may be surprised at how noticeable the diminished strength is. Dr. Smith explains:

"The basic idea behind applied kinesiology is that we all have an electrical field of force around us, much like the earth with its north and south poles, and the magnetic field. Because every cell in our body carries an electrical charge, the sum of all those little batteries creates an electromagnetic force around our whole body. If something gets near us that is a negative force, the electrical fields will indicate a change. The kinesiologist can test the muscle to find these changes."[89]

Like muscle resistance testing, electro-acupuncture relies on the observation that allergic foods disrupt the body's energy fields. "It involves connecting the patient with a wire from an acupuncture point on his finger to a machine where extracts of the foods being tested are inserted into the circuit. Reactions are shown on a dial."[90]

**NAET Treatment** This is a relatively new, and for me highly effective treatment. The modified acupuncture technique calls for the patient to hold a small vial of the allergic substance while the practitioner uses a chiropractic stimulator down the spine twice. Then six very thin needles are barely inserted into the skin at six places around the arms and feet for fifteen minutes. (This does *not* hurt!) Alternatively the practitioner may massage or mildly shock the points. The patient avoids the substance for the next 25 hours. Upon reexamination, if the reaction is not completely eliminated in relationship with all of the body's organs and chemicals, then the patient is retreated.

The theory behind this treatment is twofold. First, the treatment corrects the brain's perception that the substance is a threat and allows the brain to be reprogrammed in its relationship to the item. Secondly, the treatment removes blockages that inhibit energy flows from reaching the body's organs. On the first point, Dr. Nambudripad explains that the genesis of a food allergy may be an unrelated trauma. She describes the case of a woman who was eating a peach when she learned that her son had been shot. Within hours, she developed an allergic reaction to peaches, even though she had already learned that her son was fine.

Dr. Nambudripad feels that during a trauma, the brain loses its powers of reasoning. It only knows that a threat is present. It cannot sort out which elements of the immediate scene might be the source of the threat. In the case of the peach-eating woman, the brain identified the peach as a threat and when the woman ate a peach again, the brain tried to warn her of the threat by making her sick.[91] Dr. Nambudripad's acupuncture technique retrains the brain to accept the substance.

---

89  Smith, Lendon, H., M.D., *Feed Your Body Right*. 54.

90  *Ibid.* 50.

91  Nambudripad, Devi S., D.C., L.Ac., R.N., Ph.D. *Say Goodbye to Illness*. Delta Publishing Company, Buena Park, CA. 1993. 82.

My own experience supports this theory.    The dinner table at my family of origin was at least occasionally traumatic.  I think we started every meal with low glucose levels which meant that we were irritable.  Fighting broke out among my siblings, or my parents engaged in arguments.  In either event, my father would seek to regain order by making sarcastic comments or threatening to get out the belt.  This was painfully frightening.  I can also remember sitting down to dinner with welts from the belt already on the back of my legs.  The children at the table were pressured to eat foods that they did not like in order to get dessert.  This was traumatic for a little girl.  Perhaps it is no wonder that I tested allergic to 179 foods out of 180 possibilities.

The second theory, that energy blockages are removed during treatment, is the basis of the long history of acupuncture.  The theory is that energy blockages build up at various points in the body, possibly in reaction to injuries, illnesses, or emotional traumas.  The needles draw out the heat that the energy creates, thus removing the blockage.

Often recipients of NAET treatments are sleepy afterwards.  This is indicative of healing.  The NAET practitioner tells me that when energy reaches a previously blocked area of the body, intense healing begins which the body interprets as illness.  The body puts itself to sleep just as if it were recovering from illness or surgery.

A third theory about the relationship between food addiction and NAET treatment is that the body may not be absorbing nutrients from the food.  This may be why cravings based on vitamin and mineral deficiencies develop for a particular food.  Sugar addiction can be exacerbated by an allergy to vitamin B12.  If the body cannot use B12, it cannot absorb sugar properly.  If it cannot use sugar, the brain does not get fed and it demands more sugar.  Dr. Nambudripad has had some success in treating sugar addiction by eliminating allergies to B12.

Although I knew that allergies and addictions are two sides of the same coin, I was nevertheless filled with joy when I lost an inappropriate interest in oatmeal and fruit as a result of being neutralized for gluten and fructose.  This has also happened with soy treatment and soy milk ( which I used to want daily) and rice treatment and rice cakes.  Release from cravings based on allergies makes food rotation much easier.  Food choices become more objective, i.e. based on need instead of an addictive relationship.

> Not surprisingly, cravings disappear when food allergies are neutralized.

There are interesting advantages and disadvantages to NAET treatment.  The advantages are that the cure is permanent.  Once patients are entirely clear of allergies, they need only return to their NAET practitioner annually for a check-up to detect new allergies.  The second advantage is that the treatments are consistently effective.  About 95% of treatments result in improvement for the patients.  NAET is also the only treatment that seems to address all allergies, regardless of origin - emotional, environmental, or genetic.

The main disadvantage is simply that in the period of healing following a treatment, duration and severity of reactions are unpredictable.  The client may need prolonged deep sleep.  If allergy to a brain chemical is involved, the person may not be able to think very well.

> The time spent on NAET treatments and reactions seems small in comparison to the tremendous benefits.

When stomach work is being done, excess gas may occur.  This may only last for a few days after the treatment, but if multiple visits are required to completely clear a condition, then the length of the reactions becomes a significant factor.

Another disadvantage is that repeat visits and reactions are time-consuming.  I need to be treated for over twenty substances.  Some of them will require repeat treatments.  I am lucky that my NAET practitioner is only a few minutes from my home.  Some clients must fly in from distant homes, take a hotel room, get 3-4 treatments in a week, sleep, and fly home.  My children who are under pressure to perform in high school cannot afford to run the risk of missing school due to drowsiness or feeling 'stupid'. They have to schedule their treatments during school holidays.

Two other disadvantages is that avoiding the substance for 25 hours can be annoying, especially when the treatment must be repeated. Also, most insurance companies do not cover the treatment.

All NAET practitioners are trained by Dr. Nambudripad in basic and advanced NAET techniques as well as muscle resistance testing. Practitioners are required to attend an annual symposium to keep their skills up to date.

It is important that the practitioner you choose hold current NAET certification and that they have received at least ten treatments themselves. This is the best way to ascertain that your practitioner adheres to safe practices. Serious problems may arise if you practitioner clears items from more than one food family at a time, takes items out of order, fails to recheck for clearance with all organs and body chemicals, or uses inappropriate acupuncture sites on the body.

One last word of caution about NAET. In an odd twist, the healing that NAET produces may lead to relapse into refined carbohydrate addiction. NAET treatment may promote the idea that the addict has been 'cured' of the addiction and can start eating refined carbohydrates again. *This is not true.* Even Dr. Ellen Cutler, who has developed NAET techniques as well as related enzyme therapy acknowledges that her sugar sensitivity cannot be cured. She writes, "After careful study, trial, and error, I developed a sugar-intolerant diet for myself. I have found that eighty percent of the people who come to see me are sugar intolerant."[92]

Abstinence is the only cure for addiction of any kind whether refined carbohydrates or heroin. Read Chapter 3 "More About Alcoholism" in the *Alcoholics Anonymous Big Book*[93] (substitute the words 'refined carbohydrates' for 'alcohol') for a vivid description of how addicts hold onto the hope that they will be able to abuse their substance of choice again. For the carbohydrate addict, a return to compulsive eating is always only one bite of sugar or flour away.

To find NAET practitioners, contact:

Dr. Devi S. Nambudripad
6714 Beach Blvd.
Buena Park, CA 90621
Fax:     (714) 523-3086
E Mail:  NAET@Earthlink.net
www.naet.com

**Environmental Allergies** Food allergies are not the only source of allergy-based illness stemming from overuse of refined carbohydrates.. Because recovering carbohydrate-addicts have worn-out immune and endocrine systems, they are also susceptible to environmental allergens such as inhaled substances. These would include pollens and dust, as well as man-made substances ranging from perfumes to pollutants to pesticides. I appreciate that inhaled substances can be a drag on my system so I have switched to environmentally safe household cleaning fluids, including laundry soap. I no longer use beauty products which might irritate my respiratory membranes. I have especially moved away from nail polish (which often contains

---

[92] Cutler, Ellen W., D.C. *Winning the War against Immune Disorders and Allergies.* 437.

[93] Alcoholics Anonymous, *Alcoholics Anonymous*, any edition, p 30-39.

formaldehyde), polish remover, and heavily perfumed shampoos, conditioners, skin lotions, and make-up. Since most deodorants contain aluminum, I use instead a perfume-free first-aid spray which just kills the bacteria that cause odors.

Aside from my comfort level, there is another reason it's important to control allergies to dust, pollen or fumes, either through elimination from the environment or desensitization. "Decreasing the intensity of these allergic reactions will decrease the intensity of the hypoglycemic reaction."[94]

Because the body's filtering systems are worn down from dealing with the debris left from refined carbohydrate usage, the recovering food addict should consider the possibility of toxic build-up in the body. Blood tests and hair analysis can detect these. New therapies are available to cleanse your system if this is the problem. The production of chemicals in the United States has increased from one billion lbs. annually in pre-World War II times, to 250 billion lbs. today.[95] It seems unlikely that any of us would be completely free of toxic chemicals.

The issue of food allergies is ignored in our culture to a heart-wrenching degree. For yourself, and for anyone you feed, rotating and eliminating foods are powerful gateways to reduced allergies and to emotional and physical well-being. If practical, neutralization brings about the same great improvement in health as eliminating sugars and flours and other allergic foods. The processes are wondrous.

## VITAMIN AND MINERAL DEFICIENCIES

Another condition that accompanies sugar and flour addiction is vitamin or mineral deficiency. Rotating foods maximizes the variety of vitamins and minerals you receive, as does eliminating refined carbohydrates. But from the years of eating poorly, vitamin and mineral deficiencies have almost certainly developed. Dr. Hoffer explains why:

"Manufacturers of food have become quite skillful. They have developed palatable food substitutes such as soft drinks that provide water, carbon dioxide and harmful synthetics but no protein, fat, carbohydrate, minerals or vitamins. Millers have taken apart the wholeness of grains. They separate the endosperm of wheat (white flour) from the germ and bran. Sugar manufacturers give us pure sucrose from beets and sugar cane. Soft drinks, white flour bread, and white sugar are examples of the many foods that provide malnutrition in the form of naked or empty calories.

Empty-calorie foods are deficient in nutrients. They cannot be used in the body without vitamins and minerals and other foodstuff. If the nutrient factors do not accompany naked-calorie foods, they must be taken from other food. This means that a diet heavy in sugar or other naked calories must inevitably lead to multiple vitamin and mineral deficiencies."[96]

Even though your diet is improved, foods contain fewer mineral and vitamins today because they are grown in depleted soil. New tests are available to detect problems in these areas. As we have seen in the chapter *Medical Theory*, specific organs may be worn out from eating reactive foods. Specific supplements can support recovery in these organs. Again, your health care professional can help you. Vitamin and mineral deficiencies can be detected through hair analysis, and through the applied kinesiology or muscle resistance technique described above for allergy testing. They can even be detected through a smell test. If the vitamin or mineral smells

---

[94] Hoffer, Abram, M.D., *Putting It All Together, The New Orthomolecular Medicine*, 68.

[95] Null, Gary, Ph.D., *Nutrition and the Mind*, 194.

[96] Hoffer, Abram, M.D., *Putting It All Together: The New Orthomolecular Nutrition*, 17.

good or does not smell at all, then it is probably needed. If your stomach has been damaged by refined carbohydrates, it may not be capable of absorbing supplements taken orally. Injection may be a better alternative. Also, alkalinity imbalances can interfere with absorption. Dr. Lendon Smith suggests smelling the acidifier ammonium chloride to test for alkalinity/acidity balance. If a person is alkaline, it smells good.

Dr. Abram Hoffer makes several important points about vitamin and mineral supplements. They do not replace food. They are only to be taken after food has been optimized.[97] He also notes that all people have different requirements. The range of doses required is huge depending on whether a condition is being prevented from developing, or whether the condition already exists and is being cured. Sex, physical stress, psychological stress, lactation, pregnancy, diseases, and use of drugs all effect dosage requirements. Vitamins can be taken safely for a lifetime, but excess minerals can accumulate in the body. Get with a good health care professional to determine your needs.

In my research for this book, a set of recommended vitamin supplements for hypoglycemia reappeared several times. Experts recommend that daily amounts be broken down into several doses per day. If you use this information to treat yourself, you are within your legal rights. However, input from a trained professional is recommended.

---

[97] Hoffer, Abram, M.D., *Hoffer's Laws of Natural Nutrition*, 122.

## SURVEY OF VITAMIN AND MINERAL SUPPLEMENTS FOR HYPOGLYCEMIA

| Amounts per day | Lick the Sugar Habit[98] | Nutrition and the Mind[99] | Putting It All Together[100] | Nutrition Made Simple[101] | Feed Your Body Right[102] |
|---|---|---|---|---|---|
| L-glutamine | 1,500 mg | 500-1,000 mg | * | 500-1,000 mg | * |
| GTF Chromium | 50 mg | 200-600 mg | * | 200-600 mg | * |
| zinc and copper | | | * | 25-50 mg of zinc, balance with copper | |
| Vitamin A | | | | * | |
| B vitamins | | 50-75 mg | B3, B6, B1 | * | * |
| Pantothenic acid (Vitamin B5) | | 500 mg | | * | * |
| Vitamin C | | 3,000 mg | | * | * |
| Calcium | | | * | * | * |
| Potassium | | 500-1,000 mg | | | |
| Manganese | | 10-20 mg | * | | |
| Magnesium | | 200-400 mg | * | * | |
| Ginseng Extract | | | | * | |
| Raw adrenal | | | Adrenal cortical extract | | * |
| Proteolytic enzymes | | | | | * |
| Royal jelly | | | | | * |
| Carnitine | | | | | * |
| Bellargal | | | * | | |
| Antihistamine | | | As needed* | | |
| Cysteine | | | | | * |

*Recommended, but no amount given

[98] Appleton, Nancy, Ph.D., *Lick the Sugar Habit*, 179.

[99] Gary, Null., Ph.D., *Nutrition and the Mind*, 51 and 84.

[100] Hoffer, Abram, M.D., *Putting It All Together*, 68.

[101] Crayhon, Robert, M.S., *Nutrition Made Simple*, 200.

[102] Smith, Lendon H., M.D., *Feed Your Body Right*, 136.

L-glutamine or Glutamic acid has some of the properties of glucose, but is not as destabilizing as glucose. It is the only substance other than glucose that can fuel the brain.

Chromium, zinc, manganese, and the B vitamins aid in metabolizing carbohydrates. Calcium is often needed because its absorption is disrupted by sugar, so the possibility of damage from osteoporosis needs to be addressed. Magnesium absorption is also disrupted by sugar and so it needs to be replaced. Adrenal supplements are desirable to give the over-worked adrenal gland a chance to rest and repair itself. Other supplements are aimed at improving digestion, stabilizing insulin, and reinforcing the immune system. Check with your knowledgeable health care professional before settling on the combination of supplements that will work for you.

Fortunately, a whole new breed of medicine has emerged to work on allergies and vitamin and mineral deficiencies. It is called clinical ecology. One of the most prominent clinics is in Dallas, Texas under the direction of Dr. William Rea. Dr. Rea has also taken over the Chicago clinic of the late Dr. Theron Randolph who was the founder of clinical ecology. We should be very grateful to these doctors for their courage to stand up to the established community of allergists. Their work proved that environmental allergies are much more extensive than are normally revealed in traditional skin tests.

How to choose? One good bet is to look for medical personnel who are familiar with alternative medical practices. The American Academy of Environmental Medicine will send you a list of their members. Send a stamped self-addressed envelope to PO Box 1001-8001 / New Hope, PA 18938.

Your NAET practitioner can also identify vitamin and minerals which your body cannot absorb. Treatment can help the body use the vitamin and minerals effectively.

I would also like to reference the remarkable book, *Molecules of Emotion*. The author, Dr. Pert, has accumulated an amazing array of solid resources for help with many problems.[103] This is just another of the many reasons to read this book.

Also, the field of nutrition is producing nutritionists by the dozens. Vitamin and minerals supplements are flooding the market as consumers realize the limitations of traditional pharmaceuticals and the problems of depleted soil. See *Nutrition Made Simple*[104] for a good set of interview questions to qualify the nutritionist for you.

You can always ask your general health professional if they have had any training in nutrition. When I put this question to my pediatrician who recently graduated from a very prestigious medical school, I was taken aback when he said he had not had one course in nutrition. This doesn't mean I will stop going to him. But it does mean I will be selective about the conditions on which I consult him. I would feel comfortable with his advice on such issues as injuries, vaccinations, and one-time infections. For illnesses such as allergies, stomachaches, headaches, fatigue, and recurring problems, I would seek the advice of my environmental ecologist or NAET practitioner.

In 1995, one third of the American population spent $13.7 billion to seek unconventional therapies. Don't be afraid to venture out into the world of complementary or alternative medicine. Just be sure to get references. To a large degree, the type of healer you chose will depend on who is practicing in your environs. Listen closely to friends' stories of finally finding the right professional to fix their problems, not just mask the problems. Question stories carefully about the specifics of the 'cures' before making an appointment.

---

103 Pert, Candace, Ph. D., *Molecules of Emotion*, 324-345.
104 Crayhon, Robert, M.S., *Nutrition Made Simple*, 265.

# STRESS AND TRAUMA

After handling the mechanics of the food plan itself, facing the emotional revolution that comes at the end of food numbing is the recovering addict's greatest challenge. Along with hidden food allergies, uncovered and unaddressed emotional angst is a potential source of relapse.

Do emotional problems create addiction or does addiction create emotional problems? It hardly matters. All addicts have emotional problems to work out by the time they get off their substance of choice. Sugar and flour addicts are no different.

If your layer of fat was protective armor against predators, then unless you can find out what it was protecting you against and heal the fear, your life as an attractive, thin (at least in this culture) person may be very scary and bring you to relapse.

If there were traumatic incidences from childhood which made numbing essential for survival, painful memories can surface which unless healed, may be an avenue to relapse.

Stress leads to overeating for numbing effects. If the addict uses food in this way, she will need to learn other coping mechanisms. The 12-Step program is the most obvious place to start. It is free (small voluntary contributions) and it is effective. It is, however, not a replacement for therapy.

Healing emotional wounds without the reverberations of sugars and flours is very effective because of the absence of the capricious fears and sadness that refined carbohydrates and other reactive foods create. The links between feelings and causes are easier to establish. Memories are more clear. The courage to face painful truths is more reliably abundant. The process of emotional recovery bears many rewards.

With a body that is free from reactive foods, you have a better chance of getting accurate signals about your condition from yourself. You may need therapy or an experiential program to resolve childhood traumas and achieve emotional peace. If you or your family are recovering from reactions that affected behavior, you may need some counseling to learn appropriate behavior, i.e., behavior that is motivated by the situation and not by biochemical reactions. Support groups as well as private therapy provide answers. Radix is a type of therapy that addresses blockages in the body. If bad food can be considered an assault on the body, then a therapy which delves into physical blockages seems like it would be especially useful.

Deep descent workshops such as Woman Within (for women) and New Warrior (for men) heal wounds over a week-end. The week-ends are often helpful in addressing wounds and blocks which may be too deep to reach in the therapist's hour. Call 800-732-0890 for information.

Two authors which have helped me understand the process of healing from addiction are Marion Woodman who has written many books, among them *The Owl Was a Baker's Daughter, Addiction to Perfection, and the Ravaged Bridegroom*. She is a poetic, mesmerizing speaker so her tapes are also very worthwhile. She herself is a recovering anorexic, so her Jungian background provides especially pointed and evocative images for the recovering food addict. Her studies trace with clarity the emotional origins of eating disorders to negative parenting, both maternal and paternal. Her insights into the repercussions of repressing the feminine resonate with truth. She is especially interested in the devastating consequences of perfectionism. She sees it as crushing because it is a set-up for incessant failure. It grows from critical parents and is very painful. Marian Woodman also runs intensive healing sessions. She can be reached in Toronto, Canada.

Linda Schierse Leonard's book *Witness to the Fire, Creativity and the Veil of Addiction* is a brilliant discourse on the kinds of personae that control addicts. Understanding the archetype that dominates an addict can be the key to breaking destructive behaviors.

As an aside to therapists: I would encourage you to ask if your food addicted clients are coming to sessions 'drunk' on carbohydrates. My own therapist will not treat an alcoholic who is drinking. She requires the client to be sober and attending AA meetings. I believe this approach is useful to treating food addicts as well. Progress in therapy for me was slow until I got 'sober' from refined carbohydrates. If you are frustrated with your food-addicted clients, you might try recommending that they get through withdrawal from refined carbohydrates and augment their therapy with 12-Step work.

Spiritual healing can also be effective here as well as meditation, yoga, exercise, massage, etc. Meditation can also speed the healing of organs. Find a clear anatomy book and look up images of the stomach, pancreas, adrenal gland, and liver. Imagine the immune system sending white blood cells, macrophages and peptides to these organs to heal the ravages of food abuse. This guided imagery helps focus the brain on the tasks of repair.

Your lifestyle may be too stressful to be cured even with a very good food program. I cite the example of my friend the airline stewardess who has numerous sensitivities which a food program has not been able to diminish. She misses two nights of sleep per week while flying international routes. She is constantly jet-lagged. She is not yet ready to give up her schedule, so she may expect to see only limited improvement in her condition.

## SKELETAL ALIGNMENT

Skeletal issues may seem pretty tangential to recovery from food addiction. The topic is included here because a misaligned skeleton can produce some of the same symptoms as food allergies, particularly in the spine. As we saw in the chapter *Medical Theory*, allergies result from a worn-down, side-tracked immune system. The immune system gets many signals from the nervous system. So, if the nerves in the spinal cord are worn and irritated from rubbing against misaligned vertebrae, they themselves can cause pain and they may also send incorrect signals to the immune system about problems such as swelling.

I had frequent headaches and swollen sinuses which improved dramatically when I eliminated refined carbohydrates from my diet. But the sinus pain began to come back. Over the course of the years of following the food plan, I was still experiencing an attack about once per month. I was confused about which foods might be causing the headaches because I could not establish a correlation. I really felt that I had eliminated all allergic foods, increased my vitamins and minerals, cleared my house of fumes and toned down my lifestyle to the point where these were no longer factors. Fortunately, about two and a half years after I eliminated reactive foods, I was referred to a local chiropractor as a source of help with food allergies.

Since I was having the headaches in spite of well-managed food, my chiropractor suspected a spinal problem. Indeed, upon reviewing x-rays, he found that an old bicycle fall, combined with many hours of head-bent-over-books, had left my neck misaligned. Adjustments followed by maintenance stretching, solved the problem and also resulted in unexpected improvements elsewhere. Asthma and attitude were among the areas of relief. I am grateful to this inquisitive, thoughtful, analytical chiropractor and to the doctor who referred me to him. I try to think of ways to educate my doctors in prestigious institutions who never mentioned the possibility of skeletal misalignment as a source of respiratory pain and distress, much less food allergies. I try not to think about the days of excruciating pain that their lack of education caused me.

# OTHER

In addition to skeletal misalignment, Other diseases can present symptoms similar to hypoglycemia and food addiction/allergy. Incessant hunger can be caused by a thyroid or pancreatic problem, parasites, a mold allergy, or an emotional trauma.[105]

High blood pressure can be caused by tobacco and food allergies such as chocolate, coffee, bananas and citrus.[106] This correlation may further explain by blood pressure is lowered on the food plan since all of these substances are eliminated except citrus. Fatigue may be the result of impaired thyroid, toxic build-up, impaired liver, lack of sleep, parasites, and inadequate exercise. These possibilities are in addition to the factors already covered, i.e., food allergies, vitamin and mineral deficiencies, and yeast infections.[107]

Malfunctioning thyroids produce a surprising number of symptoms, both emotional and physical, and are often missed in testing. Other diseases which mimic food reactions are cystic fibrosis and celiac disease.

Patience is also required. My doctor has told me that it takes one month to heal from each year of an illness. I view the years that I ate reactive foods as years of illness. Since I was 43 years old when I started this food program, with the help of vitamin and mineral supplements, and allergy neutralization, I don't expect to have a fully functioning set of organs in much less than four years. I feel very blessed to have the prospect of full recovery and to have received so many benefits already.

In our culture, finding people who consistently maintain a sense of well-being is rare. Anxiety and depression accompanied by some kind of physical illness are the rule. Fixing food will give any journey toward consistent well-being a huge lift. Many other self-disciplinary practices will grow from a food plan based on loving the self. We become more attracted to situations based on mutual regard. We exercise from love rather than fear of looking bad. Making good food a priority causes shifts in other priorities. It's harder to enjoy spiritually deprived activities. They just don't feel right anymore. The meaning of enjoyment shifts away from abusive acts to caring ones. It's possible by many means to start the healing shift from an angle other than food. But with food issues at rest, healing in other venues becomes a matter of course.

---

[105] Rapp, Doris, M.D., *Is This Your Child?*, 94.
[106] *Ibid.* 227.
[107] Crayhon, Robert, M.S., *Nutrition Made Simple.* 156.

## Chapter 23
### ACTION PLANS

### TOP TEN WAYS TO GET STARTED

1. Enlist a friend to support you. Find or start a support group.

2. Photocopy the list of the names for sugars and flours and keep it with you when you shop.

3. Photocopy and enlarge the Pick-One-From-Each Column page and tape it up in your kitchen. Also make one for each person for whom you buy food.

4. Sit down with any adult members of your household for whom you buy food. Go over the rules in the chapter *Bringing Your Household on Board*. Distribute the Pick-One- From-Each-Column pages to them and ask them to cross off any foods they do not like. Set aside cabinet and refrigerator space for the adults who want to continue to buy reactive foods.

5. Cut out the summary card at the end of this book and keep it in your wallet.

6. Call your health care providers and tell them that you are starting on a food plan that may swiftly improve a number of your symptoms, especially high blood pressure, cholesterol, and diabetes. Ask what adjustments you may need to your medications. (Be prepared to hear them pooh-pooh the likelihood of benefits of the food plan, but stick to your guns.)

7. Practice learning the names for sugars and flours by going through your cabinets and throwing away any foods that contain these addictive/allergic substances.

8. Write a food plan for the week. Use the lists of favorite meals provided in this book for inspiration.

9. Do a *complete* shopping based on your food plan. If you don't have a plan, take the Pick-One-From-Each-Column chart with you to the store and buy only foods that appear on that list.

10. Call your five favorite restaurants and ask them which dishes contain no sugars or flours of any kind.

### TOP TEN WAYS TO MAINTAIN YOUR FOOD PLAN

Undertake these actions as often as you need. Do them more often if you are not happy with results and you are relapsing.

1. Attend support meetings.

2. Write on the Twelve Steps.

3. Tell an experienced friend what you are eating.

4. Weigh and measure food to make sure you are not drifting.

5. Spread the word about carbohydrate sensitivity.

6. Pray for divine help.

7. Reread and add to the various work pages in this book.

8. Write down benefits in a place where you will see them often.

9. Check to see if you are eating a variety of foods.

10. Give thanks for divine guidance at every meal.

Cut out and paste onto a business card for quick reference.

Basic shopping for one person for one week:
28 servings of protein (eggs, meat, poultry, fish, beans, buckwheat, quinoa, tofu)
14 servings of dairy (milk, yogurt, cottage cheese) or 7 more servings of protein
14 servings of fruit
28 servings of vegetables
14 servings of starch (grain, potato, sweet potato, squash, beans, buckwheat, quinoa, tapioca) plus 7 additional servings of starch if you are eating a starch at lunch.

BREAKFAST: Starch, fruit, and 1½ protein
(or starch, fruit, dairy, and protein)
LUNCH: Protein, raw vegetable,
cooked or raw vegetable, (starch optional).
DINNER: Protein, raw vegetable,
cooked or raw vegetable, and starch.
EVENING SNACK: ½ protein and fruit or dairy and fruit.

# Chapter 24
## A PRAYER FOR THE READER

Dear Reader, I have thought about you daily during the years of writing this book. I have prayed that God's will for you would be conveyed through this writing. I would like to close the book with a prayer for you.

Dear God:
Please watch over the people who are reading this book.
Keep them from feeling overwhelmed.
Show them the tiny steps that lead to recovery from refined carbohydrate use.
Please make them aware of the divine comfort that you provide for the asking.
Give them the courage to seek hope through the experiences of fellow-sufferers.
Show yourself through their triumphs.
Help them be mindful of the voices that would keep them bound up in fear.
Cleanse their eyes so that they may see your glory in the food that they prepare.
Clear their palettes so that they might taste of your good-will for them.
Answer their prayers for cessation of aches and pains.
Reveal your glory through their clear heads and bodies.
Walk by their side when negative forces threaten their recovery.
Carry them through dark passages of relapse.
Dear God, be as generous with each of these readers has you have been with me.
For this, I am grateful.

ADDITIONAL READING

I do not agree with every detail of the food plans proposed in any of these books.  However, each of them has added substantially to my understanding of the dynamics of reactions to food.

Al-Anon. *Al-Anon Faces Alcoholism.* New York, Al-Anon Family Group Headquarters, Inc. 1986.

*Alcoholics Anonymous.* New York: Alcoholics Anonymous World Services, Inc., 1955.

Alcoholics Anonymous. *Twelve Steps and Twelve Traditions.*  New York: Alcoholics Anonymous World Services, Inc., 1953.

Appleton, Nancy. *Lick the Sugar Habit.* Garden City Park, NY: Avery Publishing Group. 1996.

Clark, Dawn. *Gifts for the Soul.* Houston, TX: Aarron Publishing. 1999.

*Co-Dependents Anonymous.* Phoenix, Arizona: CoDA Service Office, 1995.

Cutler, Ellen W., D.C. *Winning the War Against Immune Disorders and Allergies.* Albany, New York: Delmar, 1998

Crayhon, Robert. *Nutrition Made Simple.* New York: M. Evans and Company, 1996.

DesMaison, Ph.D. *Potatoes Not Prozac.* New York: Simon and Schuster, 1998.

Dufty, William. *Sugar Blues.* New York: Warner Books, 1975.

Hoffer, Abram, M.D. *Hoffer's Laws of Natural Nutrition.* Ontario: Quarry Press, 1996.

----- and Morton Walker. *Putting It All Together: The New Orthomolecular Nutrition.* New Canaan, CT: Keats Publishing, Inc., 1996.

Leonard, Linda Schierse. *Witness to the Fire, Creativity and the Veil of Addiction.* Boston, MA: Shambhala Publications, Inc., 1989.

Null, Gary, Ph.D. *Good Food, Good Mood.* New York: St. Martin's Press, 1988.

-----. *Nutrition and the Mind.* New York: Seven Stories Press, 1995.

Pert, Candace. *Molecules of Emotion.* New York: Scribner. 1997.

Philpott, William H. and Dwight K. Kalita.  *Brain Allergies.*  New Canaan, CT: Keats Publishing, 1983.

Randolph, Theron G., and Ralph W. Moss. *An Alternative Approach to Allergies.* New York: Bantam Books, 1981.

Rapp, Doris. *Is This Your Child?* New York: William Morrow. 1991.

Sheppard, Kay, LMHC, CEDS. *Food Addiction: The Body Knows.* Deerfield Beach, FL: Health Communications, Inc. 1993.

Sheppard, Kay, LHMC, CEDS and Barbara Caravella. *Recovery Cookbook.*  Palm Bay, FL; Kay Sheppard. 1998.

Smith, Lendon H. *Feed Your Body Right.* New York: M. Evans and Company. 1994.

Starks, Charles A. and Peggy B. Starks. *Disease Concept of Food Addiction (the workbook)* Ft. Myers, FL: Fairwinds Institute, Inc. 1995.

Vayda, William. *Mood Foods.* Berkeley, CA: Ulysses Press. 1995.

Wittenberg, Margaret M. *Good Food,* Freedom, CA: The Crossing Press. 1995.

Woodman, Marian. *Addiction to Perfection.*  Toronto, Canada: Inner City Books. 1982.

-----. *The Owl Was a Baker's Daughter.* Toronto, Canada: Inner City Books.1980.

-----. *The Ravaged Bridegroom.* Toronto, Canada: Inner City Books. 1990.

## ABOUT THE AUTHOR

Joan Ifland was born in Beaver Falls, Pennsylvania. She received her B.A. in economics and political science from Oberlin College, Ohio. After a stint on the fiscal staff of the Wisconsin Legislature, she earned an M.BA. from Stanford University Graduate School of Business. She worked in corporate finance for five years for a Fortune 100 company.

After forty-three years of declining physical and emotional health, Joan began eliminating refined carbohydrates from her diet. It was the miraculous recovery from numerous illnesses for her and her family that prompted her to share her experience and knowledge of how to manage a life free from refined carbohydrates.

Today, Joan is devoted to spreading the word about recovery from carbohydrate sensitivity. She lectures, coaches, and holds seminars. She lives in Houston, Texas. She has been married since 1978 to her husband, an investment banker. Their two daughters were born in 1983 and 1984.